Acknowledgments

Some of the incidents in this book are based on historical events—in particular the river blowout—but they have been adapted to suit the purposes of fiction.

I would like to thank sincerely the New York Transit Museum in Brooklyn, for allowing me access to their archives; the Schomburg Library in Harlem; the New York Public Library; and the American-Irish Historical Society. I would like to thank the many sandhogs who gave me access to their hearts and memories. Thanks to the men and women of Harlem who gave me their time and remembered with such honesty. A very special thanks to Sean and Sally McCann, Roger and RoseMarie Hawke, Captain Bryan Henry, Barbara Warner, Ledig House, Terry Williams, Jean Stein, Christy Cahill, Darrin Lunde, Rick Ehrstin, David Bowman, Billy "The Mule" Adare, Shaun Holyfield, Shana Compton, Leslie Potter, and Ronan McCann, many of whom read the manuscript in its early stages and provided invaluable advice. Also to Arthur French, who graciously helped me with many sections of dialogue. My sincere gratitude to all and sundry at Metropolitan Books and Henry Holt and at Phoenix House. I'm blessed with two very fine editors, Riva Hocherman and Maggie McKernan.

Of course, this book would never have been written without the love, advice, and support of my wife, Allison. To her, all thanks. And for Isabella too.

Finally, my thanks to the men and women of the tunnels of New York who allowed me into their lives and their homes, most especially Bernard and Marco. Neither of them are in this book, but it would have been impossible to write without them.

REICH'S DEVELOPMENT, 1922–1934

When Wilhelm Reich graduated from the medical school of the University of Vienna in 1922, he had already practiced psychoanalysis for three years and been a member of the Vienna Psychoanalytic Society for two. Absorbed by the basic question "What is life?" and convinced of the central role of sexuality in it, he had been drawn to the work of Sigmund Freud by Freud's understanding of sexuality as a developmental process that begins at birth and by his hypothesis of the existence of a psychic-sexual energy, the libido theory. In addition, the technique of psychoanalysis provided the young physician with a practical tool. But there were many unsolved problems, many unanswered questions in psychoanalytic theory and therapy and in the relation of this new discipline to the world in which it was growing. During the years from 1922 to 1934, Reich would struggle to protect and extend Freud's original clinical formulations and, in so doing, come into conflict with Freud himself.

The neurosis was originally understood by Freud as the result of a conflict between instinctual sexual drives and a negating society that prohibits and suppresses them. Symptoms observed in patients were considered to be expressions of these instincts that, for some unknown reason, had broken through in a distorted form from an unconscious psychic level. Implicit in the instinctual drives was an energy function Freud called "libido." Its reality had yet to be proved, although Freud conjectured that it might be of a chemical nature. On the basis of this formulation of the neurosis, Freud had developed a therapy he hoped would "cure" neuroses. Using the technique of free association, in which the patient was to say anything but do nothing, psychoanalysis sought to get the patient to remember the events and feelings that had been repressed, to make the unconscious impulses conscious so they would be available to the individual's control and could be rejected or sublimated in some socially acceptable activity. Just here, in the goal of psychoanalytic treatment, lay the seeds of the conflict between Reich and Freud, because the demand for rejection or sublimation implied a moral judgment that the biological instincts are "bad" and society is immutable.

Reich had come to psychoanalysis with a grounding in basic science. He had studied astronomy, electronics, the quantum theory, and the physical theories of Einstein, Heisenberg, and Bohr. While his psychoanalytic colleagues tended to focus on the content of their patients' memories and its interpretation, Reich was absorbed by questions of energy, the economic, quantitative factor in the neurosis. He would search for the energy source of neurosis, its somatic core.

Little was known about the nature of mental illness. The individual neurotic symptom was viewed as a foreign body in an otherwise healthy organism. Freud had said that symptoms must disappear when the unconscious was made conscious, but success was limited, and he later acknowledged this, stating that they may disappear. But, Reich asked, what led from "may" to "must"? What else besides making the unconscious conscious was necessary to assure the disappearance of the symptom? These questions were not generally asked, but Reich struggled with them in his practice. He began to investigate fantasies accompanying masturbation and to pay close attention to the types of masturbation engaged in by his patients. He found that the form of the fantasized act offered an approach to unconscious conflicts and infantile experiences. In addition, he observed that some patients' symptoms would disappear if they were able to have a satisfying sexual experience, whether through masturbation or intercourse. The symptoms would return after several days but again disappear with sexual gratification. Increasingly, Reich focused his attention on the genital function and its central mechanism, the orgasm. In November 1923, he reported on "Genitality from the Viewpoint of Psychoanalytic Prognosis and Therapy," asserting that the genital disturbance was an important, perhaps the most important, symptom of neurosis. His proposition was received with hostility by psychoanalytic colleagues who claimed that many patients were genitally healthy. What then constituted "genital health"? Reich investigated it more closely. He had his patients give exact descriptions of their behavior and sensations during the sexual act and, in the case of men, discovered that even with erectile potency they experienced little or no pleasure. Nor was there any involuntary behavior or dimming of consciousness. The meaning of sexual potency was now at issue. "The concept of sexual potency," Reich stated, "has no meaning at all without the inclusion of the economic, experiential, and energy aspects. Erectile and ejaculatory potency are merely prerequisites for *orgastic potency*. Orgastic potency is the capacity for sexual surrender without any reservations, the capacity for complete discharge of all dammed-up sexual excitation through involuntary, pleasurable convulsions of the body. No neurotic is orgastically potent." The somatic core of the neurosis had to be dammed-up sexual energy that could only be adequately discharged in the orgasm. Hence the study of orgastic impotence became the central clinical problem of Reich's research and orgastic potency the goal of his therapeutic efforts. Becoming aware of the repressed sexuality must go together with the capacity for orgastic discharge. Reich had expanded Freud's concept of cure with the addition of the economic energy factor, and he began to use the term *sex economy* to describe it.

Reich's conclusions had been drawn not only from clinical experiences with private patients but also from careful observations on disturbances of genitality among working-class people at the Vienna Psychoanalytic Clinic, where he was given access to a wide variety of serious pathology not seen in private practice. These disturbances were not sexual in the more general sense of Freud but specifically genital in the strict sense of orgastic impotence. The disturbance of genitality was not *one* symptom but *the* symptom of neurosis.

During these years from 1922 to 1926 when the orgasm theory was being formulated and tested, Reich was deeply involved in efforts to understand and improve psychoanalytic technique. Psychoanalysis depended on free association, but few patients could free-associate. Improvement relied on random breakthroughs that were not understood. In 1924, Reich assumed the leadership of the Psychoanalytic Technical Seminar that had been created two years earlier at his suggestion. The problem was to work out a technique to find and eliminate all pathological attitudes preventing the establishment of orgastic potency. He designed a plan for systematic reporting of cases that would focus on resistance situations and emphasize technical problems rather than case histories. Gradually, it was learned that most analysts avoided negative reactions in their patients and were helpless in the face of resistances. In addition, psychoanalytic therapy was burdened by Freud's changing views. In 1920, he had hypothesized the existence of a death instinct and assigned it equal importance with the sexual instinct. At the Psychoanalytic Congress in 1922, he spoke of an "unconscious feeling of guilt" and, in discussing the so-called negative therapeutic reaction wherein the patient gets worse just as he is getting better, he said there must be a force in the unconscious ego that opposed getting well. The idea of a death instinct gradually changed the whole concept of neurosis, which was now formulated as the result of a conflict between sexuality and the *need* for punishment, instead of between sexuality and the *fear* of punishment. To Reich, this contradicted all clinical experience and would make any therapeutic efforts pointless. He viewed the psychoanalysts' growing adherence to an unsubstantiated death instinct with alarm and shared his concern with Freud. Freud assured him that it was just a hypothesis, not clinically founded. Reich felt momentarily relieved, but Freud did nothing subsequently to stop the misuse of his unfounded speculations. Only Reich resisted. He continued to struggle with practical therapeutic problems.

At the Psychoanalytic Congress in Salzburg in 1924, Reich introduced the concept of orgastic potency, directing particular attention to the clinical difficulties in achieving it. Only rarely, he had found, did the liberation of genital excitations from the patient's symptoms lead to orgastic potency. Where else, then, was sexual energy bound? Psychoanalytic theory offered no solutions. It even contradicted Reich's observations that there is a fundamental qualitative difference between genitality and pregenitality. Only the genital apparatus can provide orgasm and discharge sexual energy completely. Pregenitality can only increase tension. It is obvious that these divergent viewpoints would lead to incompatible therapeutic conclusions, for if genital excitation is a mixture of pregenital excitations, the therapist's task would be to shift the pregenital onto the genital. On the other hand, if genital excitation is biological, then it must be freed from any mixture with the pregenital.

Sharp discrepancies in psychoanalytic theory were also apparent in terms of the central problem of anxiety. Freud's original assumption was that if sexual excitation is barred from perception and discharge, it is converted into anxiety. But no one knew how this conversion takes place. In wrestling with this question therapeutically, Reich observed the relation of anxiety to the vegetative (autonomic) nervous system. "There is not conversion of sexual excitation into anxiety," he concluded. "The same excitation which appears as pleasure in the genital is manifested as anxiety if it stimulates the cardiovascular system." Sexuality and anxiety represent opposite directions of vegetative excitation. Reich presented this finding to Freud toward the end of 1926. To his surprise, it was rejected. At the same time, in *Inhibition, Symptom, and Anxiety*, Freud retracted much of his original formulation about actual anxiety. Anxiety, he wrote, could be considered no longer as the result of sexual repression but as its cause. It would now become more difficult for Reich to defend the position that anxiety results from a damming up of sexual energy, i.e., sexual stasis, and that its basic mechanism is the overburdening of the vasovegetative system with undischarged sexual energy. Reich was observing physical mechanisms. "Sexual energy" was becoming increasingly real. But as he drew closer to the physiological, the breach with Freud and the psychoanalytic community widened, despite Freud's dictum that someday psychoanalysis must be given a biological base.

Reich continued to work with the reality of technical problems. Why were some patients inaccessible? Why did all his efforts rebound as from an impenetrable wall? The patients appeared "armored" against any attack. The entire person resisted. Gradually, he realized that the obstacle to recovery lies in the patient's whole being, his or her "character," which forms a unified, automatic resistance. The character armoring protected against unpleasure, but it also inhibited the capacity to experience pleasure and to function rationally. There was a stratification of armoring, a layering, which revealed a specific structure in each case, corresponding to its development. What had been repressed last lay closest to the surface. Systematic analysis of these layers of resistance provided an orderly way to reach the patient and revealed that the experiences of the past were alive in the character attitudes of the present. Reich tried to convince the other analysts, who paid little attention to character, that only the removal of the characterological basis of the symptoms could really bring about a cure.

One of the major problems in psychoanalytic theory was the question of the origin of the destructive impulses that were found in every patient. Was it biological? Freud wrote an article on "primary masochism" in which he again modified an earlier concept. Previously, masochism was viewed as the result of a destructive impulse toward the world that was turned back on the self. Now, according to Freud, the destructive impulses were expressions of a primary masochism, as was the patient's resistance to cure and the unconscious feeling of guilt. Freud was extending the death instinct theory into the most essential areas of psychoanalytic practice. Yet there was no clinical evidence for the existence of such an instinct. On the contrary, Reich found that, carefully examined, every psychic manifestation that might be interpreted as "death instinct" proved to be a destructive impulse that gave way to a sexual one. The destructive aggression bound in the character was nothing but rage over disappointments in life and, in particular, the lack of sexual gratification.

In May 1926, Reich gave Freud a copy of the manuscript of his first major work, *The Function of the Orgasm.** Freud, to whom the work was dedicated, received it coolly. "So thick?" he said. More than two months passed before Reich received a formal response from Freud, which seemed to reject the orgasm theory. In December 1926, Reich spoke on character-analytic technique in Freud's inner circle. "The main problem I presented was whether one should interpret the patient's incestuous desires in the presence of a latent negative attitude, or whether it was better to wait until the patient's distrust had been eliminated. Freud interrupted me: 'Why do you *not* want to interpret the material in the sequence in which it appears? Of course one has to analyze and interpret the incest dreams as soon as they appear!' I had not expected this. I continued to substantiate my point of view, but the whole idea was foreign to Freud. He did not understand why one should work in the line of the resistances and not in that of the material. This contradicted things he had said in private conversations about the technique. The atmosphere of the meeting was unpleasant. My opponents in the seminar gloated over it and pitied me. I grit my teeth and remained silent."

But the pain of these two bitter disappointments in Freud took a heavy toll. Reich contracted tuberculosis, a disease that had previously claimed the lives of his father and brother. In January 1927, he went to a sanitarium in Davos, from which he returned, cured, three and

---

* Revised by Reich and published as *Genitality in the Theory and Therapy of Neurosis* (New York: Farrar, Straus and Giroux, 1980).

a half months later. Work in the technical seminar proceeded, bringing some system into therapeutic practice. Reich continued to feel that he was applying analytic principles to the study of character, a task consistent with psychoanalysis.

During these formative years from 1922 to 1934, Reich was married to a woman named Annie Pink, who had been an analytic patient of his when he was a medical student. They had agreed, upon marriage, that they would remain together as long as they loved each other but would separate when either one no longer loved the other. Reich therefore felt it was essential that Annie have her financial independence. Wanting to be able to share everything with her, he encouraged her to become a physician. But according to Reich, Annie resented his insistence that she have her own career. She wanted to be taken care of and felt that he was not willing to provide for her. "I believe she never forgave me for the fact that, with my economic and emotional support, she became an independent physician and actually stood on her own feet twelve years later when we separated." Nevertheless, the first six years of their marriage, he said, were happy. A daughter, Eva, was born in 1924 and a second child, Lore, in 1928.

Although Reich worked with Vienna's destitute in the psychoanalytic clinic and was in touch with social issues and events as they were reported in the newspapers, neither he nor Annie was particularly interested in politics. However, Reich was faced with the growing contradiction between his clinical experiences and the psychoanalytic cultural concepts, which demanded renunciation and the sublimation of sexual impulses. Whoever was incapable of this was considered neurotic. Yet Reich found that, the more successful the therapy, the more difficult it was for the patient to renounce happiness. You could divert one interest to another, but you could not divert a physical tension that pressed for gratification. Furthermore, he observed that people who were genitally satisfied were more productive in their work. The psychoanalysts carefully avoided the question of what happens to physical excitation when it is free. They equated free sexuality with chaos and disorder. The patient was supposed to be abstinent during treatment; marriage and family were not to be touched. But if the goal of therapy was orgastic potency, this was impossible. Where does sexual repression and suppression come from? Reich asked. And what is its function? These questions drove him to study ethnology and sociology.

Then in July 1927 Reich witnessed a strike by thousands of workers in Vienna. The police fired indiscriminately into the crowds, killing one hundred people, while the Social Democratic defense troops, whose function was to protect the workers, walked away from the conflict and returned to their barracks. Reich could scarcely believe what he saw. This was not "class warfare"; working-class people were fighting each other. The police behaved like "senseless machines," "mechanical men." The crowds were helpless and submissive. Why? Was this culture? It was assumed that people are capable of freedom once the external oppressing force is removed. But are they? Can the masses build a free society? And what is the relation of politics itself to the real life of people? Freud could provide no answers. They could only be elicited from practical experience. After the strike, Reich joined the Austrian Communist Party and became a politically active physician.

He also studied the work of the great socialists and, in particular, that of Karl Marx. In his discovery that the value of a commodity is created by the human work power, or energy, invested in it, "Marx was for the science of economics what Freud was for psychiatry," Reich wrote. "Both claimed that social life was governed by factors independent of conscious human will. For Marx, it was the economic conditions and processes. For Freud, it was psychic, instinctive forces. Both sciences had been built on as yet undiscovered biosocial and biological laws." But these common factors were overlooked at the time Reich became involved in political life. Psychoanalysis and Marxism were considered separate and irreconcilable. "Two basic objective biological functions of the living, work and sexuality, were treated as two separate scientific systems."

Between 1927 and 1930 Reich formulated a sociological critique of psychoanalysis, utilizing Marx's methodology of dialectical materialism. It was presented in a series of publications. With Freud's approval, he founded six sex-hygiene clinics for workers where psychoanalytic sex-economic knowledge could be applied on a broad social scale. Character analysis was also developed and Reich published his findings in individual clinical articles. These writings included a clarification of the problem of masochism and a refutation of the death-instinct theory. But inevitably all psychiatric work led into the social sphere, and Reich became increasingly involved in the turbulent politics of the time. He watched the Austrian Social Democrats fail and the Christian Socialist and German Nationalist parties grow in strength. There were only about three thousand Communists in Austria, mostly among the unemployed. Reich spoke on problems of mass hygiene at meetings for the unemployed and was active in all the Communist demonstrations. But he recognized that between the wretchedness of people's real lives and the goals of social revolution there was a gap that no slogans or propaganda could bridge.

When he first started his sociopolitical activities, Reich spoke to various organizations about psychoanalysis, the Oedipus complex, castration anxiety, and so on. He soon realized that these theories had no practical use for people. They sounded ridiculous. He began to speak about human problems that affect everyone: marriage, family life, sexual difficulties, distress in adolescence. He solicited written questions from his audiences, answering every one, no matter how personal. Again and again, the discussion of real problems in people's intimate lives would lead to general social issues, and people began to develop social goals of their own. For instance, the lack of privacy in housing stimulated ideas on new architectural designs. A discussion of marital distress might lead to consideration of marital legislation, the experience of the Soviet Union, to nature, the church, belief in God. Reich's lectures generally lasted about forty-five minutes, but questions and answers continued for hours. They dealt with common life interests that cut across party and class lines. And it was precisely this that the political parties would find threatening. Their strength lay in people's helplessness. Reich was stimulating people to think and act for themselves. Instead of attacking outside oppression by the law or the state, he would suggest tasks that the people themselves could undertake to alleviate their misery, such as the organization of children's clinics.

The Socialist and Communist parties had largely ignored the problems of youth. Reich made contact with young workers and adolescents from the working class. Gradually winning their trust, he uncovered the connection between their restlessness or hostility and their genital frustration. This forced a decisive correction of a basic psychoanalytic concept. "True," he wrote, "the Oedipus complex causes the puberty conflict, but it is the actual negation of adolescent love life which causes the child to fall back into the infantile neurosis in an intensified form." The only possible solution was a full, satisfying sexual life for adolescents.

It became clear that the repression of sexuality has the function of making people susceptible to exploitation and suppression. The longing for happiness was everywhere, but so was sexual distress. Between them lay sex-negative education in childhood, denial of sexual fulfillment in adolescence, and the demand for monogamy in marriage. How could things be changed to help everyone? Little could be done medically. Individual treatment was senseless from the social point of view. But Reich still believed in the possibility of change through political action. Working within the Socialist and Communist parties, he created a movement for radical sexual reform based on the principles of sex economy. It would be called "Sexpol." He devoted himself to this cause, giving all his money except that needed to support his family. He organized meetings, founded revolutionary cells in factories, spoke almost daily at gatherings, and answered hundreds of letters. Throughout, he assumed that the socialist parties and his psychoanalytic colleagues would react positively and would want to help in this, or any other, serious social effort. He was wrong. The Marxists began to complain that Reich's emphasis on the sexual problem might divert working-class people from the class struggle, and the psychoanalysts were becoming increasingly uneasy with Reich's determination to draw the logical consequences from Freud's basic formulations and to focus on the need to prevent neurosis by changing social conditions.

By 1929, Reich had begun to realize that the basic conflict between pleasure and moral denial is anchored physiologically to muscular disturbances. Excitation is bound in chronic muscular spasms. This relation was manifested with particular clarity in masochism. Whereas the psychoanalysts maintained that the disorder resulted from a biological need to suffer, Reich's clinical research showed that masochism is the expression of a painful inner tension that cannot be discharged, the result of an imbalance between inner pressure and surface tension. Reich considered the analogy of the female egg that divides when internal pressure and surface tension reach a certain level. Since the human organism cannot do this, it can only become masochistic, pleading to an outside source for relief of tension, if it is unable to allow the orgastic discharge of pent-up energy. This organismic energy appeared to move in two directions: out of the self, toward the world, and back into the self, away from the world. The movement of expansion from the center to the periphery was expressed in sexuality. The reverse direction, from the periphery to the center, was functionally identical with anxiety. Reich hypothesized that there is one process of excitation, within which an antithesis of sexuality and anxiety is manifested in the opposite directions of biological activity.

Reich's emphasis on the function of energy was reflected in his developing technique of character analysis. Since most patients could not free associate, he used everything the patient did as a point of departure. How the patient acted and reacted became more important than what he or she said. The *form* of the communications became more important than the content, because the form was now understood as an immediate expression of the unconscious. Following the path of his clinical work, Reich discovered that correct dissolution of the psychic armor always led to a liberation of anxiety, and once this anxiety was freed, there was a chance to recover free-flowing energy and genital potency. If the capacity for genital surrender was attained, it was observed that the patient experienced feelings of current in the body, described as "streamings," and exhibited fundamental changes in behavior, a different kind of morality based on the organism's ability to regulate its own biological energy rather than on any externally dictated compulsion. The individual functioned according to a self-regulatory principle and, in so doing, exemplified precisely those characteristics of rational activity, gentleness, and strength that society reveres as ideal. Yet Freud insisted that culture depends on the suppression of instincts. That might be true for the existing culture, Reich reasoned, but does culture per se depend on this suppression?

In December 1929, Reich gave a talk to Freud's inner circle on the prevention of neurosis. It was essential, he maintained, to destroy the sources of neurotic misery. He pinpointed major areas of concern: the authoritarian family, marriage, housing, the need for economic security, and, above all, the puberty problem. The sexual happiness of youth was central to the prevention of neuroses. Freud opposed Reich's views, insisting that, even though natural sexual pleasure is the goal of life, it must be renounced. Man must adjust to the "reality" of culture. Human structure was basically unchangeable, as were social conditions. This was abject hopelessness. Reich could not understand how Freud could believe that his discovery of infantile sexuality would not effect changes in the world. "He seemed to be doing a cruel injustice to his own work. The human longing for pleasure could not be eliminated, but the social regulation of sexual life could be changed. I had grasped the biological goal of human striving which was in conflict with existing human structure. Freud sacrificed the goal to the existing structure." Reich determined to retain the goal and study the laws by which human structure develops. Sooner or later, all the political, social, and scientific forces would reject or attack his efforts. But Reich persisted, always stressing the vital connection between the social and the sexual. "Human structure is determined by the way in which the social organization influences the biological sexual energy. Hence, the sexual problem is a major aspect of social politics."

Reich's continuing involvement with social issues and his criticism of bourgeois sexual reform not only strained his relationship with Freud and the Viennese psychoanalysts but also affected his marriage. Annie shrank from Reich's radical politics and the conclusions his medical and social experiences led him to draw about marriage and the family. She forced herself to participate in the sex-hygiene clinics, but Reich sensed her hesitancy and thought she did not share his goals, especially as she expressed doubts about any new thoughts he had. She also opposed him in matters regarding their children's sexual education. Although she might agree with him intellectually, Reich felt, she could not deal with manifestations of their daughters' sexuality. Annie was better suited to the milieu of psychoanalysts like Anna Freud, who considered all children little wild animals who had to be tamed. Gradually, according to Reich, he and Annie began to long for others. Reich had an extramarital relationship with a woman he had known when he was a medical student. Annie, too, became involved with someone she had known previously, and the marriage deteriorated. Although they were not divorced until 1934, the relationship was basically over when Reich moved to Berlin in November 1930.

There his work flourished. The German psychoanalysts were more advanced in social issues, and the orgasm theory was better understood. Reich came in contact again with Otto Fenichel, with whom he had attended medical school, and Fenichel agreed to help him organize young psychoanalysts for practical social work. Reich lectured to student organizations and gave courses on "Marxism and Psychology" and "Sexology" at the Marxist Workers School, which distributed his writings throughout Germany. Communist demonstrations were more militant than those in Vienna, but the party line was the same. Very few of the leaders tried to analyze opponents and none had read Hitler's *Mein Kampf,* despite the alarming growth of the National Socialist Party since the collapse of the German banks in 1931.

There were about eighty sex-political organizations in Germany, with a total membership of approximately 350,000. They supported birth control and legal abortion and opposed the punishment of homosexuals. However, the organizations often fought among themselves, and there was no basic thinking about sexology or political organization and no mention of youth problems. Reich wanted to unite these groups under the Communist Party and train leaders in sex-political principles. Once again, the party functionaries felt threatened by the inclusion of emotional issues and maintained that Reich wanted to replace politics based on economic issues with sex politics. Reich withdrew from a leadership role and tried to set up a pilot group, but the demands were too great and the functionaries too frightened. The whole movement bogged down in organizational politics. Then, in 1932, the police intervened and the united congress of the organization was dissolved. Reich continued to teach and concentrated his efforts on youth groups, at whose request he wrote *The Sexual Struggle of Youth.* The Communist Party refused to publish it. So Reich established his own publishing house, Verlag für Sexualpolitik, and paid for the publication of the book, as well as his ethnological work *The Invasion of Compulsory Sex-Morality* and two books for children. They were received enthusiastically by the young, but on 5 December 1932, the party banned their distribution, claiming that they had nothing to do with "proletarian class morality" and that they "corrupted youth's fighting spirit." The young people continued to distribute them.

Reich's effort to understand how people experience the social process and to bring their sexual lives into that process was meeting increasing hostility from both the Marxists and the psychoanalysts. To the former, it was "unproletarian." To the latter, it was "unscientific adventuring." Reich said later that he was often tempted to give up the mass-psychological work, but his burning interest in human responses held him.

Between 1930 and 1933, he watched closely as the National Socialist movement gained power. Reich recognized that Hitler's program mirrored the prevailing human character structure. The masses' longing for sexual happiness and freedom was opposed by their fear of it. Hitler freed them from the struggle to resolve this contradiction and to assume responsibility for their own lives, the task to which Reich had devoted himself. His classic work on the mass psychology of fascism was written in 1932 and published the following year.

While the various socialist party leaders squabbled among themselves, Reich called for unified action against the planned fascist seizure of power. On 28 February 1933, he returned to Berlin from a trip to Copenhagen, where he had lectured on race and fascism to a Danish student organization. That night the Reichstag was burned. He only escaped immediate arrest because he had not held an official position. But soon afterward, a newspaper article on his youth book appeared and he had to leave Germany. He returned to Vienna, where he found little understanding of the German disaster and increasing personal hostility from his psychoanalytic colleagues. The year before, Freud had insinuated that Reich's work on masochism, which refuted the death instinct theory, was influenced by his communist ideology. Efforts were made by the president of the psychoanalytic association to curtail Reich's teaching activities, and he was told to stop lecturing in socialist and communist organizations. When he refused to submit unconditionally but agreed to consult with the committee before accepting speaking engagements, he was told that he could not attend any psychoanalytic meetings. His contract with the psychoanalytic press for *Character Analysis* was canceled "because of the political situation," and later Reich had to borrow the money to publish it himself. Members of the psychoanalytic association were advising physicians not to study with Reich. He asked the executive committee to take an official position on his work, but the secretary hedged and all Reich's efforts were futile. Finally, a young Danish physician suggested that Reich come to Copenhagen to train physicians. He was given a six-month permit by an uneasy Danish bureaucracy, which was concerned about the lectures he had given there earlier. Having borrowed the money for the trip to Copenhagen, Reich left Vienna at the end of April 1933. Annie and the children were to join him later.

In Denmark, Reich continued with his therapeutic and teaching activities, but he soon found himself in conflict with the Danish Communist Party, which ignored starving German refugees unless they were party members and angrily rejected Reich's contention that Hitler's triumph was a defeat for the German working class. In addition, there was controversy over an article by Reich that had been translated and published by an intellectual communist journal called *Plan* before he came to Denmark. Certain words relating to a child's penis had been poorly translated, and the journal editor was accused of pornography and sentenced to sixty days in jail. The party blamed Reich. It also disapproved of the interest generated in his meetings and lectures by the discussion of sexual issues. On 21 November 1933, he was excluded from the Danish Communist Party (to which he had never belonged). At the same time, conservative psychiatrists complained about Reich. This, combined with the uproar over the *Plan* article, caused the authorities to deny Reich a residency permit. One of Reich's students wrote to Freud, asking for his help, but Freud refused, acknowledging Reich's stature as an analyst but criticizing his political ideology. Despite these overt acts of hostility on the part of communists and psychoanalysts alike, Reich continued to feel himself a part of both organizations, "a badly treated and misunderstood opposition."

He arranged to move to Malmö, Sweden, in January 1934, hoping his students would be able to continue their work with him there. But first he met Annie and the children in the Tyrol after a seven-month separation and visited with analysts and exiled German communists in England, France, and Switzerland. He found no real understanding of events in Germany. No one grasped the real issue of mass psychology, the irrational reactions of the masses. On his return to Denmark, Reich passed through Germany, spending three hours in Berlin. He found it frightening: soldiers everywhere, people moving tiredly, furtive glances, the seemingly incomprehensible fact that many communists had become fascists. He was joined in Berlin by Elsa Lindenberg, a dancer and political activist he had met at a communist demonstration in 1932. They had established a personal relationship, and now she returned with him to Scandinavia.

In Malmö, Reich continued to work with his students, and he founded a new journal, *Publication for Political Psychology and Sexual Economy*. However, he was primarily occupied with plans for laboratory experiments to attempt to confirm his hypothesis that sexuality is identical with a bioelectrical charge and that the orgasm is fundamentally an electrical discharge. Intrinsic to this assumption was his clinical observation of a four-beat process in the orgasm which he called the tension-charge (TC) or orgasm formula: mechanical tension→bioelectrical charge→bioelectrical discharge→mechanical relaxation.

Meanwhile, the conflict within the psychoanalytic movement was intensifying. Reactionary analysts were gradually taking over the German organization. All Jewish members, whatever their orientation, were removed from leadership positions, and it was even suggested that they could or should retire. A group of young analysts who opposed the death instinct theorists and adhered to the possibilities of Reich's sex-political work gathered together as "dialectical-materialistic" analysts. They considered themselves an opposition group within the international organization. When Reich left Berlin, Otto Fenichel had assumed leadership of this group. He tried to run it as a secret organization, writing long, gossipy letters which were supposed to be burned after they had circulated. He carefully avoided mention of Reich's sex-economic viewpoint and his critique of psychoanalytic social concepts, and he determined to keep Freud out of the conflict. In fact, he stated that nothing new had been learned about sexuality since Freud. For all intents and purposes, the orgasm theory did not exist or was "old hat."

In May 1934, Reich's residency permit in Sweden expired and he was denied an extension. No reason was given. Once again, Freud refused to help. Reich returned to Denmark, where he lived illegally under an assumed name. Then, on 1 August 1934, three weeks before the International Psychoanalytic Congress in Lucerne, Reich received a letter from the secretary of the German association, advising him that his name would not appear on the list of German members. This had no particular significance, he hastened to add, as Reich's name would soon be listed among the Scandinavians. When Reich arrived at the congress on 25 August, however, he learned that he had been excluded from the German association in a secret meeting the previous year and thus automatically excluded from the international association. He tried to find out why this step had been taken and why he had not been informed, but the only reply he received was a shrug of the secretary's shoulders. Suddenly, a wide space separated him from his colleagues. The dialectical-materialistic analysts who had previously grouped together with him in opposition to Freud presented their papers, which were often based on Reich's work, without mentioning his name. Ernest Jones told Reich that he could not attend the business meeting and could only give his scheduled lecture as a guest. Leading analysts, including Jones, Federn, and Eitingon maligned him, saying that he seduced all his female patients and was a psychopath. With Annie's help, this slander would grow into the rumor that Reich was insane and would be repeated mindlessly to this day. The executive committee tried to convince Reich to resign, but he refused. He maintained that the orgasm theory and the concepts that grew from it did not contradict clinical psychoanalysis, but, in fact, represented its legitimate scientific development. Since the executive committee rejected these concepts, he would proceed alone and call his work "sex economy." Only the Norwegians were supportive, assuring him a place in their organization and offering him the opportunity to continue his work and use the physical laboratory at the Psychological Institute in Oslo.

Finally, on the fourth day of the conference, Reich addressed the International Psychoanalytic Association for the last time.

M.B.H.

1934

"Like fishermen, we scientists sit, perfectly ignorant, on the banks of the stream of life and cast our hooks more or less at random. Sometimes one of us pulls out mud and weeds, another fishes out a piece of gold, but a third one comes up with something that will change part of the world."

My dear colleagues!

Having been a member of the International Psychoanalytic Association for fourteen years, I am speaking to you for the first time as a guest of the congress. One year ago, the Executive Board of the German section of the organization decided to exclude me; neither I nor the Executive Board of the IPA heard about this until four days ago. Since the Executive Board approved my exclusion, it is now my strange task to give as a nonmember a report to the congress on the current status of my scientific position. It is customary for such exclusion from an organization to be carried out or to be accepted with protestations, mutual repudiation, and other unfruitful types of behavior. Since the majority of those present do not understand the exclusion, because neither my scientific views nor my political convictions nor the remarks of those responsible revealed any reasons for this action, I believe that I can best serve the cause of psychoanalytic research by trying to disclose the background to these differences. I have frequently done this in the past in various areas, but I believe that the papers presented at this congress have proved, as never before, that the gap between two irreconcilable tendencies, which I discovered some eight years ago and which has in the meantime become unbridgeable, does indeed exist, and that my exclusion means simply that one of these tendencies is currently responsible for the field of psychoanalysis. You will already have guessed that I am referring here to the gap between the representatives of the death instinct theory and the theoreticians of the libido theory.

At this point, I do not wish to set forth in detail the fundamental differences. Instead I will try to demonstrate the direction that consistent pursuit of the problems associated with the libido theory has taken me . . .

31 August 1934

LECTURE NOTES

FURTHER PROBLEMS AND SOME CONSEQUENCES
OF CHARACTER ANALYSIS

Origin of the "ego-drive" energy, with clinical case histories. Fear of falling and superficial association. Fear of object loss and characterological contactlessness. Vegetative reactions after dissolution of character armor. Muscular rigidity and character block. Some psychophysiological borderline questions.

TO LOTTE LIEBECK *
10 November 1934

Dear Lotte Liebeck:

Your letter was a great pleasure. I might have many things to say, but will have to be brief because I have little time.

While my concept of masochism, in character analysis, wrests the problem from the metaphysical realm of the death instinct, it is still far from complete. Nevertheless, it can be comprehended; one merely has to dig deep down into the analyses to reach the anxiety about the "bursting" of the genitalia. I have now finished my congress lecture and was able to expand on the relation between masochism and orgasm. Should I eventually send a copy or galley proofs to the group, for critical comment?

With Otto Fenichel the situation is *very* difficult! This friendship and inclination to understand the orgasm theory, combined with a structural inability and unconscious hostility, is a complicated problem for me. I am glad that you could judge this for yourself when you were in Sletten.

You have good reason to be deeply moved by Freud's books; he was

---

* German psychoanalyst and student of Reich's. Translation by Therese Pol.

a wonderful man. But I was even more affected by the subsequent break in his work. This is tragic. I am curious to know if you will discern it before it becomes openly manifest. It goes back to the earliest writings (predominance of symbolic interpretation over questions of dynamics, economy, genitality, etc.). But this can only be discovered ex post facto. Enjoy yourself, then, and good luck in your work.

Tomorrow will be the first decisive meeting with the physiologist.* Am very excited.

Best regards to all the colleagues and to yourself.

12 November 1934

People are armored! One feels this in every attempt at progress. This coldness and professional disinterest!

Finally had a session with Nordbo† yesterday—extremely difficult.

14 November 1934

After 1¾ years of roving, a place to live again. In Oslo, thirty-six hours from the children. Hard being without children—this active life. My vision has cost me wife and family, but it does contain an inherent logic, which is irresistible.

TO ANNIE REICH
17 November 1934

My dear Annie,

Your letter was very refreshing, and I am happy to respond to your request that I tell you more about my life. I am going through a

---

* Reich was seeking a physiologist's help to design an experiment with which he could test his clinical hypothesis that sexual excitation is functionally identical with an energy charge that can be measured at the skin's surface. Cf. *The Bioelectrical Investigation of Sexuality and Anxiety* (New York: Farrar, Straus and Giroux, 1982).
† Norwegian physiologist.

difficult, a terribly, inordinately difficult period. I came to Oslo with
some firm agreements to carry out my experiments, but as usual I am
running up against people's unsociability, indifference, and feigned,
profoundly paralyzed willingness to help. It will take a lot of effort to
overcome all this. At any rate, by a stroke of good fortune, I have
found myself an apartment to rent. Somehow or other, I will get by.
But your question about my current life is more general in nature.
Let me have a go at it. You see, Annie, about thirteen years ago when
I described to you my absolutely rotten mood and met with rejection
on your part, I did not know, and did not even suspect, that I was
experiencing in myself the much maligned vegetative longing, the
feeble vestiges of life, the ruins of the yearning for happiness on which
reactionary mysticism is based. There are three possibilities in such a
situation: one can become a resigned or melancholic cynic like Céline
(whose book I am now reading); one can be destroyed by it, like all
psychopaths in the world; or one can fight against the misery of the
world and thereby run the risk of being thought a Don Quixote.
Without realizing what I was doing, I chose this last route in becoming
a sexologist and discovering the function of the orgasm. My choice
has proved as bitter as it was unavoidable. I have so far fought my way
through many difficulties and achieved quite a lot, but the task is
immense and there is no end in sight, no matter how much I would
like it to be otherwise. The problems continue to spread like fire. Let
me give you some examples. The tension-charge law, which I see as
the basis of orgasm, seems to control the mitotic processes of cell
division; you will already have read that the sexuality-anxiety antithesis
leads to a unitary view of the vegetative apparatus. It is not my fault
that I happened to make an observation that has unearthed such an
enormous amount of material for discussion. Like fishermen, we scientists sit, perfectly ignorant, on the banks of the stream of life and
cast our hooks more or less at random. Sometimes one of us pulls out
mud and weeds, another fishes out a piece of gold, but a third one
comes up with something that will change part of the world. You must
understand that I am deeply immersed in the subject matter and, as
a consequence, I can sense perspectives long before someone less well
versed and less interested in the topic can see them. Often, such a
person regards me as a psychopath. Whether and to what extent that
is a true description of me will become clear one day, thirty or three

hundred years from now. I am not a megalomaniac, I just have agonizingly good intuition; I sense most things before I actually comprehend them. And the most important "intuitions" usually turn out to be correct, like the belief I expressed in Seefeld in 1923 that an erection is identical with the reaching out of a pseudopod, that anxiety is a retreat into oneself. Now, eleven years later, a whole new area of physiology revolves around that. You will be reassured to know that this has been confirmed to me by a physiologist.

Sometimes I feel like despairing. There are so many difficulties on all sides that I often wish I had dealt with the biophysiological aspect of the problem first before tackling the sexual-sociological side. Hostility upon hostility, conscious or unconscious, wherever I turn. People cannot stand being told that they are throwing away their lives for nothing, that they have lost their lives. This is not just sexual resistance on their parts. They are afraid of perceiving their own vegetative longing. That may sound romantic to you, but romanticism, or what is at its root, is, after all, a reality that brought Hitler to power. Is that not sufficiently material? So I am still fighting on and could not turn back even if I wanted to. Please believe me, finally, that I am not opposing Otto [Fenichel] out of masochism or for some frivolous reason. I dread the thought of it. But the man is so unthinking, for all his awareness. He has badly misunderstood my orgasm theory and everything connected with it; he is so tied to me and at the same time so hostile, jealous, nervous that I am afraid I will soon have to deal forcefully with him. If only he would just sit there quietly and call himself my personal friend but not my champion. I got on well with Barbara Lantos* in Paris, for example, after she told me that she was not interested and would not fight for the cause. I also get on with you better since you openly declared where you stand. But Otto circulates these silly letters, plays like a small child at being an organizer, and has no idea what it is all about. I would also be willing to let him go right ahead as he is doing were it not for the fact that he is already obscuring the painfully gained clarity about the method and character of dialectical-materialistic psychoanalysis, is making stupid compromises, and is a coward. It is better to have an openly declared enemy than an unconsciously hostile friend. Otto is an example to us all.

---

* German psychoanalyst who had contact with Reich in Berlin.

But there is more involved. I had to get away from your world of doubts, precisely because I loved you. I had to fight against Freud, put my good position at risk, abandon the children, make enemies with so many people. I often yearn for calm and quiet and peaceful work, but I know too much. In Scandinavia I have a group of about twenty very smart, educated, dear people. One of them said to me once: "It is almost unbearable to have a better understanding of so much, to understand so much more about human longing." The age and the society in which we live are currently against us. We work like the devil and encourage one another to hang on. We are not utopian dreamers; we proceed step by step, from detail to detail, with a basic view of life that we constantly verify. We may end up destroying ourselves, but we may also achieve a breakthrough. That is how I live.

Elsa is a major part of all this. She understands me without flattering me; on the contrary, she is sharply critical, but in a structured way. She is, however, suffering from a severe neurosis, and I am afraid that we will not be able to remain together if she is not cured. She has bravely borne all the misery of the last two years of nomadic life, but she suffered during that time and could not develop anything for herself; she relies on me, which is very difficult for her to accept as someone who is striving to be independent. Perhaps now we will get some peace. But the fact that we were stopped by the police at the Swedish border is proof that the political reactionaries are keeping an eye on us. Stockholm had notified them. And yet, I have done nothing public for one and a half years. No, these people know what it is all about.

Very often I waver and start to doubt things that once appeared as solid as a rock. But then, so many new confirming facts come streaming from newspapers, from movements like the Oxford Movement, and from thousands of details, that I cannot keep up with it all. I am suffering a great deal, but on the whole I am in good spirits and I am happy to be a pillar of support for a large group of people. (Incidentally, most of them have not been analyzed by me, i.e., have not been hypnotized.*)

It is not clear how long I will remain in Oslo. Probably one year if the experiments are a success and develop further, but most likely I will stay longer unless I manage to continue the experiments in Paris

---

* Reich had been accused of having hypnotic power over his patients.

or Vienna. Perhaps institutes in other cities will let me conduct the experiments there. But I doubt it. I would very much like to go back to Vienna. I don't know whether I will be allowed. I want to, if only because of the children. I suffer terribly from being separated from them. After all, I have only experienced a part of their growing up, and I love children so much. I will definitely have more children of my own. Later.

Perhaps, dear Annie, we will get on better with each other one day. Somewhere you have it in you, like everybody has. But this damn wall, this armor. I now understand everything much better and regret a great deal. I am not only older but also wiser, and all in all I have calmed down.

I probably will not come down at Christmas. It costs too much and right now I need an enormous amount of money for the publishing business and also for the apartment. But it's extremely difficult for me to accept the idea that I will not see the children again until Easter. What do you think about allowing Eva to come here for Christmas? I realize that it would be difficult. Think about it carefully and tell me what I should do.

How did you like the last issue of the journal? Sometimes I feel that we are talking into a great void without getting an answer but that the walls have ears that are listening attentively. Can you try to gather up a few people in Prague willing to donate about 10 Danish kroner a month? That would be a great help. We are starting to organize circles of friends. But I am not clear as to what form the future organization will take. For the time being the main work is purely scientific. All polemics against political parties have been stopped. We are now also analyzing the mass psychology of films. It is tremendously interesting and important work. One can learn a lot in the process. The work is being done by a woman in Copenhagen, an industrial artist.

Write again. It makes me so happy. Living here one feels "totally alone in space."

TO PSYCHOANALYSTS IN DENMARK, NORWAY,
AND GERMANY WHO ARE IN CONFLICT
WITH FREUD
16 December 1934*

Dear Colleagues:

My exclusion from the International Psychoanalytic Association resulted from a chain of circumstances that served the interests of my opponents. The German association did not actually want to exclude me and had taken it for granted that I would automatically become a member of the Scandinavian section. I was asked by numerous colleagues from various local groups to rejoin via the Norwegian organization, and three of its members, who were attending the congress, assured me of acceptance. I could not make up my mind at that time and wished to consider the matter. When I moved to Oslo to carry out certain experiments concerning my sexual theory, people collaborated with me as if I were a member. The close connection of my work with the IPA group, and renewed assurances from colleagues in Oslo, prompted me to reapply for membership. No one had expected that Dr. Fenichel would bitterly oppose me and use his influence against me. A few days earlier, I had asked Fenichel for his opinion, but he merely shrugged. The reason for his opposition is as follows: he said I harmed the cause of natural scientific (dialectical-materialistic) psychoanalysis; it would be better if I remained outside and if the cause were even dissociated from my name and person.

1. *Chairman Prof. Schjelderup's† stand*: Schjelderup personally favors my readmission and only wished to bring up two questions for discussion: First, are we factually (orgasm theory and character analysis) in agreement with Reich? (His other activities do not concern us.) Second, are we willing to take the risk connected with Reich's admission—for instance, exclusion of the whole group?

2. *Fenichel's function*: I must recall briefly that before I moved to Berlin in November 1930, Fenichel had neither called himself a dialectical-materialistic analyst nor been connected with the cause in

---

* Translation by Therese Pol.
† Harald Schjelderup, Norwegian psychoanalyst and student of character analysis, whose position as a professor at the Psychological Institute of the University of Oslo had made it possible for him to offer Reich a position at that institution.

any way except through my writings, which he had reviewed. In Berlin, there formed a small circle of analysts, among them Fenichel, who were interested in my scientific concepts. Since the situation in the association soon became difficult and the confusion in the field of libido theory and death instinct theory was enormous and since I had no time myself, I asked Fenichel to keep the interested colleagues continually informed on the status of the problem. I soon had the uncomfortable feeling that, although Fenichel reported on my concepts very ably and at first openly championed them, he increasingly—in direct ratio to the growing difficulties—tried to bridge contradictions, to water down concepts—in short, to reconcile all sides. In my paper "Dialectical Materialism and Psychoanalysis" I had clearly shown which of the scientific views I had always advocated were held in common [with Freudian theory]. But the contradiction between death instinct theory and orgasm theory, between the biological and the sociological concept of sexual repression, between the bourgeois-metaphysical and the dialectical-materialistic ideology had to be worked out equally clearly. I know from experience that there is no better way to serve Freud and psychoanalysis than to separate the scientific from the nonscientific within the doctrine of psychoanalysis. This is the right way to gain adherents to psychoanalysis in those circles that matter. Fenichel never wanted to commit himself unequivocally to my scientific platform. He did not want to be just one of the "Reich group," but neither did he do anything on his own to oppose the death-instinct theory and everything connected with it. Instead, he based the struggle on purely organizational questions and presented a childishly stubborn opposition. I was always against it and tried to make clear to him that a struggle within a scientific organization must be conducted along factual and professional lines, excluding political and even organizational factors. I told him that if we aroused the professional interest of our colleagues they would be more likely to commit themselves politically and organizationally. At the congress, colleagues who were friends of Fenichel's and had no connection with me made the same criticism, and when the board resorted to all its diplomatic wiles, Fenichel caved in completely. The true reason is that he never intended to risk exclusion. However, he should have come out and said so instead of hiding behind the excuse that one first has to have greater influence. How? By avoiding all controversy, by soft-pedaling one's work, and by alienating all sympathies with such timorous attitudes? Look how differently the non-Marxist Schjelderup behaved, purely instinctually! And look how much sympathy the Norwegians gained from his stand! Although I suffered an organizational defeat at the congress, sympathy for me had never run so high. It was Fenichel's job to use this as the basis for his own work. Instead, because he felt I was becoming more and more of a burden, he turned against me, became vindictive, and finally, as I have said, opposed my readmission—always on the pretext that he was protecting the "cause" from me.

3. I would ask you to note that I deeply regret having placed any confidence in Fenichel and seeking his help. I cannot entrust the dialectical-materialistic theory of psychoanalysis, which I have worked out over many years despite the gravest trials, to anyone else, nor can I dissociate myself from it. I have no quarrel with anyone doing exactly as he pleases, but I must defend myself against usurpers and other such services of friendship. Responsibility for the "cause" of "dialectical-materialistic psychoanalysis" and its core, orgasm theory, must still be reserved for me alone. Naturally, one may hold different opinions on what I have called dialectical-materialistic psychoanalysis and sex economy. But when I describe my orgasm theory as its primary criterion and when Fenichel, as has been shown, will not accept it or misunderstands it, we are back to the unhappy confusion of terminology and concepts. I therefore find myself faced with the unpleasant task of summarizing my scientific position. Basically, it consists of three main parts:

a. *The concepts held in common with Freudian theory* (the materialistic dialectic already developed by Freud).

b. *Orgasm theory* and *character analysis* as consistent extensions of Freud's natural science and, simultaneously, as representative of those theories that I oppose to death instinct theory and the interpretive technique. Part *b* is still in the realm of psychoanalysis.

c. My own concepts of sexuality, based on orgasm theory and transcending the sphere of psychology (sex economy and sex politics). Part *c* has merely points of contact with psychoanalysis. It forms an independent field: the basic law of the sexual process.

Whoever expounds a "dialectical-materialistic psychology" without explicitly expounding its very core, with the risks and sacrifices this entails, has simply made up his "own" dialectical-materialistic psychology and is at liberty to teach it. There is nothing we can do about the nuisance of activities named at whim.

I realize that these comments on the nature and particularity of the scientific trend I represent will continue to be misunderstood by those who have not experienced with me the developments of the last twelve years. I can only ask you to have patience until the planned comprehensive presentation is submitted. The basic principles worked out in special fields are set down in my published writings.

The fact that I dissociate myself from imprecise, nebulous concepts should not be held against me any more than I hold it against people that they react to my concepts cautiously or negatively. It was from my teacher Freud that I learned the art of waiting and keeping my ideas free from undesirable interpretations and mongrelizations. I prefer to have fewer relationships and, instead, more order in my work.

I would not like for this letter to be misconstrued as an attempt to alienate Fenichel's "circle" and his friends. Every colleague is of course free to identify himself with Fenichel's brand of dialectical-materialistic psychoanalysis and to declare himself against my concept. But my task can only be to continue developing the trend I have established and to keep those groups that are interested continually informed on the progress of the work. I am also grateful for every suggestion and constructive criticism.

Finally, a few comments on the struggle for the scientific trend in psychoanalysis. I do not believe that this struggle can be won without a clear-cut, courageous, and factual differentiation of common features and differences. Whoever fears exclusion—which is not so reprehensible—cannot take part and is much more valuable as a quiet sympathetic bystander than as an active fighter. It is self-evident, however, that the victory of the scientific over the metaphysical trend in psychoanalysis will be more easily attained and secured if we succeed in revealing to those groups that have plainly demonstrated their scientific orientation the various consequences inherent in the raw material of their own work. The commitment to the dialectical-materialistic trend in psychoanalysis in no way entails a similar commitment to the political trend of communism. There is no doubt that the person who is a valid scientist in his chosen professional specialty is to that extent safe from the influences of political reaction. And scientific integrity carries infinitely more weight than political commitment. Such natural scientists will someday become the decisive force of social progress. They should merely recognize the origins of the error in their work.

1935

"I happen to have a 'prejudice' in that the orgasm problem might hold the key to the most basic questions, provided we are sufficiently capable of mastering it."

1 January 1935

People are rejoicing like children because they're a year older—or more adult. The National Workers Party celebrated New Year's Eve. Strange, this mixture of narrow-mindedness, bourgeois nationalism, and revolutionary sentiment.

One should have special Sexpol groups that do nothing but carefully examine sociological events on the basis of revolutionary and reactionary content. I measure the "real" far too much by the standard of the "pure revolutionary idea" but at the same time am extremely dependent—within myself, secretly—on the opinion of the communists and the others. In the end I have usually proved to be right where I held out stubbornly—not where I yielded. The issue is: *Adhere to the principle without isolating oneself!* One must not be so revolutionary as to lose touch with the world.

Great joy: once again much pleasure with Elschen. A dear woman—and beautiful! Wonderful night! But separation is unavoidable! She won't see it through.

3 January 1935

In the Soviet Union they have supposedly proved the electrical nature of living matter! I wonder whether they also discovered the law of tension and charge. That would be wonderful, although it would annoy me a little—or maybe a lot.

TO ANNIE REICH
5 January 1935

My dear Annie,

Thank you for your kind letter, which I did not find offensive in any way at all, although you seem to assume that rational criticism cannot get through to me. Long ago I tracked down the sources of all my faults and you are right: it is indeed terrible to be materially dependent on me, but for a different reason than the one you suspect. Not because I cannot tolerate commitment. My whole being and life is one single *voluntary* commitment; I make an enormous number of sacrifices and I carry a heavy load of obligations, more than I would expect of any of my critics. I only resist taking on irrational, useless commitments, namely those that hamper me, or that might one day hamper me, in performing my principal tasks. The problems with Elsa have nothing to do with the fact that I now find her a financial burden; instead, I wish to avoid a paralyzing future. If, in fact, her neurosis does not subside, then—and I know this from my own life and profession—I will be destroyed along with her, inwardly, that is, because of an obligation I can no longer bear. Can you see that? I never felt that you were a material burden either; my analysis proved that beyond a doubt. Instead, I was reacting against the inner paralysis that emanated more and more from the relationship and was connected to your dependence on me. You write that you can speak freely with me as long as you do not want anything from me. You have hit on the truth. Experiences that I have had in recent months with other people who are financially dependent on me have finally helped me solve this riddle. The underlying problem is not that I am miserly or unwilling to give. Instead, male and female friends react in a strange way, which up to now I had not perceived, to another, entirely healthy trait in me. I heap far too much love and trust on anyone from whom I expect anything, whether personally or materially. *My armoring is inadequate.* Consequently, I provoke the other person into behaving toward me as if toward his or her own mother, with all the ambivalences that this involves. I put too much of myself into everything, and that is why the other person cannot stand it. When I then withdraw, after being disappointed, it is terrible, sometimes brutal, because I do also have the ability to detach myself. Usually it happens very late. I trust too much and expect too much. That is *my* fault; I merge with the other person. Without this, events of the kind that have occurred with Fenichel would be impossible, I should never have permitted him to use my work to fortify himself for so long and then to behave the way he did. That is my most important and disturbing failing. I love far too much and then have to hate and to hit out all the harder. I really do possess a different structure, one that does not fit into this world, and I have many fellow sufferers. I surrounded Elsa (as I did you in the first few years) with "tender care and love," holding back nothing of myself. That was the mistake. You are all much more reserved, both when you love and when you hate. The characteristic I have just described enables me to grasp the real processes of life much more easily and quickly than the average person can, but I pay for it by suffering much, much more. For example, I do not know how many people currently recognize, feel, or notice, as I do, every little sign of the destructive catastrophe that is coming our way in the form of the socialist movement. Exactly the same ability allows me to sense others' emotions before they have manifested themselves; that is what made me a character analyst. That's the point. I have very low tolerance for irrational behavior, including in myself. I detect the slightest signs of such behavior and I often think about this strange ability I have. Sometimes it makes me uneasy because it is unusual, "unnormal." This, and nothing else, is the malady. It is true that I face the threat of personal (not objective) loneliness, but that is the nature of my research work. That is, if you like, the fate that comes with making a great discovery.

I am fully capable of working, hating, and loving, and I fear only being tied to a neurotic situation that could drag me along with it. On the whole, I am very calm and the only thing I am fighting against is the need to armor myself. I am afraid that in the process I will lose my best intuitive qualities. That's serious!

I am pleased to hear that you are happy with Thomas,* and I myself would love to know the secret of how to love somebody without provoking the mother ambivalence in them. Please pass along my kindest regards.

At present I am working on the Soviet Union question ("The Sex Economy of the Soviets"). This is a very difficult and risky matter. I hope, nevertheless, that I will be able to master it. After seven years of collecting material and examining the basic ideas, I am slowly approaching the time when I should actually put something down on paper. This was another case where I had an uncanny feeling, namely, when my embryonic theories from the years 1927 to 1929 proved compellingly and consistently right. The misunderstood and aborted

---

* Thomas Rubinstein, Annie's second husband.

sexual revolution in the Soviet Union is central to resolving some very basic problems. * If you were not convinced by the most recent events, then perhaps you will be by those that are still to come.

You would be best off ordering "Dialectical Materialism and Psychoanalysis," like everything else, directly from Copenhagen. I have nothing here except the copies I am working with.

Much love and all the very best to you.

8 January 1935

I am gradually beginning to understand what makes for people's sluggishness. It is their tie to a reactionary social environment. If the environment were revolutionary, they would be equally bound to society but would be rushing forward. Consider how many problems must be solved, how many scientists there are—and what they are doing. Their veneer is false modesty. Their core is vanity. Afraid of taking a stand, they discuss trivialities and avoid the main issues—and rattle on about objectivity. It's enough to make you puke! I suggest factual decisions and they barricade themselves behind bureaucratic formalities. Man is neither good nor evil, he's just helpless. There is no greater lie than the statement that work is man's fulfillment! Not in our times! Not as long as work is an obligation! Shall we succeed in replacing membership in formal organizations by identification with a cause?

Engels sensed the necessity of that substitution.

---

* Cf. *The Sexual Revolution: Toward a Self-Regulating Character Structure* (New York: Farrar, Straus and Giroux, 1974).

TO LOTTE LIEBECK*
15 January 1935

Dear Lotte L.:

Ever since I decided to stick strictly to my work, I've begun to perceive the emptiness, waste, and injustice of the entire conflict. You're right in pursuing a straight line by working through Sigmund's theory. The only constructive thing one can do today is to analyze the nature and origin of the "split" with complete intellectual honesty and independence. I've done my part—and that's the end of it. I scarcely have time to carry on this controversy. The experiments are about to begin, the character-analytic seminar is starting, and, besides, I have other things to worry about: it will be very difficult to work out, unaided, the abundance of problems presented by the clinical aspects of character analysis. Every day I run into new technical questions, which in turn give rise to new theoretical questions. I realize more and more how sinful the death-instinct theory really is. What a choking-off of life itself! Meanwhile I've had my congress lecture, "Psychic Contact and Vegetative Current," typed up. Could you study it together with your colleagues and gradually start the collective work by making constructive criticisms before I publish the paper? That would be a real beginning. I intend not to publish one comprehensive paper on the problem but to work it out successively in monographs. Thus I hope to establish, in the foreseeable future, a detailed basis for my concept of the two kinds of work performance whose differentiation is so important.

One more thing: Nic Hoel† had the idea that we should start thinking about ways of protecting character-analytic technique from unwelcome distortions. What do you think? How should we go about it? I think it's important to start soon—this is bound to become a fad. We would have to establish definite training requirements. I'll never permit the work to get out of my hands; it is my strongest weapon. Please write me about this. It is also in the interest of the younger colleagues. Under no circumstances will I allow the IPA, after the way they treated me, to "practice" their own character analysis.

* Translation by Therese Pol.
† A Norwegian psychiatrist and student of Reich's.

I completely share your opinion about the *Three Contributions,** with two exceptions: genitality is completely left out, and I consider his theory of constitution to be inaccurate. By the way, our circle has translated the book into Danish. I've written the preface for the translation.

I would like to know who in your circle would be a serious candidate for the rigorous problems of character work and the orgasm theory.

TO FELIX DEUTSCH †
21 January 1935

Dear Doctor:

I am extremely sorry that I did not recall the paper you sent me. But please remember the difficult conditions under which I have had to work over the past two years. In my paper (which is only part of a series of contributions on "personal sex economy") I was not interested in taking a stand on the concepts of psychophysical interrelations. I would not presume to undertake such a critique. The way I see it, my only task is to develop my orgasm theory in whatever direction the facts will take it. So, for the moment, all I can do is exact research. As for the available literature, I can only say—and this also applies to your paper—that it does not deal with the orgastic function. Now, I happen to have a "prejudice" in that the orgasm problem might hold the key to the most basic questions, provided we are sufficiently capable of mastering it. But we are still far from it. I did not even succeed in arousing any interest in it for use in clinical psychoanalysis. If I may be permitted to point out characteristics of my work that distinguish it from other pertinent literature, I would first of all call attention to the connection between sexuality and vegetative anxiety rooted in the orgasm function, which I stressed as early as 1926; furthermore, the

---

* Liebeck had stated that Freud's *Three Contributions to the Theory of Sex* contained "just about everything that can basically be said on the subject! Everything else strikes me as mere elaboration."

† Internist interested in psychosomatic research. Translation by Therese Pol.

conscious application of dialectical-materialistic methodology to psychology and physiology. I know that the concept of psychophysical functional identity is gaining more and more ground. However, I postulate a different concept: *identity and, simultaneously, antithesis,* which is a problem for dialectical materialism and will have to be developed from concrete facts. In a forthcoming paper I carry this thought into the characterological field. You will no doubt be interested to learn that Oslo's physiological and psychological institutes have expressed their readiness to help me master these problems. Beginning next week, the hypothesis of the electrophysiological nature of the orgasm and of sexuality in general, developed from the clinical application of analysis and character analysis, will be tested experimentally. I think it is important not only to assert that both psychophysical parallelism and the mechanistic interaction theory are wrong while the unitary (plus antithesis) concept seems to point in the right direction. Above and beyond this we must prove experimentally what this unity *demonstrably* consists of. I believe I have been successful with respect to the detailed functions of the parasympathetic and sympathetic systems (sexuality and anxiety). But under the circumstances I do not see how today's psychoanalytic concept of anxiety is at all tenable. Perhaps I am mistaken in this respect.

I would appreciate any criticism or suggestions, also for a review of my work in a scientific journal. The problems on which all of us are working together will require much more effort and will not be solved without overcoming a great deal of confusion.

20 January 1935
So Elschen is going to Berlin—I am faced with miserable loneliness. What sacrifices this mess requires! She thinks she'll be back soon. No, it's too difficult here with me. And I can't stand lukewarm relationships. Either the contact goes without saying or. . . . In a way I am *very* angry that she is leaving me. I demand too much.

We, E. and I, were living outside time! E. has escaped back into time.

All this is gibberish. I am simply afraid of tying myself down to an

unhappy situation—can neither let E. go nor chain her to me completely.

28 January 1935

If only Elsa would get well! Fenichel's patients are deserting him
following my first lecture on "Character."

TO ELSA LINDENBERG
3 February 1935

My darling girl!

Today I received two letters at once and I was overjoyed. I sent you
the flowers not with sinister intent but just because I needed to, because I was thinking of you and dreaming of spending a happy future
with you. It is good for me to be in contact with you in this way. I
believe, in fact, that you have loosened up quite a bit.

Now to something else: I am very sorry that I did not compose my
last letter with more care. You must have had the impression that I
was applying pressure or trying to force decisions. But all I wanted to
do was to tell you once more what has to be decided so that you have
a clearer idea and can give your analyst a better sense of the current
situation. But rest assured that I am not interested in putting you under
pressure; on the contrary, I would not expect to get anything out of
that because I know that neither of us would benefit if you returned
without the inner readiness to do so. You know that it is difficult to
fool me, except perhaps where faithfulness is concerned. So I am all
in favor of your taking your time, no matter how difficult that may be
for both of us. We will get used to it, even if we do not exactly like
it. Let me stress again that I would advise you to take six hours of
analysis a week. Pay for it out of the support payments, and the rest
I will make up for now. There is still time to decide whether your
analysis should take place entirely in Berlin or whether you want to
continue it here later. At any rate, we both know that our relationship
deserves to be very well cared for and protected. Neither of us would
benefit if you came reluctantly or out of duty. Perhaps one of us will

be overcome by longing and will commit a little faux pas. But please, let's not have any "principles"!

Today, I skied all by myself in the Normarka. It was wonderful. I felt fine all alone like that. I shall go out again tomorrow. These past few days I have been working a little less hard, perhaps due to a lack of "sex economy." But things will be all right. The only strange thing is how completely the recent difficult weeks have disappeared from my consciousness. I can barely recall them anymore. That proves a great deal: namely, that you are still my darling girl or, if you prefer, you are my darling wife (don't be afraid; you are not committed to anything; in the psychoanalysis think of your fear of totally committing yourself and the resulting tendency to flee). Your photograph is still smiling at me. I love it very much.

Please, if you have a dress made for yourself, make sure that it is of simple, smooth material—good silk—and clings tightly to your breasts. Below the hips the skirt should be full and hang loose; it should be high-necked or have a nice little neckline. Wear it just for me. Let other people be looked after by somebody else. I am not a weakling or a masochist.

So far, I just could not find it in me to be unfaithful to you, simply because I did not (yet) have the need. You still live on too vigorously inside me.

So, my girl. Hold your head up. Everything will turn out fine!!

I kiss both your sweet little breasts, which for the time being are still *mine*.

TO ELSA LINDENBERG
5 February 1935

My dear girl,

By now you will no doubt have received both my letters. I did not write for two days, yesterday and the day before, not because I was out but because I am actually going through a state of change and do not know which way to turn. Forgive me if I have unloaded serious problems on you. You need rest and time for reflection; but it is wrong

of you to say that you have conflicts with me. Your conflicts are with
your mother, and just about everybody else, and you have merely
transferred them to me. I am just the scapegoat. In the present situation, all I can do is wait helplessly. Professionally, I am doing better
than ever. But I've been through this before. Whenever I create a stir,
that is usually precisely the moment when a major storm blows up.
There is a lot of talk of hostility, or so I was warned by a woman who
is a friend of Philip's.* Yesterday I had a long conversation with a few
of my closest friends. Some of them had already realized for themselves
that the attacks to which I am exposed are nothing more than the
reactions of people to my research work. Whoever cannot see that has
absolutely no understanding of anything. In fact, I am even wondering
whether I should continue to give my university lectures. There is no
need for me to say anything dangerous. The topic alone and my ability
to present it, which the people here find so striking, are sufficient
provocation. This is all very unpleasant. But there is nothing I can do
about it except to be very, very careful. There is a reason why I am
writing this to you. And I was unable to write these past few days
because I did not want to alarm you; I wanted to give you time first
to come to terms with yourself. At all events, in reaching your decisions, you must take into account the nature and consequences of my
work. You and I would both prefer to part while the memories we
have are sweet and dearly cherished rather than to have you become
nervous again so that I feel you are holding me back. In fact, you only
do that when you are confused, but it's not good when it does happen
and I would like to be fond of you as long as I live, even if we separate
now. My dear girl, please only come again if you can be *totally*
committed, not just so-so or because you feel compelled or out of
other considerations, including financial ones. Please don't be angry
at me when I put it like that. I am trying to be, and indeed I feel,
completely honest. I could lead that sort of existence with any other
woman, but probably not with you. We are not made for that. That
is not "asking too much." But you and I can only tolerate coolness
between us, certainly never hostility. Another thing: I did not really
want to write and tell you this yet. Advise me what I should do. I will
probably not be able to bear a long period of separation without be-

* Tage Philipson, Danish physician and student of Reich's.

coming numb and indifferent. I feel that one simply cannot accept a pointless separation for longer than two weeks without losing interest. One could perhaps make a go of it, but it would be a struggle and involve a great deal of sacrifice. Sometimes I have the feeling that you will soon be there for me again.

Somehow, I'm running out of breath now. I don't know what more to write. Ah, yes! I am ashamed to say it, because I know that it is not good to say it. Nevertheless, here it is: I am fighting against feeling angry at you. I know this is stupid, but you know how often my mother left me when I was very, very small. And things like that leave their mark. In the past I tended simply to turn away from them. Ever since I have clearly understood the problem, I have been able to control myself. Nevertheless, I have genuine reasons for not wanting to remain alone for a long period of time. I simply cannot do it. This does not mean that I want you to come back as soon as possible whatever the circumstances and no matter how you feel. It is a part of my health that I can sense when someone is truly there or when it is only compulsion. I would just like to know whether and how long I must wait and whether and when I should let go.

Although I realize the urgency of your conflicts, I also have to tell myself that I cannot remain hanging, nor can I carry everything myself. In a nutshell: I do not know what to do. It would not help if you were to come back the same as you were when you left. You are right in saying that it is better for us both and in the interest of our continued relationship if you stay away. But I am not a little lamb that will wait patiently to see what is going to happen to it. Please, my dear girl, for goodness' sake do not take that as a reproach or an attempt to apply pressure. But with whom else should I discuss my needs? For the time being, it has to be with you. It is also quite impossible for me right now to get used to another woman. Just the thought of it makes me sick. And even if I did find someone nice, I would always feel it would be unfair to "send her away" if you ever decided to return. This really is an awful situation.

How is life for you right now and what are you doing in general? Are you visiting old friends? How do you spend your day? Do you exercise? Are you reading anything?

Please, Elsa, if I have to write to you two weeks, two months, or four months from now that I cannot go on like this, and if you can't

either at that time, then don't be angry with me, but go on loving me
as before and understand me. Why am I writing this now when it is
not yet relevant? Because I feel great conflict in me and I know that
in the near future it will have to be resolved if I am to have the strength
to continue.

All our friends here send you their fondest regards. They know
nothing about what is happening. They regret that circumstances have
forced us apart and they would dearly love to see you come back.

There are a lot of discussions and lectures going on here now; there
is a bit more life than just before and during Christmas.

One more thing, my darling! I have such vivid memories of your
body and your sweet nature that for that reason alone I balk at the
mere thought of seeking love elsewhere. I don't want to. If it were not
for your neurotic problems you would now be my dear wife, even
without a marriage certificate. But you don't want to be. And I know
that you are in the same state as I am and that it will be a long, long,
very long time before either of us can embrace another. So it is understandable that the most deep-felt love is the most determined to
break apart.

Please excuse this letter. Perhaps I won't write again for a while
because I can only write what I feel, and it is not always best to put
such things into words.

At the end of this month I will deposit two hundred kroner for you.
I don't think I can manage any more than that, not unless I borrow.
This month, in fact, I also have to borrow to help pay off 1,800 kroner
worth of promissory notes that have come due. But in three months
it will all be over. Don't have any scruples about it.

Greetings to your mother and everybody else.

When you lie in bed on Friday at twelve midnight, focus your
thoughts on the two of us, together. I'll be doing it as well.

Much, much love and kisses. I must not indulge in yearning, nor
must I do anything silly.

18 February 1935

I see it all clearly! First, it's not my aggressiveness but my lenience
that is wrong. Second, I appeal to people, they feel attracted, are afraid

of becoming involved, and then run away. I don't use force on people but I awaken the fear of being ensnared.

TO ANNIE REICH
26 February 1935

My dear Annie,

To be alone is horrible but also very useful. It occasions many thoughts and discoveries. This epidemic of neuroses is the plague of modern mankind. Elsa collapsed because of all the uncertainties and had to go to Berlin for analysis because there is nobody here for her; but she will probably be back in about two weeks and we will do our best to accommodate her here. We are facing the difficult question of whether to make our relationship a permanent one. We would both like to make it permanent, but we are both all too familiar with the miseries of marriage. It is not an easy thing to decide.

I have also learned to accept injustices without bearing grudges. The fact that I have not been allowed to see the children for a whole year is not surprising, given the circumstances. But it is unnecessary for all kinds of doubts and reservations to be immediately put in my way whenever I try to overcome this constraint. And you and your father are behaving in a somewhat dictatorial way. Let me worry about the money. The question of what to do this summer depends mainly on whether or not I can get away from here. And that in turn depends on the Character Analysis Summer School that we wish to hold. If some of the students decide to go with me to the Tyrol, then I will be very happy. If not, then it is impossible for me to come, because four weeks is not enough for such a distance and I could not stay away any longer for financial reasons. If I cannot get down there, then the children must come up here, or we will not be able to see each other for another whole year. Is that good for them, particularly for Eva? In short, I have in mind to come down to you. Elsa also advised me to do that. I myself would love to see Austria again. We must start giving some thought to the place. Grundlsee, Zell am See, or somewhere in the vicinity (I would like to go swimming), possibly Ötztal, would all be acceptable. Why don't you also suggest some places? I would need two single rooms because Elsa would probably come with me. We would get on with each other this time; and if we don't, we can be careful. Would you start having a look around for something now? In any case, there is always the possibility that I will not be able to get away from here. And it is wonderful here. You would really enjoy it.

As far as Eva's puberty is concerned, I am much more worried than you two. I understand it a little differently than does Bertl.* In particular, if the child adapts too easily or shows any sign of coldness, that is in my opinion a pathological condition. It is quite clear to me that Bertl has not understood Eva, and you should by now be able to trust my judgment in such matters. But I can do nothing and I am just a little worried about this child and also about Lorchen. It is not true that I am neglecting Lorchen. I always write her extra letters. But she very seldom replies.

All in all, it is not a good situation. Only my work here is going very well.

I was very, very happy to hear that you have finally found some work, something in which you can be independent. You are a smart woman. Would we be able to understand each other better after all those terrible years? I have only just realized, fully realized, what was wrong with us. Out of love for me, you should have made an effort to understand my work, and I should have tried to be tolerant. But I was so alone and struggling desperately. In addition, I now realize that people are simply afraid of me because I am "too seductive." After all the many disappointments, I have become much calmer but also colder and more indifferent toward others.

Please write soon about this summer. I am looking forward to it.

The work on Russia is going ahead full speed. We will have a lot to discuss about it. Give my best wishes to Thomas and tell him that I am also looking forward to discussions with him.

With kindest regards and kisses.

---

* Berta Bornstein, with whom Eva was in psychoanalytic treatment.

TO ELSA LINDENBERG
28 February 1935

Dear Elschen,

Your letter of Sunday night did not reach me until this evening. I do not think that it would be useful right now to go into all the points you raise. We will have plenty of opportunity to do that later.

Accommodations: Whatever happens, I have given my notice here effective 1 June. I would have liked to have a second apartment in the building, but the swine did not want to go down to 250 kroner for both apartments. Not much is lost, because you need a larger room in the city anyway. In any case, I shall rent a large apartment with four or five rooms, or I will take two separate apartments. I have now set up an office with a secretary, and I need an extra room for that.

I am not in favor of your coming here any later than the ninth. I fully understand your wish not to travel right in the middle of your monthly period, but it is more important to think of the other matter. Each additional day later makes it more difficult to get the work going. I have everybody and everything fired up here and it would be wrong to let it all cool down again. Apart from Raknes,* who has written to you, Hoel† is also getting in touch with some people from the theater. With the permit from the institute, you will be able to do everything you want, probably even appear on the stage. When I see how relatively easily everything is falling into place, I am a little sad that we could not have had all this with a little less pain. What I am doing for you now is no more than what I have always wanted to do, but you never wanted to accept it. Since nobody praises me, I will have to do it myself: There are few people around who can match my self-discipline in understanding and tolerating other people. I hope that I will have as good a friend around one day when I collapse. But then everybody will run away, or they will give me cheap advice, telling me to be less aggressive or to stand there and let myself be slaughtered. I no longer get into a rage when I think of this rotten kind of "friendship."

Now, Elsa, I am very, very happy that you have gained some clarity. Briefly I thought you had gone past the point of no return, but I think

* Ola Raknes, Norwegian psychoanalyst.
† Sigurd Hoel, Norwegian writer and husband of Nic.

your earlier ability to experience pleasure has returned. And that is enough for a start. You will, of course, continue with your analysis here in Oslo, so that you get completely and entirely out of the mess. Unless you provoke me too much, my love for you will enable me to find the necessary patience. But in the last few days I have been through a bit of a crisis again, and it has changed me somewhat. Once more I got rather mad at the fact that I cannot, and am not allowed to, be myself, that people treat me in such a way that I have to be unnatural, tactical, calculating. In short, I am not happy. You will find me somewhat changed and pensive. Do not let that frighten you. These past seven weeks will not have been easy for you. I also had to struggle with deep nagging doubt, and I am still not over it entirely. You will probably have to doctor me a little bit with your dear ways of loving to make up for the last few weeks. After all, I am not made of wood and I certainly have sensitive nerves. But I have coped well with all the devilry. Don't forget the serious disappointments I have had to quietly overcome these last several months: Fenichel's meanness; the disappointment in people who make me promises that they cannot keep; it was very tense and difficult. All my work seemed to be going to pot. But I didn't let it. Then there was you with your problems. You who have meant everything to me. It really was not an easy time. And there was nobody to whom I could turn. I had to help myself. It was good training. As a result I have become a bit more mature and wiser, but not yet older. One more thing: Even though I also recognized what was wrong with me, that doesn't mean that my friends' behavior is or was correct. If I am guilty of giving too much of myself, then it is the fault of the others that they do not know how to take. In short, my love, there has been quite a bit going on and we should spend a quiet evening together discussing it all. Then I will find out whether my little Elsa is still able to empathize as well as she used to. I think she can.

You will not have to wander around again in the near future. I intend to remain here for quite some time. And, if it has to be, Elsa, then you will have learned something and built something up so that you can also live without me if you cannot share the load. We must find a way to lead a married life without being married, to live together but independently. I still have to get rid of a few of the problems that have afflicted me recently. I am afraid that I cannot return all that soon to a harmlessly naive and natural state. I have learned to be careful. I believe that the only way I can ever again find the strength to overcome all these problems is by experiencing clear, unequivocal love. Perhaps you can help me. I would like to be my old self once more. Also, do not forget that it is only since you fell ill that you have found my love insistent; before that you were fully able to accept it. Remember also that I did some silly things out of fear that our relationship might be ruined. Now I have learned to adopt a more distant attitude, perhaps just a little too much so.

Today I received a very kind letter from Malinowski.* He is very enthusiastic about the *Invasion*.† He is singing its praises everywhere and is using my theories in his lectures. He wants to introduce the book into America. It was a very nice letter. Things are slowly starting to pick up, and all this tremendous effort might turn out to have been worthwhile, possibly even before I am too old to enjoy it.

I shall expect you, then, on Saturday morning or evening. It is good that the following day is a Sunday. Make good use of the last few hours and get as much done as you can. Our young lives deserve it. Do be sure to book a sleeper.

TO ELSA LINDENBERG
1 March 1935

Dearest Elsa,

I should really be more restrained because you don't like my stormy nature, but I don't wish to deny it; I want to live it to the full and if you don't want to have that side of my character, then it will just seek out another loving woman. (Now I am being nasty!) In short, Elsa, I have been rather silly. We now have a small house I am renting from one of my patients. I might even buy it. On the ground floor there is a very large, bright room with a fireplace and balcony. Behind that,

* Bronislaw Malinowski, Polish anthropologist.
† *The Invasion of Compulsory Sex-Morality* (New York: Farrar, Straus and Giroux, 1971).

on the road side, there is another room, nice and large. It looks out onto forest. The house is near the fjord where Drammensvejen and Bygdöalle meet. The front faces south. There are stairs leading up to two large rooms and two smaller ones. I have divided it up as follows. Downstairs you can have your workroom and your own bedroom. Upstairs I will have my waiting room, workroom, and office for the institute. Bath, hot water—everything is available. There is a rose garden out front. In short, it is a very nice little new house. It would cost 150 kroner a month if I decide to buy it. Actually, what that means is that most of the money is paid by some lousy bank that then charges interest (120 kroner, 30 for water, etc.). I would make an arrangement with the seller to pay her in the form of psychoanalytic sessions. If we rented, it would be more expensive, namely 250 kroner a month. Buying is therefore better, because then I could also sell it myself later on. I am becoming quite a bourgeois in my old age. But Bert Brecht has also got a small house. Mine is not as grand, though. I have made the deal conditional on your liking the place. You would be right in the middle of the best area and you would have a wonderful workroom. Look how quickly and simply everything goes when one is happy, in love, not suffering from neurosis, and the sun is shining.

How would it be if you came *before* the ninth, i.e., before your monthly period. The few days do not make a great difference, and then everything would get under way here. I'm all in favor of that! Secretly, so are you; but Elsa has got principles. I know.

I wanted to take a trip up into the mountains recently, but I am saving it to do with you.

Yesterday I gave a brilliant lecture on the character of children. The members of the audience all told me that they were very happy with it.

Just imagine. Fenichel intends to write an article criticizing me and Kaiser;* in one of his papers Kaiser had officially declared his support for my technique. Fenichel has therefore placed himself at the head of the "movement," but of course as a friend. My colleagues gave him a very hard time at the last meeting. I shall not lift a finger in this respect. The whole thing is very sad but hardly affects me anymore. I am very calm and working extremely well.

* Hellmuth Kaiser, a psychoanalyst.

The days are crawling by slowly. I think affectionately of you almost every day; once again I feel you so extraordinarily alive. Spring is coming. It is still light at six in the evening. The surroundings are marvelous. I hope Elsa will bring her dear face with her—the one from before. She ought to. And if she doesn't, then I shall just withdraw again.

Elschen, be a darling. Pack up your things as if you were preparing for a trip, get on the train, and come. Be bold!!!!!! I am curious to see whether you are capable of doing it.????!!!

With sweetest kisses.

TO ELSA LINDENBERG
6 March 1935

My darling, my Elschen,

I am in a great mood again. I just arrived home at 1 a.m. from a seminar evening at which Schjelderup gave an excellent report on a character-analytic case. It was the first time in the twelve years that I have been fighting alone for my technique that another person has reported on a case in a manner in which I recognize my work, my battles and struggles. To be quite honest with you, I was a bit touched. Afterward I heard that Gerö, * without having written to me first, had announced that he would give a talk at the IPA on Friday. I am used to people's lack of gratitude, but it annoys me nevertheless. How strongly people depend on organizational structures, and how unwilling they are to stand by one in true friendship.

I am sitting here now full of anticipation at the thought of seeing you again. I am listening to the radio, drinking whiskey, and feeling quite sentimental. I am waiting for you *with all my love*. I do not want to think about whether I will be disappointed or not. I am already imagining kissing your thighs, your mouth, your sweet breasts. I love you very much. And if you disappoint me, I will crawl away into a corner and weep. But I would not fall apart, my Elschen. I have so

---

* George Gerö, a psychoanalyst and student of Reich's.

much to tell you about myself, about us. I am fantasizing a great deal about having a child, *our* child. I want a child by you, particularly you! You won't run away again, will you? And if you do, then I will wait again. Ah! Elsa, how willing I am to love you, how very much I want to give you pleasure—to you—to us both.

I am very excited.

I am looking forward to the evening when we will talk to each other, look into each other's eyes, and hold each other's hands. I feel your beautiful body, my body in you. Elsa, woman, take me completely, be my Elsa, hold to me as I will to you, as your friend and comrade. I know that we belong together, I know that our child would be a dear, beautiful child. I want a child by you! And you want it too—I know that also!

You wrote that you have me "the whole year—but Berlin only once a year!" Elschen, I understand that but *I* would give up Berlin if I could have *you*. Ah! I am just a silly young boy, quite silly. I yearn for your arms. Do I love you more than you love me? What a silly question! I want to build a life with you. I am so filled with longing and there is no other for me but you. My dear, sweet girl, if you come, love me, be gentle, be a mother and a lover, understand me. I deserve it.

I am looking forward to having you here *so very much*, with a wide-open heart like the wind blowing over mountain slopes or causing the telephone wires to sing, like flying all alone in the vast expanse of space. The world is so immense. Part of it is our love, part is my love for you. I embrace you.

8 March 1935

Tomorrow my Elsa is coming. What a great fool I was. I want to live with this woman and have children. It will work out. When I kissed my first wife for the first time, I asked her to marry me. Since then my fears have prevented my offering another woman a lasting commitment.

But Elschen is my woman—to a certain extent she was justified in being angry with me.

TO LOTTE LIEBECK*
11 March 1935

Dear Lotte L.:

I feel you're doing character analysis an injustice if you believe that it is merely catharsis, combined with a thorough working-through, that makes it something new. The old could only be freshly re-created because I succeeded in discovering *the armor* and its structure as a fact. I've come to realize more and more not only that the orgasm theory has established a new branch of science but—above and beyond this—that many old concepts either have become untenable or must undergo complete revision. This could well be discussed at length and in detail. I can't deny that I sometimes feel dizzy when I gaze at the new vistas and at the uncertainties surrounding the mastery of the tasks ahead. A while ago it occurred to me that I might tackle the problem of the prevention of neuroses concretely, in a kindergarten where I would study by direct observation the emotional freezing of children and find ways to prevent it. This seems to me entirely feasible.

TO ALFRED PINK†
15 March 1935

Dear Father,

We will probably never agree on the education of the children, and in particular not where Eva is concerned. You single out for praise the way in which she currently wants nothing to do with sexual topics, but this is precisely what makes me extremely worried, and remember, I have had almost twenty years of very painful experience in this field. However, it would be going too far to explain and prove here in great detail just what problems a child experiences on entering puberty and how that child starts to shut him- or herself off from the problems if they are too much to cope with. The present calm is, I admit, pleasant,

* Translation by Therese Pol.
† Annie's father.

but it is a potential source of many dangers that will show up at a later date. But I have learned that I should not try to make either the world or my own children happy in any way, and by myself I can do nothing to fight against the present ideology. One day, things will be different. I hope very much that Eva is strong enough to get through puberty bravely despite all the problems, the atmosphere, and the various influences. My experience in life has made me grow used to the distrust of my medical, sexual-psychological, and pedagogical views, which comes through all the time in your letters. So far, however, it has usually—I almost wrote "unfortunately"—proved to be the case that I was right after all. I realize, too, that I will never see eye to eye with Annie on this topic either. Before closing, let me give you the following analogy:

When plants growing in a garden that has never been watered— i.e., where the natural conditions for development do not exist—get into difficulties and someone comes along and waters them because, let us assume, it has not rained for a long time, someone else will come along and say, "Let the plants develop in peace."

Yes, I would let Eva develop in peace by herself if it were not for the fact that the entire social situation in which she is growing up is lethal. I am doing nothing more than occasionally giving some water to a plant that needs water but never gets any. I am aware that this is only a surrogate. I am also clearly aware that some time from now, perhaps even within a hundred years, people will be appalled at the way in which we deal with the sexuality of our children and they will compare our methods with those of the Middle Ages. You do not know that in a somewhat different atmosphere, namely in Sletten, Eva read the Malinowski book* and discussed it calmly and sensibly with me. And if Malinowski sends her the book, then he knows what he is doing. However, if Eva feels that Berta Bornstein, you, Annie, and all the others are upset because "she is reading such a book," then obviously her conscience is going to trouble her. But neither Eva nor Malinowski's book is to blame for that.

* The Sexual Life of Savages.

TO ANNIE REICH
25 March 1935

My dear Annie,

Thanks for your welcome letter. Why do you just let life "take its course"? I try to shape it the way I want it, as long as I can. I know that the age in which we live is against this and that the situation will grow worse in the coming years. But I do not want simply to give up. The fact that we have drifted apart is not so terrible after all, but it is hard that we can see each other only infrequently. Still, we have remained the very best of friends and I feel that you now understand me much better than you did before, as I do you. We would have been spared so much if we had both started out with the knowledge we have today. Are we getting old? I don't think so. Not yet! I, at least, feel very young, but I have become just a little too wise. When I think of how I set out on 6 October 1928 with 250 companions to take on 30,000 others in riots in Wiener Neustadt, how I said goodbye to you and the children, etc., then it strikes me as odd.* But I do not regret these acts of "stupidity." They were extremely instructive and there are many things that I would understand much less well today if I had not allowed myself this foolish behavior. But now that is all in the past, probably and . . . unfortunately!

It is just so dreadfully sad, so utterly terrible, to watch with one's own eyes as people march straight toward death, without zigzagging as much as possible before they get there. This does not make the time any shorter, but the path is longer and more interesting. The war is probably just around the corner and it will be bad.

Yesterday the apparatus finally arrived.† It is a tremendously clever piece of equipment and I stand small and stupid alongside it, not understanding a thing about it. And the physiologist is as stiff as a rod. I am filled with despair. I feel like an untrained tourist with mountain

---

* Reich refers to an experience in which a small group associated with the Communist Workers Defense Organization set out to prevent a march of the Austrian Fascist Party's Home Defense Force and to lead the Social Democratic troops in destroying it. This incident is described in *People in Trouble* (New York: Farrar, Straus and Giroux, 1976).

† Reich refers to the oscillographic equipment to be used in his bioelectrical experiments.

boots on my feet and an ice ax in my hand standing at the foot of Mount Everest. I do not know whether I should learn how to operate the machine (it would take at least two years) or whether I should have an assistant come here from Germany. That would cost a lot of money. And what if the whole thing is a flop?

So, I should go to Grundlsee? I am giving it a lot of thought! I don't know how I can simply take off for six weeks and not earn anything in that time. When exactly will you be on holiday? I suggested a possible solution to Father today. Ask him to tell you what it was. I am too tired right now from dealing with a difficult patient to describe it all over again. (I am slowly beginning to understand the phenomenon of psychic dulling. Strange.) Is it totally out of the question for you to come here for a few weeks if it turns out that I really can't make it to you? That's only a maybe. I have heard nothing from the children for a long time now.

On Saturday, right on my birthday,* we drank a toast to the new apparatus. It was a nice occasion. Despite all the hopes I have that my work here will be successful, I am still giving a great deal of thought to returning to Vienna after about a year unless there are reasons not to—for example, a war in which I would have to take part. It is not all that bad here, merely too far removed from the rest of the world. I am after all a restless spirit. Are you thinking of staying on in Prague forever? How is your practice and what about your private relationships? Do you get to meet a lot of people? Do you know Gunnar Leistikow from Copenhagen? He is now in Prague. The *Neue Weltbühne* is supposed to have commissioned a series of articles about my work from him.

I think about us both frequently and with a great deal of nostalgia. It is not easy just to wipe that all out. That's good.

Farewell and look after yourself.

---

* Reich was born on 24 March 1897.

TO LOTTE LIEBECK*
30 March 1935

Dear Lotte L.:

This is my first chance to answer your letter in detail. Your letters are a great pleasure. You and Schjelderup are the first analysts— may I say, character analysts—whose results show the true nature of character-analytic work. What you described in your cases has long been familiar to me although up to now I haven't been able to master all of it theoretically: the shattering insight into the previous wasteland of living and just existing; the tremendous fear of happiness; the reactivation of the deepest—I would say, almost biological—reactions, such as bursting; the timidity in coming to grips with reality in a healthy way, etc. From the end phases of clinical cases I first came to understand the world's fear of the orgasm theory and, even more, its lack of understanding, which reflects a repression of its better judgment. Life doesn't become any easier when one begins to feel things might be different.

I would appreciate it if you would elaborate your criticism of Freud in detail. The other day, for the first time in a long while, I looked through the *Three Contributions*, and I was amazed by some of the passages, especially on genitality. I've done myself a grave injustice by working for so many years under the impression that my theory of genitality was rooted in Freud. This was merely due to my father fixation. Someday I hope to make a clean break.

Yesterday Fenichel presented his "criticism" of my technique and everybody was against him, including most of his own analysands (Nic Hoel, Raknes). Did you know he's leaving Oslo? Things have been hard for him lately because the superiority of character analysis had become obvious to all. He's going to Prague. Unfortunately, he believes that this will solve his problems. The whole Norwegian group has sided with me, except for someone who doesn't know what it is all about, and two people who are honestly trying but are structurally incapable. Since the last discussion I haven't been to the psychoanalytic association, but all of them are attending my lectures and my seminar on character.

* Translation by Therese Pol.

Now, about the equipment: I have to start very slowly and work my way into the electrophysiological technique. It will be very hard but looks most promising. The apparatus is among the most modern there is. It may soon be necessary to have a professionally trained assistant come from Germany because the local physiologist merely wants to "help," but that's not enough. The first experiments (recording of potentials at erogenous zones) will start soon. Further experimentation, however, will have to develop from whatever course the work takes. Please try to find an unemployed electrophysiologist who is well versed in work on oscillographs and knows about the physiology of the skin and the vegetative nervous system.

TO LOTTE LIEBECK *
1 April 1935

Dear Lotte L.:

This is no April Fools' Day joke. The apparatus has stirred up the public here, and as a result the physiologist got scared. There is nothing further I can do with him, and now "I'm up a tree." Since the equipment cost me about 1,000 marks and since I also don't want to give up, I'm looking for a way out. I was thinking of the following possibility: if I could hire, perhaps for eight weeks, a young physiologist from Berlin who happens to be out of work, then I could get started. A physiologist will not understand the problems involved, but he can handle the technical end of it. These are quite complicated electronic matters. I need at least an introductory textbook on radio technology (tubes, amplifiers) and a good book on electrophysiology dealing with oscillographs. Might I ask you to make inquiries and send me suggestions? Could you talk to Kraus, † and am I asking too much of you? All this is so difficult, and I have so much work. I know I will succeed eventually, but I'm annoyed about *this* world. People here are very

---

* Translation by Therese Pol.
† Friedrich Kraus, Berlin internist who, on the basis of pioneering experiments, had ascertained that the body is governed by electrical processes.

agitated and curious and are telling one another the wildest things about this undertaking. It may even be necessary to guard the equipment from damage.

The collapse of everything is ghastly. I'm always reminded of the war, which also came to an end.

14 April 1935

I need some time to collect my thoughts:

1. Is it worthwhile to make such great personal and financial sacrifices? Popularity isn't gained by speaking one's mind.

2. Where to concentrate? On Sexpol—or the experiments?

3. Best to be free of *all* tradition!! It is senseless to expect others to be interested in what doesn't concern them.

I need children around me!

15 April 1935

Surely life is bearable under simple, everyday, natural conditions! One lives detached from the world—can't live in it and can't live outside it, in new realms!

TO ALFRED PINK
15 April 1935

Dear Father!

I am terribly sorry about this mess with the money. I had actually deposited the cash at the end of March. It is the fault of the other parties involved. But I have now threatened to break off all relationships from which only others derive any advantage. I have also arranged for a larger sum to be sent to you all at once just in case the April amount has not yet been paid in; altogether, therefore, 700 kroner. That's 200 kroner each for April, May, and June and another 100 kroner for the lawyer.

I was somewhat depressed by the latent reproaches in your letter. I really don't think that anyone can complain about me. Despite the total breakup, I have been paying for the children since May 1933, and I think that is no mean achievement; certainly another father, with a slightly different attitude, would not have managed it. It is regrettable that Annie cannot contribute a little bit more. You should not forget for one moment that because of my many good "friends," and thanks to some important discoveries that are rocking the world, I would be a dead man overnight if I did not work so hard to guarantee the publishing house and my publications. The fact that "the children must come first" is all very correct, but if I did not assert myself in a purely ideological sense through the publishing house, I could not send anything at all for the children. Therefore, in purely financial terms, it is actually my work which has to come *first*. Please do not go on reproaching me, because I do not deserve it. At any rate, I am still the one who is doing the most for the children and yet, if it can be measured at all, I get the least out of them. For example, I am afraid that I will face problems when, for financial reasons, I try to have the children come here in the summer. On the one hand, I would be saving two months' cost of a children's home, and on the other hand I could go on working here. Annie should really bear that in mind. Finally, not even the Civil Code says that a father has only obligations but no rights. In my opinion, things are not all that bad; so, as I said, I do not want to hear any more reproaches.

A complaint: So far I have refrained from saying anything, but I think that people could show a little more concern for me as a father. For example, you could have dropped me a few lines when you were all together last Easter. I managed to write to Annie as well as to the children when I was on holiday. It is also not good for the children when Annie behaves like that, because they will definitely notice it and worry about it. Even if you do not want to have any contact with me for personal reasons, you should at least maintain some sort of appearances just for the children's sake. I realize that there was no sinister intention behind your actions, but from a distance I am beginning to smell an attempt, albeit unconscious, to alienate me from the children. Even Berta has not found it worth the trouble to reply to my letters. Life has taught me not to react to such things, but I would not like our various lives to move too far apart. I hate stupid problems. I am writing this to you so that you can try to exert some "gentle pressure."

TO H. LÖWENBACH*
15 April 1935

Dear Dr. Löwenbach,

After glancing rapidly, and only very superficially, through your works, I realize that on purely technical grounds we would understand each other. I am conducting experiments with an oscillograph that was made in Denmark (four-tube amplifier), the purpose of which is to obtain information on surface potentials. I have already written to Prof. Fischer† that the problems cannot be described in a letter. The subject matter is essentially new and presupposes certain theoretical assumptions that differ from the usual ones. I think you will be interested in it. I believe one of my students gave Prof. Fischer a copy of the article entitled "The Basic Antithesis of Vegetative Life,"‡ which explains some of the points. You may also want to get in touch with Dr. Liebeck. She, too, can tell you something of my work. But unless you have been familiar with the problems for a long time, I do not think that you can really penetrate the subject matter. I would therefore suggest that we take a risk and go ahead with the project, for the time being in the manner I proposed. I have already made inquiries. You can live comfortably in a guesthouse for about 130–150 kroner per month. Any final details will have to wait until you are here. To start with, therefore, you could spend about four weeks, without any obligation on your part, just orienting yourself. Unless you change your mind, I will expect you here on 2 May. The work will be performed

---

* A Berlin physiologist recommended to Reich for work with the equipment for the bioelectrical experiments Reich planned.
† Albert Fischer of the Rockefeller Institute in Copenhagen.
‡ Included in *The Bioelectrical Investigation of Sexuality and Anxiety* (New York: Farrar, Straus and Giroux, 1982).

either in the Psychological or in the Physiological Institute, as required. If possible, I might even set up a small laboratory. I can tell you right now that, if the first series proves positive, the experiments will soon lead into the biological sphere. We will be working for the most part on the living organism. Negotiations are under way with an insane asylum here that will supply us with catatonic patients. The matter holds great promise, but in the beginning there is no doubt that many difficult problems, including those of a financial nature, will have to be overcome.

You will certainly be pleased to know that the surroundings of Oslo are beautiful. We will leave everything until we meet and can discuss matters personally, but the discussion will have to be thorough. Please write and let me know whether you can come on 2 May or at some other time convenient to you.

TO SIGMUND FREUD*
20 May 1935

My dear Professor:

I am enclosing a pamphlet containing my lecture at the XII Psychoanalytic Congress, in expanded form. I was able to give this lecture only as a guest of the IPA.

Several years ago, when I reported on the role of the orgastic function in the psychic economy, you told me that I had either regressed to the preanalytic level, with its denial of pregenitality, or, if this was not the case, that I would someday have to carry the heavy burden of psychoanalysis alone. I do not know if you remember this. I was extremely impressed with your comment. Since the first part of your observation does not apply, the second has all the better anticipated a glimpse of the future.

I would appreciate it if you would convince yourself, by reading my pamphlet, that I have sincerely tried not to turn the grave injustice I

* Translation by Therese Pol. There is no indication that Freud replied to this letter.

suffered into grounds for a personal and irrational reaction. I hope that, at least in this respect, I have succeeded.

I also believe that in this paper I was more successful than before in explaining the clinical reasons that compelled me to clarify the contradictions that today dominate the doctrine of psychoanalysis. Furthermore, I feel that I was able to find a constructive formulation for the common roots as well as for the theoretical differences inherent in these contradictions.

With best wishes.

27 May 1935

The experiments were completely successful—the electrical nature of sexuality has been proved!

13 June 1935

Facts, conclusions:

1. The surface of the skin possesses a potential that is significantly larger than the EKG.

2. The range of diversity in the skin potential is very large. Erogenous zone potential larger than nonerogenous. Genital zone potential larger than nongenital.

3. There is obviously a *resting potential* (RP) that must fluctuate within certain limits in one and the same person.

4. The change in the resting potential that is caused by nonerogenous stimuli (pressure, irritation) is minimal compared with the magnitude of the deflection.

5. Simple pressure does not change the potential.

6. The potential goes on increasing slowly when a tickling/itching sensation is experienced (*preorgastic potential*).

An observer can recognize from the apparatus whether a tickling sensation is experienced or not.

7. Sexual sensation obviously builds up *above* the RP as an *increase* in excitation in contrast to pressure or shock.

Further problems:

1. There must be a difference between the electrical charge that corresponds to all friction (mechanical process) and the electrical charge that signifies *biological excitation*.

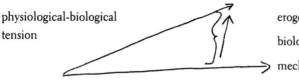

physiological-biological tension — erogenous excitation / biologically specific reaction / mechanical excitation

2. For orgastic excitation the apparatus will first have to be modified—*sooo much*.

3. Main point: Passive stasis _____
                        vegetative excitation = life

4. How can psychic inhibition be eliminated during erection tests? (Let the test subject himself do the test!!)

5. Attachable electrode for remote testing—female physician—female test subject

TO WILHELM HOFFMANN [*] AND
H. LÖWENBACH
6 September 1935

Dear Dr. Hoffmann,

Dear Dr. Löwenbach,

I am still in the grip of the experiment that we witnessed together the day before yesterday, and I would like to summarize the results of our subsequent discussion.

You are aware of just how much time and money it cost me to obtain funding for the experiments on my orgasm theory. In one of the conversations I had with Dr. Löwenbach, he advised me not to pursue the matter experimentally anymore because it would be financially difficult to carry out and the clinical evidence is sufficient in

---

[*] Physiologist.

itself. I saw his point, but I had to follow a certain indefinable urge that told me that without experimental evidence, at least as regards the central question of the so-called mechano-electrical leap,* the clinical theory is only half proved. And we had agreed that an electrical theory of sexuality possesses sufficient weight to warrant every effort that promised in any way to be successful. I can vividly imagine that what we are experiencing is no different from the feelings of a mountaineer who can see the summit of Mount Everest in clear outline but soon realizes that the final assault (and that would be equivalent to carrying out the central experiment, measuring the potentials in a state of full sexual excitation) is fraught with insurmountable technical difficulties. Since I have no technical training, I had no real idea of just how complicated these difficulties are, but I got a glimpse last Wednesday. We had finally agreed that proceeding via catatonia is a roundabout route and can even be very unreliable. If the erogenous zones of catatonics have so far failed to yield any special results, this does not disprove the validity of the assumption, because we know, clinically, that catatonics suffer from reduced libidinous functions or lack them altogether. A negative result in the case of catatonia would of course immediately provide full confirmation if only it were technically possible to reproduce in healthy persons those test conditions that permit full vagal sexual excitation, which according to my theory always ends in orgastic excitation. Despite the gloomy outlook, we agreed to continue the catatonia experiments for the time being and to look for those influences that yield fluctuations in potential outside the realm of vagal excitation.

From our later discussion it became clear, to me at any rate, that the crucial point is to prove that a leap takes place from the state of mechanical expansion or tension into the state of electrical charge (nerves and muscle excitation). I believe that one could overcome this problem on simpler objects than the surface of the skin, and you shared my opinion. When I looked once more through a summary description of cardiac function, my view was strengthened that faster progress could probably be made by examining preparations of heart and bladder tissue. In view of the facts that I have now collected, I would therefore propose that we have a thorough discussion of this possibility. I have

* Reich refers to the change from mechanical tension to electrical charge that he had postulated in the orgasm formula.

to admit to you that I was assailed by doubt as to whether the main effect of the vegetative change in excitation would be discovered at the surface of the skin. I hope you will not hold this "wavering" in my hypothetical assumptions against me. Such uncertainties are part and parcel of this kind of work. The question therefore is whether, in addition to examining the skin potentials of healthy people and catatonics, it might also be possible, simultaneously or very soon, to detect the mechano-electrical current by examining preparations of heart and bladder tissue. As I have repeatedly suggested in conversations with colleague Löwenbach, this work will require two things: (1) extremely accurate utilization of all the experimental facts and technical methods that have so far become known, and (2) while the study is being conducted, the setting aside of all theories and assumptions based on these facts. I am sure that you will agree with me that, when one tests the validity of a particular assumption, other assumptions and hypotheses are merely confusing in the initial stages, although later it is essential that they be used for control purposes. It was also clear to me that in order to detect the antithetical functions of vagus (sex) and sympathetic (anxiety), one must first concentrate on what is typical and normal and, for the time being, leave to one side anything that is atypical or that complicates the issue. It is impossible for everything to be explainable and solvable all at once. I was very happy that we were able to eliminate a disturbing misunderstanding. Löwenbach and I initially meant something quite different by mechanical tension. I saw expansion or tension rather like the phenomenon that occurs when a hose is filled with water; on the other hand, Löwenbach saw the tension of the muscle prior to convulsion. In Löwenbach's terminology mechanical tension *follows* the electrical excitation, while in my terminology it is the other way around.

Motesiczky* offered to repeat the central experiment he conducted before. Please let me know where and when this could be done. As soon as I have finished compiling all the facts on heart function and EKGs, I will let you know. I would like to add that I have rarely had an opportunity like this last time to discuss these matters with such objective and understanding partners. Let us hope that our efforts will one day bear fruit. The "risky" nature of the work is somewhat irritating, but for me at least this also represents a certain attraction.

---

* Karl Motesiczky, a student of Reich's.

TO EVA REICH
18 September 1935

My dear Evchen,

I assume that you are already fully immersed in your work and also back in analysis. I am taking a half hour off from my own work to chat with you, in particular about your analysis. You wrote me recently that you no longer intend to be obstinate. That is very good. Obstinacy never gets one anywhere. I would like to discuss your attitude toward your analysis. You know that I have never interfered, but now I really must give you some advice. You told me that there are many things that you do not want to, or cannot, tell Bertl. Now, it makes no sense at all to go into analysis with that kind of attitude. I would advise you to think about what I am going to say and discuss it with Bertl. If one cannot or is unwilling to reveal one's most important secrets during the analytic sessions, then the only other possibility is to discuss in detail with the analyst the reasons why it is not possible to speak openly. One should not force oneself to speak, but it is essential that one understand the reasons one cannot speak. You told me that when you are asked to speak, you feel as if you were all alone in a large empty room. We have to find out what exactly this image means. Then perhaps your block will be cured. Up to now, analysis has done you a lot of good and you should take advantage of it during the next few months. So don't discuss with Bertl the things that you cannot say but instead talk about what is holding your tongue. I assume that it is your general shyness and specifically the cramping that occurs at the mouth and neck when you speak. Write me about it afterward, if you want to. We'll see then what we can do.

TO HARALD SCHJELDERUP
26 September 1935

Dear Professor Schjelderup,

Yesterday you certainly got a very good impression of the kind of difficulties the experiments have encountered up until now. The purely technical problems involved in creating suitable psychic situations are in themselves enormous. But I do not wish to talk of these. Instead, I wish to address the other difficulties created by Dr. Löwenbach's basic theoretical attitude.

We arrived at a decision yesterday: we will wait until the end of October and then either abandon the matter altogether or resolve to carry on. After careful reflection I have concluded that in this form our decision does not take us a single step forward. From the standpoint of orgasm and affect theory, we are looking for the specific sexual, sensual "feeling of current." According to the theory, the act itself and ejaculation are meaningless unless they go together with the specific subjective sensation of orgastic current or "streaming." In the preliminary discussions about the experiments and in the report on the initial results, I tried to make it clear that only this clinically well-founded hypothesis, and nothing else, can be the starting point of the tests. When I now look back over the work that has been performed since 1 May of this year, this is what I find:

1. In the first tests, which were performed with the silver and then with the potassium chloride electrode, there were some phenomena that clearly indicated the accuracy of the hypothesis. Dr. Löwenbach did not mention these phenomena in his report but admitted them later.

2. Since June the experiments have been continued on catatonics in Dikemark but from the standpoint of a theory that is totally irrelevant to the problem we are investigating. The workers there measured only the resting potentials. The technique was modified for that purpose. But we are not looking for resting potentials. What we are interested in are the potentials that exist at the peak of sexual excitation. It is clear right from the start that an electrode firmly attached to the nipple, no matter how correct it may be, tells us nothing about the specific orgastic sensation occurring in the glans penis, even if it obtains positive results. The problem is thus how to adapt the technique to the requirements of investigating local excitation peaks.

3. Dr. Löwenbach went to Dikemark with the specific intention of verifying the tests already conducted at your institute (tickling test, masturbation test, passive stasis test), this time using the best available technical methods. At the same time he was to compare the results obtained in studies conducted on catatonics. As already said, the tests

on catatonics were performed on an entirely different basis, but not even the slightest effort was made to check the results obtained from May on at your institute. This was without doubt due to the fact that Dr. Löwenbach does not have a real conception of what we call orgastic or preorgastic excitation. As far as I have been able to ascertain, absolutely nowhere in the literature on physiology is there even the slightest hint of any attempt to examine the sexual area, and this has been confirmed by Dr. Löwenbach himself. That is the only way to explain why, in the paper he presented on Sunday, Dr. Löwenbach said that nothing could be expected and indeed that even positive observations would be meaningless. We had agreed that one cannot accept the fluctuations of potential discovered by Tarchanoff but deny the opposite fluctuations in the case of sexual excitation.

4. The argument that pressure phenomena are responsible can be refuted as follows: (a) The character of a change in potential when pressure is applied differs significantly and visibly from the slow wandering of the light strip when sexual excitation increases and from the phenomenon, which was clearly observed once, of the potential shooting from about 40 mv to about 120 mv and then dropping again to 0 *at the moment of climax.* (b) It is unlikely that pressure itself would be effective so precisely at the moment of climax. (c) The record of the May tests shows that the KCl electrode (handheld electrode) yielded uniform values, always in the 30–40 mv range, when the tests were repeated at nonerogenous points on the skin. In order to distinguish the pressure phenomena from the erogenous phenomena, it is first necessary to have observed and recorded both phenomena. I find it an unnecessary complication, and it slows down the work, if one examines pressure phenomena before recording the basic phenomenon that one wishes to observe. I therefore propose that one should first carry out the masturbation test using a well-insulated handheld electrode and that the pressure effects should be verified *afterward.* It should not be done the other way around, because then there are no possibilities of comparison. It strikes me as much more advantageous to observe the problems in connection with the main phenomenon.

5. Dr. Löwenbach declares that the first tests undertaken with both the silver electrode and the KCl electrode were useless. I do not share this view, for the following reason: if these electrodes were or are so unverifiable, then it is impossible to understand how, as is evident

from the records, we were able to obtain uniform results at various points on the skin. If the electrodes contain a source of error, it would also not be possible to obtain exactly the same phenomenon in repeated tests—for example, using tickling stimulation—while at all other times the phenomenon is missing. I would never rely solely on these first experiments. But they must be checked and repeated. The phenomena discovered in the process must be followed up. I therefore propose the following: carry out one masturbation test with a handheld KCl electrode and another with the silver electrode (possibly an improved electrode). If, in both cases, we were to see exactly what we observed in the first silver electrode tests—namely, the sudden rise and fall in potential at the moment of climax—then there would no longer be any reason to doubt the existence of the phenomenon. It is not important at this point to determine the absolute magnitudes or details, as Dr. Löwenbach wishes to do; but for the time being all we need to do is record in its entirety a phenomenon that has already been seen once, and then we can discuss the problems and the sources of error and also analyze the phenomenon itself in precise detail. So far, Dr. Löwenbach has ignored, failed to follow up, or tried to place a different interpretation on any observed phenomenon that appears to confirm the hypothesis. But we are not concerned here with drawing theoretical conclusions about what has happened. The only thing that concerns us is to obtain a photographic record of what we have seen: first the excitation at climax, then the possible pressure phenomenon.

Dr. Löwenbach denies all possibilities and after many months has failed to advance technically from the basic premise of our problem. We therefore find ourselves faced with the possibility of temporarily abandoning the project. But before we do so, the first series of tests performed at your institute absolutely must be repeated and photographed with all the sources of error. Similarly, the records from the May tests must be stored and studied. I would be forced to withdraw immediately if the principal test itself were not to precede a check of the sources of error; the same would apply if Dr. Löwenbach were to persist in his point of view that the first tests conducted with the silver and KCl electrodes should not be repeated. I would then prefer to wait for better circumstances at a later time. If the experiments were repeated and the phenomena were photographically recorded in October, the apparatus could of course be made available for continuing the tests on catatonics. My attitude is based, last but not least, on my heavy financial burdens.

To Löwenbach's objection that it is "nonsense" to repeat these experiments I can only reply that he himself has noted that of 500 studies performed by others on skin potentials, about 490 were incorrect. I was able to convince myself that infinite confusion reigns, especially in this area of physiology. Why should one struggle so hard to avoid committing another stupid act in such an important matter just before the whole business is abandoned? One piece of stupidity more or less no longer makes any difference.

TO HARALD SCHJELDERUP
30 September 1935

Dear Prof. Schjelderup,

Yesterday the first electrode tests took place in Dikemark. It was found that, with the exception of some small, almost negligible, rapid fluctuations between 1 and 10 mv, neither warmth nor friction nor touching the electrode at different points nor any pressure on the liquid-filled glass produced even one of the phenomena we had observed during the first tests. This coming Wednesday or Thursday the electrode will be tried out on a sick person. It will be redesigned. I shall keep an exact record of what is done. Dr. Löwenbach expressed such serious charges and doubts that I am now absolutely determined to conduct the control tests with the utmost accuracy. Yesterday he himself disproved his main objection that my observations were due to condenser effects because the effects soon disappear again completely. I don't believe that Löwenbach is bringing enough objectivity to bear on the matter; instead, it looks as if he deliberately did everything he could to slow the experiments down. I am subjectively interested in seeing the experiments succeed. Hoffmann, with all his fabulous objectivity, has not yet gained the appropriate insight into the problems we are dealing with. I therefore ask that you be present, if at all possible, at the next control tests in Dikemark. One gets an entirely different view of the initially observed phenomena once one sees the difference in the other physical phenomena and realizes that the electrode cannot be influenced.

30 September 1935

Löwenbach is a schemer. Tried to rile up Hoffmann with lies. The schemers of this world have it easy. You can only confront them with straightforwardness, but for that you always pay the price.

During the electrode experiment with Hoffmann, Löwenbach didn't have a single argument to advance. Hoffmann had no impressions of the initial experiments—the "wandering," etc.—and so he was taken in by Löwenbach. Löwenbach is a typical fart, one of those scientists who for decades examine the finest little fibrils on a leaf when they are supposed to find out what a tree looks like and how it thrives and grows. Along comes someone who describes the tree as a whole, and then they become exact—and belittle him.

17 October 1935

Only pleasure yields the positive manifestations of life. Fear, pressure, etc., all negate.

19 October 1935

The world is growing darker and darker! Mankind has literally gone mad. I have a hunch that Sexpol will someday—when?—bring movement, life into this world. It is all so self-evident—life, growth, pleasure. Fear of pleasure kills everything. And the insane are doing their diplomatic dances on the backs of the apolitical.

But mankind even survived the World War. It sometimes seems that a humanitarian mass culture will only become a part of world history in the coming decades or centuries.

22 October 1935

Elsa is a dear comrade—I would like to have a son with her. Poor Evchen, Lorchen. Shall I ever be with them again? Children are life itself! I want to have them around me! But my work won't allow it.

Sexpol is making progress everywhere. I'm concerned that trained personnel won't be available in Holland, England, Switzerland, Denmark. We are forging ahead everywhere.

29 October 1935

Friends advised me to concentrate on science and not encumber it with politics. They said I would accomplish so much more. I can't agree with that. I can't work scientifically far removed from the socialist struggle. The future of science lies in the hands of the revolutionaries and in the simple man's sense of life. Nothing else is worthwhile; the future of mankind is at stake.

TO LORE REICH
14 November 1935

My dear little Lorli-girl!

It was all just a bad dream that the little girl had dreamt!!! Her father hadn't disappeared at all. Instead he had never grown up but remained a young boy who had wandered off into the big wide world to ask all the parents who were nasty to their little girls and boys and who scolded them and bawled them out to cease and desist. He thought a lot about the little girl back home and he sometimes wept a silent tear and looked forward to the day when he would return to her. He had a lot of things to do on his journey; all the little boys and girls were happy when they saw him because he understood them so well—all their lovely games, all the pouting and sulking, the hopping and skipping, and going off to play tiger in the forest. One day, he was very sad because he had asked the little girl to visit him; but she did not want to, because she thought he no longer loved her as he loved the other girls and boys. But that was simply not true. Then he got a bit angry too and went into a forest and spent a whole hour jumping from tree to tree like a squirrel. Then he did three somersaults, called out five times "karuzi-tapuzi-marana-padu," and everything was all right again. Then he went to see the little girl. At first she was very grumpy, but the next day she ran to him happily and they played together in the meadow near the lake, and he taught her how to swim better, so that she didn't just flop into the water like she always used to do. But then he suddenly had to go away again, and he waited with great longing in his heart for a letter from the little girl telling him where and when they could see each other. But he did not have to wait long, and look what happened.

(The little girl now continues the story.)

10 December 1935

After a talk with Eva: It is clear that my work will cost me my children; the world is stronger. After all, they're right—what is accomplished by dragging the others along? They want to be left in peace. Loneliness seems inevitable. If things continue as they are now, Eva will soon be so transformed that she will no longer understand me. She said, "I was furious at you. You shouldn't call so often. It costs too much. And you shouldn't write me letters like that. I have never been honest with you."

That was not Eva speaking! How the world shapes a person after all.

11 December 1935

I am very wary, justifiably so. People understand only to a limited extent. I am unjustified only in reproaching them for (1) resisting any disturbance, (2) not knowing that they are cheating, deluding themselves, and making more promises than they are willing to keep.

18 December 1935

It is awfully hard to bear the fact that, for the sake of the cause, one must become increasingly lonely, that one can't just exist as a human being among other human beings! Over and over they tell me that I take too much for granted and that my innovations have become too self-evident to me! It's true!

1936

*"The better one understands the world and
mankind, and the greater one's involvement, the
further removed one is, because man does not
understand himself and hates and murders
anyone who tells him what he really is."*

20 January 1936

Electrical sex research—monograph #1* finished at noon! Then ski tour to the Kuytha-Hytta. Beautiful!

With the exception of Lotte, Nic, Sigurd, Aenne,† and Elsa, no one understood the report, I mean really understood it. Sex radiation—if each body radiates, then the sexually excited organ must radiate as well. It only has to be discovered, but how?

5 February 1936

A complete readjustment is necessary. Science—Biology

TO ROGER DU TEIL‡
27 February 1936

Dear Professor,

Through Dr. Victor Bauer** I am sending you a copy of the manuscript on the experimental results of my work, which is now ready for press. I have heard from Dr. Bauer that you are taking a great deal of trouble over the matter; thank you very much indeed. I certainly hope that one day I will have the opportunity to discuss the ambiguities with you in more detail than was possible during our brief meeting.

At the moment, I am making all the necessary preparations to examine the problems relating to the charge and tension process and the expansion and contraction phenomena in mollusks. It is not an easy matter to create all the necessary technical conditions here. In

---

* *Experimentelle Ergebnisse über die elektrische Funktion von Sexualität und Angst* (Copenhagen: Sexpolverlag, 1937). Included in *The Bioelectrical Investigation of Sexuality and Anxiety* (New York: Farrar, Straus and Giroux, 1982).
† Aenne Morseth, a student of Reich's.
‡ Professor of philosophy at the Centre Universitaire Méditerranéen in Nice.
** An active member of Sexpol in Nice.

addition, in the course of the preliminary testing, so many new and strange phenomena have shown up that I have to take great care not to lose my way in the undergrowth.

I shall take the liberty to keep you informed of the further progress of the experiments. For the time being, I prefer to report only the actual observed results before I publish the general theories that derive from these data. Dr. Bauer has probably given you a reprint of the article "The Basic Antithesis of Vegetative Life," in which, about three years ago, I summarized the clinical-theoretical preconditions for the tests on the basis of experiments carried out by other authors. I would be extremely happy to hear what opinions you have formed about the entire matter.

TO IRMGARD STRAUSS *
28 *February 1936*

Dear Irmgard,

Many thanks for your letter of the 24th. Please do not hold against me my inquiring how seriously the academy matter should be taken. †
I have suffered too many disappointments. Yesterday I sent you a finished manuscript. Major changes were made only in sections A and D. Section C has been newly added because it contains the most important control experiments. Both of you will be interested to learn that in the meantime I have succeeded in reproducing in sound, using a simple radio set, the same phenomena that are converted into light phenomena by means of the oscillograph; that is to say, in the same way that the light phenomena in the oscillograph behave, the humming sound in the radio set increases when tickling or stroking is carried out. On the other hand, the sound drops when pressure is applied. I believe that this control experiment is decisively important. If inorganic

* Irmgard Strauss and Victor Bauer were helping to translate Reich's monograph on the bioelectrical experiments into French. Like Bauer, Strauss was involved in Sexpol in Nice.
† Du Teil had informed the French Academy of Science about Reich's monograph on the electrical function of sexuality and anxiety.

material is connected to the system and one then switches the radio set on, the humming sound disappears completely, in precisely the same way that the potential drops on the oscillograph. I'll leave it to you to formulate these last few sentences in an appropriate manner and to add them as a further point in the chapter on the control experiments, with the comment that a detailed description of the conversion of the fluctuations in potential into sounds will be given in a future publication.

At present I am focusing the experimental work on two aspects. First, I want to establish the differences in the resting potentials in people with various kinds of neurotic armoring. Second, I want to carry out direct observations on invertebrate mollusks. * I think I will learn a great deal from these experiments.

29 February 1936
The body differs from a charged electric sphere in that the electricity is always nonuniformly distributed in the body, while inorganic electricity is uniformly distributed.

TO VICTOR BAUER
30 April 1936

Dear Victor Bauer,

I was surprised to learn that the translation is "almost" ready. I thought it had been handed in long ago. I would like to know what will ultimately happen to the French manuscript. Will it appear in the French psychology journal, where it does not really belong, or

---

* Reich intended to set up an aquarium and to acquire marine animals in which the extension and retraction of their soft parts could be readily observed and also animals, primarily starfish and jellyfish, in which the rhythmic expansion movement was evident.

will it be sent to the academy? Please write and tell me honestly whether the suggestion that it should first be published in a (little-read) psychology journal was made because of some problem that has come up. In the meantime, I have completed all kinds of preparations to continue the experiments on worms and protozoa. Recently, for the first time, I observed protozoa that were exposed to the effect of an electric current. The tension-charge formula involves some incredible things. The whole business is proceeding much too slowly for my liking, mainly because I must first gradually acquire the necessary technology and also in part invent it myself. A short while ago I ordered a handbook on protozoa and a technical manual. If you know of any good literature, please give me the details. In particular, I need German and English literature, not about structure and reproduction but about how protozoa come into being. I must have accurate information on all the theories related to this topic. Meanwhile, I have also carried out an initial test with the surface charge of worms. It seems to have worked, but that is a very rough assessment. A German friend of mine has presented my institute with a beautiful binocular microscope capable of up to 2,000–3,000 magnification. In the near future I shall probably bury myself deeply in these matters, and I just hope that I can find someone who will free me from the political and, in particular, the organizational work.

6 May 1936

Freud's 80th birthday. Ten years ago, when I presented him with *The Function of the Orgasm*, he remarked, "So thick?" At the time he warned me against believing anything people said. Nothing, he said, had been accepted! He was right! And how do things stand today?

My outlook on life has shifted completely.

It is difficult to make progress. People fail. They abdicate long before they are aware of it. Those who tried to save themselves are understandable. Will the tension-charge formula be validated? How to proceed? The detail technique that has developed has erased all tracks leading to the vital source of life. It must be a *very simple* matter— the *origin of life*—or an overrated idea? A feeling of certainty that my thinking is correct is directing my work. I experiment as if I were in a trance. Do amoebae (motile plasma) really originate from the swelling, formation, and dissociation of inorganic matter? Stay calm, wait, be cautious. Mistakes don't matter—just don't get upset. Scientists have chopped life up into pieces. They isolate the details and then want to reconstruct a whole from the isolated details, like a machine from its parts. And yet the Orient did see one aspect correctly—namely, that living matter is not a machine capable of being constructed.

The leap from mechanical to electrical must prove itself correct. Can I hold out? I think so! Even if they say I'm mad.

17 May 1936

Living earth! The preliminary stages of life discovered!

[Undated]

Experimentation reveals that boiled, sterilized earth undergoes vesicular disintegration; the vesicles are motile, highly charged, the so-called germs (a) for "bacteria" (rods, vesicles), (b) for amoebae (vesicular structure).

Rotting plants undergo vesicular disintegration. Rot is *not* caused by "rot bacteria," but swelling organic matter undergoes vesicular disintegration and creates "rot bacteria." *Vesicular disintegration of inorganic and organic matter + swelling → life.*

Protozoa are the result of reanimation of organic material that has become inorganic!!??

In earth heated to incandescence, all "living matter" is killed but at the same time, through vesicular disintegration, new life is generated when *swelling* also occurs.

Dialectic of death and life

1. When the metazoan dies, the protozoan appears.
2. As the unicellular organisms coalesce, so the multicellular organism is formed.
3. Life can form through the gradual swelling of matter.
4. It can form through the effect of sunshine. Spring.
5. It can form by boiling dried-out material.

6. Inorganic material organizes itself through swelling and the buildup of charge into organic material.

15 June 1936

There is no question about it: The motile structures have nothing to do with "germs" or the like, but instead are inorganic matter *that is coming to life*. It is necessary gradually to put things in order.

1. Immediately after being produced, a mixed preparation of protein yields numerous motile *vesicles* = decomposed protein—the typical lecithin structures appear right away!

Conclusion: The formation of life must take place not only "quite simply" but also at an extremely rapid rate.

2. We must distinguish between *bacteria* that form from decaying organic matter by individuation, *vesicles* that form by swelling from inorganic matter, *structures* that are formed by a gel-like grouping of vesicles (amoebae).

3. Since everything is antithetically arranged, there must be *two different types* of single-celled organisms: (a) *life-destroying* organisms or organisms that form through organic decay, (b) *life-promoting* organisms that form from inorganic material that comes to life.

4. *Cancer brings together the vesicles*, organizes them, but disrupts their motion. Cf. the general, combining, paralyzing function of cancer.

Fish feed on the products of decaying material in the water. These decay products are without doubt the vesicular grains, energy units. Probably the same thing happens in the course of digestion: the food is broken down into energy vesicles.

How is the absorbed energy processed in the blood? Directly, generally?

Sedimentation reaction of the red blood corpuscles in the case of disease = decolloidization.

TO NIC HOEL
2 July 1936

Dear Nic!

Since we both cherish clarity and openness so much in everything, I will give you my frank comments on your article "Psychoanalysis and the Workers' Movement." I disagree entirely, both personally and in terms of the policy of the movement, with the manner in which you have written the article; and furthermore, I regard the direction you have taken as extremely dangerous and ripe with the seeds for future difficulties. It's advisable therefore to get a clear view of the matter right now. My main objections are as follows.

1. In your article you lose sight of the order of magnitude between, on the one hand, Freud's cultural criticism in our sense and, on the other, the reactionary views that he has created and left behind for his pupils to misuse horrendously. The ratio of the former to the latter is 1:1,000. Therefore, it is not serving the cause to put so much emphasis, as you have done, on the very few, unclear, and completely buried *rudiments* suggestive of our own direction. By dangling these things before the reader's eyes, you lead him to be uncritical of the other aspects of Freud's writings.

2. The critique you give of Freud's cultural philosophy begins with the words "In response, we must raise the following objections," or something similar, and then you quote almost word for word the formulations and views for which I have fought very hard. Who is this "we"? Is it Sexpol? It is not mentioned in your article; nobody knows what it is. Are you it? Does the "we" refer to officials of the Norwegian workers' movement? In short, your words "we must object . . ." say nothing that specifically addresses the history of Sexpol. It is incomprehensible to me why you make absolutely no mention of Sexpol when you talk of revolutionary cultural criticism.

3. Furthermore, in your work you commit the error of ascribing to psychoanalysis or to Freud something for which he had expelled me, namely, "The plus that psychoanalysis (if we make critical use of its experimental materials) brings to the workers' movement is not only this but also the peculiar fact that the economic suppression inherent in our form of society makes use of sexual suppression . . ." It is not the case that psychoanalysis *plus* my cultural revolutionary criticism of it does this to the workers' movement. Quite to the contrary, it is my cultural-political criticism of Freud within the context of my opposition to psychoanalysis that is responsible. Here, sex economy and psychoanalysis are antithetical because psychoanalysis as a theoretical system asserts that sexual suppression is part of cultural development, and it denies the class-based character of sexual suppression; whereas my position is simply that satisfied sexuality is *the* foundation of cultural development and—this is one of my core theories in everything that has so far been debated—that sexual suppression is at the heart of all ideological suppression and is the means of all material suppression. What you have written therefore confuses the reader, confuses and provides no explanation.

4. (Probably because of the atmosphere surrounding it, this point is the most serious.) You write that Freud's work is being continued on a Marxist basis by Fenichel, Fromm,* and above all by Wilhelm Reich in his character analysis and sex economy. I must energetically protest this formulation and this comparison. It is totally untrue that Fenichel is pursuing anything on a Marxist basis; on the contrary, he is simply putting together a mixture of whatever can be pursued. You have far too little knowledge of the history of the movement in Germany and Austria to judge how Fromm behaved and what he did. The specific aspect of the dialectical-materialist development of the theories of psychoanalysis into a revolutionary cultural criticism is centered on the question of the economy and energetics of sexuality as the core mechanism of cultural processes. And you will find nothing about this in either of the two authors, quite apart from the fact that they are both outspoken enemies of Sexpol. It is part and parcel of Marxism in particular that one fights for a cause and is committed to that struggle—within the workers' movement, within the organiza-

* Erich Fromm, German psychologist. Like Fenichel, he had been in contact with Reich in Berlin.

tions, outside the organizations, in the street, etc. Neither Fenichel nor Fromm could be regarded as Marxists in this, the only correct sense of the term. In short, one can either refrain from writing such an article or, if one does write it, do so in a manner that is faithful to the movement for which it is or should be intended.

I very much hope that you understand me correctly. But please also bear in mind that such articles, written by a certain Nic Hoel, will be read in Moscow, throughout Norway, and elsewhere and will afford enemies of our work the means to say: "Look here, Nic Hoel is a member of Sexpol and just read what she writes; it doesn't agree at all with what that damned Reich says . . ."

I understand fully and seriously, and in friendship, some of the difficulties you have. You know that I personally support you, and you are also aware that I am very willing to allow everybody time to develop; but I believe that, within the context of the cause I represent and out of complete friendship, I am entitled and indeed obliged to inform you of the foregoing. It would make me very unhappy if you, Nic Hoel, whom we think such a great deal of, whom we hold in very high regard, should one day regret having written such things— namely, when the history of the Sexpol movement and the development of sex economy and sexual politics out of the criticism of Freud and out of the struggle against the Fenichels and Fromms of this world is made known.

A comrade who regards her- or himself as a member of the Sexpol movement and who wishes to be regarded as such cannot allow such a lapse. It is not a question of being submissive or of suspending the critical faculty; rather, anyone engaged in such difficult pioneering work as we are should not himself abet trends and tendencies that our most villainous opponents are also particularly fond of following. I know that you are one of us, and that is precisely why I wanted to tell you everything as clearly as I have.

I hope you have a good rest. Please keep in touch.

12 August 1936
Visit to Grundlsee: the children, Annie! Sad. Eva has become superficial, quiet, adjusted, Lore neurotically superficial. Annie says that

she is absolutely determined to raise the children herself. Eva situation not dead yet, but a final parting is certain. Why so many sacrifices?

18 August 1936

Grundlsee. This is getting to be ridiculous. Eva makes a wide detour around me. Occasionally, if she isn't thinking, an affectionate smile crosses her lips when she sees me.

Today when I was with them she asked me to leave.

When I am loving and patient it is interpreted as weakness. When I'm strict it adds fuel to their fire. Lorchen is visibly disinclined to react to me. The following facts:

1. Being alone with the children (a car ride) is not permitted.
2. Having the children at my house, not permitted.
3. The children do not visit me or talk with me.
4. Eva does not wish to talk with me: "I'm too cowardly."

It is horrible and ludicrous. Annie remarked today that she was unable to forgive herself for having been "tolerant" for so long. Her tolerance is precisely what infuriated me.

Strangely enough, I'm in an atmosphere of *punishment*!!

I said I would not sever the connection but could only be contacted in Oslo from now on. Support payments will be held in Oslo.

Annie is taking revenge at the children's expense.

20 August 1936

Beginning the journey back to Oslo with a thousand worries. Foremost: Will Eva see it through or give up? I can do no more. The louder the din of human destruction, the quieter the world becomes. People save themselves by simply closing their eyes.

2 August–5 September 1936

Alone by car: Oslo, Copenhagen, Gydnia, Kattowitz, Prague, Marienbad, Linz, Grundlsee, Innsbruck, Zurich, Paris, Dieppe, Newhaven, Totnes, London, Elsbjerg, Copenhagen, Oslo!!!

5 September 1936

It feels good to be back again. Laboratory, work, home! Another 6,100 kilometers, another chapter closed. A new one is beginning.

6 September 1936

And the truth must finally lie in that which every oppressed individual feels within himself but hasn't the courage to express.

8 September 1936

Stalin will become the Hitler of Russia, no doubt about it.

6 October 1936

On Sunday, Malinowski complained to me about his suffering. How miserable everyone is! With the Polish ambassador he donned his "dignity." The Portuguese ambassador and the other big wheels talked for half an hour and said *nothing*, absolutely nothing.

Revolutionary parties themselves make the mistake of showing celebrities great respect and then instilling that in the masses instead of destroying it, instead of demonstrating how pitiful and unworthy these decorous fools really are.

I see clearly a vision of a future world, but to express this vision in words would mean isolating oneself completely from the present world. It is obvious that humans are the only living creatures who deny the natural law of pleasure. Therefore war must exist. Frenzied electrical machines attacking one another—the senselessness of life is only made possible through the denial of the biology of life. Only sexuality can produce an electrical charge. *Sexuality equals life.* Its denial destroys life, which then thrives on the violation of pleasure. But all this philosophy is worthless trash. We must rescue life! But we are powerless, despite our superiority.

The better one understands the world and mankind, and the greater one's involvement, the further removed one is, because man does not understand himself and hates and murders anyone who tells him what he really is. The unfolding of new life extinguishes the old, but the old doesn't want to be extinguished, would rather vegetate.

Yes, one is completely alone—the more alone the better, and the more thoroughly one feels life pulsating. Animal life grows on plant life, just as apples grow on trees. How natural, but how "revolutionary"!

Elsa will leave me for the very reason that she loves me and cannot cope with this. My hands are tied! I see, understand, and am powerless.

11 November 1936

I ask myself whether my lot is an inevitability related to my work or whether it has arisen from a weakness within myself—namely, that in order to win my battle I make myself hard, rigid, somehow not flexible enough in my personal relationships. I'm sure I must be doing that to save myself from ruin. My question, after forty years of life, is: Were the sacrifices necessary? Annie, my children, and now Elsa, friends, organizational affiliations, etc. It must be some weakness of mine but I can't see which one! True, Elsa's reactions are severely neurotic; she impedes my work, is jealous of coworkers. And still, could I have done better? I would have *had* to find a better way, here at the summit of my work. This conflict between family-oriented and family-opposed existence can only be borne at the expense of life itself. There is no solution. I want a child by Elsa—and then what? Scenes, deceit, the ruin of a child, maybe even the ruin of Elsa and myself. It's so idiotic, now that I have everything I need to be happy. These cursed times! If only I could discover whether it is the demands of my work or a weakness of my own!

Eva wrote me a letter saying, "Don't write to me, because I am quite angry with you"—i.e., she is longing for me. Her handwriting is a scrawl, indicating severe inner strife. Poor thing! She should know that she can depend on me, that she can count on me. Someday she'll come—probably shattered.

Despite professional success I feel so miserable. Will it all pay off someday? I love Elsa, her realness, but actually everyone is magnificent and it's only the plague* that makes them the way they are.

I must be proud, very proud, without becoming hardened. I must find a way to do my work without causing people to go to pieces. I absolutely must! This struggle to be human is difficult, very difficult.

And in addition there is so much hard work—politics, biology, therapy, organization, a new problem every hour. Have to hold it all together!

TO ELSA LINDENBERG
11 November 1936

My dear Elsa,

I am writing this letter to you not only as the man with whom you have lived for four and a half years but also, and in particular, as a comrade who bears a great deal of responsibility for important work

---

* Reich refers to the existence of neuroses on a mass scale.

and for an organization. You must believe me that I am making every effort to say as honestly as I can exactly what I feel. I am doing this not to reject you but to keep you for us, for our work, and for me. I have tried in vain to say this to you face to face. There have been so many misunderstandings that I prefer to put in writing what I said last evening. The current problem is not a special case; it is typical for many of us, and many more people will have to go through it.

Before continuing, I would like to say how I and most of our friends felt and feel about you. You have enjoyed a great deal of honest, true respect in our group. This was not affected by our knowledge of your weaknesses, which you have just as anybody else does. We were all extremely happy that you enjoyed such great success in last winter's performance; we were happy that you had recovered your drive and had entered a period of unusual productivity. We all realized that you would be the right person to represent the ideas of Sexpol in your particular field of endeavor. But we also realized that you would first have to go through a certain process of development. Many of us, and primarily myself, helped you in every way possible, providing you with accommodations, knowledge, friendship, money, and real comradeship. I am saying this not to boast or to ask for thanks but to express something that will become clear later on: I did not ask for thanks, but neither did I want to be treated badly, as you have treated me and some others among us; your reasons for doing so are now irrelevant. I am merely trying to tell you how I see the situation at present.

You came into conflict with some of our friends and coworkers. I was the first person to notice it and to tell you that I would stand by you. Since that time, everyone, without exception, has recognized their irrational reactions and corrected them through long discussions and through treatment, etc. Other people also had difficulties, not just you. We were all making an effort to be human and decent. We recognized that we are going through a necessary process in ourselves; we had to go through it because to us fell the unenviable task not only of recognizing the role of the irrational in social existence but also of coping with it. In our own circle, we are experiencing, on a greatly magnified scale, a very important piece of the misery of the world. We could not do our work if we were to reject these experiences. We are simultaneously the subject and the object of the world's madness.

You have a positive attitude toward the cause, not just intellectually but also emotionally. But a pathological mechanism has interposed itself and as a result your interest is not genuine, and you have a craving to be taken seriously. In my opinion, everything else follows from this, as you are probably best able to judge from your analysis.

But the question now arises how this understanding attitude toward problems can be reconciled with the demands of real solid work. It is not always easy. The work will go on, will become more and more complex and difficult, and it is not possible to let everything come to a standstill because of this or that disturbance. Elsa, I assure you that I, and your so-called enemies as well, witnessed very clearly your honest attempts to comprehend and to organize things differently. But the form of expression and the intensity of your disruptive reactions made it impossible to rely solely on adopting an understanding attitude and calmly waiting things out. In addition, I have the feeling that doing nothing more than being understanding and patient brings with it the risk that you will not truly, deep down, and totally, grasp and eliminate the cause of the problem. My feeling that your interest and your efforts were not genuine, that there is a layer of unbelievable rigidity in the way you cling to the impossible (behind all this, it should be noted, lives a splendid Sexpol person), was confirmed the day before yesterday when you declared with considerable but sincere agitation that the entire Sexpol business is a load of rubbish, that with a few exceptions the workers are not comrades and citizens, that I am mad and full of lies, that we make such a fuss about ourselves. In the process, you cited your proletarian childhood and the deprivation you suffered. You displayed a hatred toward the Sexpol movement that shocked me but that also revealed why your true, genuine interest in the cause must find nongenuine expression: you had to suppress this hatred. It is good that it came out. Now the decision can be made whether you genuinely remain with us or genuinely go away. You have often seriously insulted me by referring to your proletarian origins and your hatred of intellectuals, but I have never held it against you. But that same evening I gave you the following matter-of-fact explanation.

You have no right to look down in that way and judge people who are working as we are, who are as committed to a revolutionary cause. I reject such judgment both in my own name and on behalf of my comrades for as long as they are working. You do not have the slightest right, by referring to a miserable childhood, to escape the obligation to fit in and to learn. A wretched existence is a misfortune, but in the absence of any enduring revolutionary contribution, it is not a reason for feeling superior. To a large extent, the problem of our age is that scientists and the impoverished middle class are mostly as bad off as the workers. It is a problem to place these strata of society alongside the proletariat. I believe that any superiority of the kind that you claimed is unjustified and politically dangerous. It cannot be permitted in our organization. You know as well as I do that large masses of, say, Scandinavian or German workers are as bourgeois as the bourgeoisie itself. You also know very well that I get on much better with uneducated workers than with bourgeois citizens or academics; this is one of the reasons for the hostility toward me. But this does nothing to alter the fact that I regard the sexual distress of a bourgeois girl in just the same way as I do that of a proletarian girl. You rant and rave about Lotte, a bourgeois girl who joined us just two years ago. What does this mean? Even if it costs me my relationship with you, I must defend Lotte as long as she demonstrates through her actions that she is working for the cause. You complain angrily about Philipson, that bourgeois. What kind of comrade are you to make demands when you have not understood that we need the Philipsons, that we must help them to develop, to come over to us entirely, to become socialist human beings. I *must* defend Philipson against your attacks—regardless of whether they are irrational or not—as long as he works for the cause. You decry Sexpol as a bunch of neurotics. You insult them as "bourgeois," as rubbish. As a founder of the Sexpol movement I must protest. All mankind is sick, neurotic, shattered, in the gutter, and you along with them. So pitch in and help, and stop grumbling. The fact that you suffered deprivations in your childhood does not give you any rights but merely bestows on you the obligation to understand things better, to make things better, to be a leader, to bring people together, to cooperate. I too went hungry, I know the rabble! I have lain in the mire. What would you say if I referred to this and started cursing the way you do?

The situation appears clear to me: I am honestly willing to wait. From the standpoint of our work, I am absolutely determined to defend any of my coworkers so long as his or her work is useful. If you finally go away, then I shall suffer in much the way I did when I lost Eva:

the sacrifice is completely pointless. For me and for all of us, become a comrade, someone who is quietly willing to learn, work, and help us in our difficult cause. Then I will be happy to have you as a wife.

Take your time! There is a great deal involved for you, for me, for us all!

20 November 1936

Saw a film on cancer yesterday, shown by the English delegation. No doubt about it. I'm right.

"Migratory cancer cells" are amoebic formations. They are produced from disintegrating tissue and thus demonstrate the law of tension and charge in its purest form—as does the orgastic convulsion.

Now money is a must—cancer the main issue—in every respect, even political.

It was a staggering experience. My intuition is good. I depend on it.

Was absolutely driven to buy a microscope. The sight of the cancer cells was exactly as I had previously imagined it, had almost physically felt it would be. Cancer is an autoinfection of the body, of an organ. And researchers have no idea of what, how, or where!!

22 November 1936
Doubts

Are the structures obtained from Preparation 6b living structures or "merely" colloid particles that exhibit surface phenomena?

They can be seen to sprout, divide, copulate, "eat"! These are all signs of life! Until now, "life" has always evoked a mystical response, as if it were something completely different, separate. But the substances do not change as a result of the mechano-electrical leap; instead they function! Is a staphylococcus a life form or a charged colloidal vesicle? It depends on the definition of life! Have I therefore created life, or structures that function as if they were alive?

7 December 1936

It's incredible how stupid and petty, how unconscious the arguments against spontaneous generation are. "Life must have a father and mother"—there must be law and order!! Science! I'm going to plant a bomb under its ass!! Abiogenesis does exist!!

How ridiculous not to be honest with oneself as well. After all, I have struggled and have accomplished so much. In fifty to one hundred years they'll idolize me.

And I would have been grateful to them for just a smattering of fulfillment in real life. On what grounds did they take away my children, my love, my wife? On what grounds do they now refuse to accept life when I have discovered its principles for them? They engage in high-level politics but they deny life and kill anyone who illuminates it for them, only to make a god of him later. Life is what I wanted, to watch my children grow, to rejoice over them—with them. I don't want to be a martyr. I'm not made for that.

Now they are preparing for war, for slaughter, while the radio blares in the background.

World, mankind, where are we headed? Children, little children, hungering for love! I love life! I don't want this!

9 December 1936

Groping along in the dark like a blind man, guided only by a sure instinct, by the knowledge that life is this and nothing else. I must concentrate on biology! One has to be capable of waiting until things and processes reveal themselves.

TO ANNIE REICH
10 December 1936

Dear Annie,

I have just been through some very difficult days. I felt as if I were seasick. It was quite awful. But now I am recovered again. I am happy that I have finally learned to accept realities, not to regard the other person's interests, even when they clash with my own, as necessarily a sign of hostility toward me and not to get bogged down in reproaches.

I completely understand that you cannot have any interest in ensuring my happiness. However, this lesson could have been a little less painfully imparted. But there are many things involved: old love and comradeship, old resentment and a little bit of revenge, deep bonds and the fact that we have grown apart; all these complications must be included in any calculation. I was very down, but I am happy that I no longer reacted angrily but simply protected myself and preserved my strength to go on working, the demands of which are heavy. I was on the point of cracking up. You've seen me when I am like that and I am happy to say that I can see a way out, so that I can go on living in peace, without interruption. What got me down was the fact that I received no reply to the letters I wrote in September, that you ignored my plan to come and visit you at Christmas. My first reaction was to smash everything around me. My attempts to remain in contact with Lore are obviously unsuccessful. Since the summer of 1934 I have seen her for a total of only six days. I do not believe that is good for her. She has written me heartrending letters: she is looking for her father, all girls have fathers except her, etc., etc. What should I do? I do not feel guilty. Neither of us is guilty. But we must be clear that the paths of our lives are moving further and further apart; the children should not be torn to pieces in the process. There is still one way out—and I say this entirely without bitterness—that is for me to withdraw completely from their lives. I know that deep inside I would not be able to accept children who were raised under the influence of Anna Freud's Weltanschauung. And they would not be able to accept me. But ranting and raging would be pointless. There is also the possibility of placing the children in a completely neutral zone where they could be and become themselves. But I imagine that this would create problems from your side. Everything is so terribly bitter, despite the enormous successes I am achieving in my work. I yearn to have children around me. Because of my work it is very doubtful if that will happen. The threat facing us is my becoming emotionally detached from the children or reducing my relationship with them to the normal kind of fatherhood. I don't know what you think about this or what you want to do. You have never replied to my repeated questions whether or not you would like to have Lore live with you. I assume that this is because you are not interested in anything that I want. I had hoped very much that our ways would not diverge so widely and that certain common interests would remain. I am neither angry nor insulted, I am simply looking for a way out. It might one day prove bad for the children, if circumstances should ever change, that they were unable to establish a relationship with me. I think we should bear that in mind right now. In view of the great distance, our difficulties, and the infrequency of the visits with the children, I think it would be important and in their interest if they were to learn a little bit about me and my life and if I were more to them than just a shadow. Believe me when I say that I am writing today without bitterness. I would not have written otherwise.

So, if you think it is important enough, please write to me occasionally to let me know how you see the future developing.

Although I am seriously willing to acknowledge your point of view as a fact, I am equally anxious to get my own viewpoint across. Later the children should know precisely what I thought and what I wanted. It is not possible to predict how things will develop. I am interested fundamentally in whether the great cause will triumph. I believe that all the major problems of our age are reflected and reproduced in these "trivial matters." Please understand my view of you, and don't be reproachful. Be a little bit more open with me. In particular it is very important that you consider carefully where I am going or where I am being taken by my work. Please do not worry that, as in the past, I still take umbrage at misunderstandings or incomprehension. I have really learned to know and to admit fully to myself what I am doing. Nowadays, I no longer become angry if recognition is denied me, and this makes my existence very much easier. Mind you, I cannot completely control my rage at certain diplomatic attitudes toward me. But recently a very smart person told me that I would never get used to such things, nor should I even try.

I know too little about your present life to judge how much you know about me. I have heard that you are retreating from politics more and more. I am being more and more deeply drawn in. A few days ago I received a letter from an illustrious university library that —and I am very proud of this—described my psychiatric works as the most *decisive* contribution to dialectical materialism since Ulyanov* (literally) and credited me with playing the main role, "later," in developing it. The first fruits are being harvested, even though the pickings are sparse. And hostilities rage against me. But I am very

* Lenin.

calm and confident in my replies. Holland and Spain are particularly strong sources of interest. This gives me strength and confidence. One becomes less aware of the razor's edge along which one has to walk.

My experiments (I am now working alone) have also, against all expectations, yielded positive results. Recently—you will laugh, but it's true—I was able beyond any doubt to take an electrophotograph of a kiss. And if I were now to lay wires to Prague and could connect you up, I would know precisely your feelings and emotions as you read my letter. It is already possible, from one room to another, to determine objectively and conclusively the slightest flicker of pleasure and nonpleasure. Soon I will turn my attention to radiation. I know that you are skeptical, but the people here are astonished and, to be honest, so am I. Look what "little Willi" has done!

But on the whole, little Willi is very sad because people are trying to punish him. Why? Annie, try to act differently! It will work.

Much love.

TO ROGER DU TEIL
12 December 1936

Dear Professor,

I am writing to inform you about the current status of the experiments that have taken place since the work with which you are already familiar. I am almost reluctant to write to you so directly and openly because a few months ago it still seemed incredible, even to me, that the results could be correct. After I had succeeded last year in confirming the tension-charge formula in electrical experiments, I set about studying protozoa and colloidal substances. Then in April, on the basis of the tension-charge formula, I was able to produce colloidal structures that behave in exactly the same manner as living cells.* I did not want to talk about this to anybody until I had convinced myself by means of culturing tests that I was actually dealing with biological

---

* Reich named these structures "bions." See *The Bion Experiments* (New York: Farrar, Straus and Giroux, 1979).

dynamisms. In the last two weeks, I have succeeded in observing the growth of cultures of cell formations that I had obtained by boiling certain substances. I can imagine that at this point you might be experiencing some distrust because the whole thing sounds mystical, and I myself did not believe for a long time that it might really be true. But the facts are so unequivocal that they can no longer be doubted, at least as far as the tests conducted until now are concerned. All the filmable tests and results have been captured photographically (16 mm format), so it will be possible to make copies available.

Two days ago, I successfully demonstrated the experiment for Albert Fischer at the Rockefeller Institute. The substances were mixed and boiled, and my colleagues detected cell-like moving structures immediately after the boiling. Giemsa staining of the preparation was positive. It will now take a long time to carry out the complete set of confirmatory and control experiments. Please be kind enough to inform me whether I might submit a provisional report, through you or directly, to the French Academy of Science for publication. A detailed report on the experimental work conducted last year would then follow in due course.

12 December 1936

The grandchildren of my bions have come to life; so that's the third generation!!

I actually have every reason to be very happy. If only this epidemic of neuroses didn't bother me!!

The cancer plague is becoming more understandable all the time.
1. The disturbed sex economy of the human being
2. The production of motile forms from disintegrating tissue
3. Mechanistic and religious thinking in the sciences

13 December 1936

Today, suddenly, the following happened. Elsa had agreed to stay away from the Sexpol meetings temporarily because analysis had intensified her frantic condition. A meeting had been arranged because of the Leunbach affair.* She was aware of this but nevertheless flew into a rage over "filthy Sexpol." Today she informed me that she was going to sleep with another man. She says everything is different now. Obviously revenge for something imagined. But it's clear that it's all over.

Monogamy is unnatural. The whole secret behind Elsa's ravings is the fact that she wanted to sleep with other men and would not allow herself to do so. What a lie this world is! She will not find peace until she recognizes the law of nature.

Nic cannot cope with Elsa's neurosis because she would like to be my wife herself, in place of Elsa.† There is nothing I can do. Elsa is the victim of an insane constellation. One cannot give in to her, but one also can't reject her. Everything is falling apart: Jörgen‡ is dying. The Copenhagen Sexpol chapter has been disbanded. The chapter here has no experience.

Honesty is absolutely necessary. One can't succeed by playing tricks. How I loved Elsa! How sensitive I was to her. How her illness destroyed everything. How I preferred her to all other women. Fate? The story of our times! In reality, what is important now is not whether she receives someone else's penis into her body but *the horrendous contrast between life itself and the forms this life assumes for those who have to live it*. The love life of the king of England was more important, more exciting than the entire Spanish Civil War. The individuals responsible for revolution don't know what they want themselves.

I cannot control the madness of life but I can preserve its logic. Where life demands that its laws be fulfilled, I can, I must fight and defend them.

14 December 1936

I just awoke from a very restless sleep with the feeling that last night, when I was overwrought and announced to Elsa the abrupt end of all politicizing, I had by no means grasped the full extent of the catastrophe that rocked my entire work yesterday.

I had before me simultaneously all the arguments that were pressing

---

* J. H. Leunbach, a Danish physician and Sexpol member, had been charged with performing an illegal abortion.
† Elsa was in analysis with Nic Hoel.
‡ Jörgen Neergaard, a young member of the Sexpol organization.

toward the inevitable conclusion that for the moment, until further notice, a continuation of Sexpol is completely uncalled for. Immediately I had to raise the question of whether I was not trying to escape from Sexpol myself in order to devote myself to my biological discovery. For the last few days I have been giving it a great deal of thought. I had serious doubts about the Sexpol organization and felt constrained to agree with my enemies, or onetime friends, who have withdrawn. The venture I had dared to embark on was mad, could only have been undertaken by a megalomaniac or an honest but naive child groping around in a filthy world. It was by no means a stroke of genius, nor was it courageous. If I had known ten years ago, had really had a perspective on what would be going on today, I would never have touched it. I merely drew naive, self-evident conclusions from my work as a physician. The death crisis for Sexpol has begun. If the organization does not withstand the attack in Copenhagen, then it ought to perish. If it survives, so much the better. It can only survive, however, by admitting, without reservations, to the real situation.

I want to summarize the reasons behind my putting matters on a yes or no basis this time. But first I'll list the sacrifices I made because I firmly believed in the soundness of my work and its consequences:

Loss of all the fruits of a decade of activity as a teacher who raised a whole generation of psychoanalysts.

Loss of the usual bourgeois career within a bourgeois life, which everyone is striving for today—striving all the more intensely and noisily the more the situation demands revolution. Am I strong enough to stem that tide?

I lost my membership in three organizations: the German Socialist Party, the German Communist Party, and the IPA. This was no "tactical" error on my part but rather a logical consequence of my utterly naive convictions, which had nothing to do with "power politics," and my combining of theory and practice. I simply drew my own conclusions without thinking where that might lead, although I was aware it might be dangerous.

I was deeply disappointed by scientists, socialists, politicians, and people in general. During the early years I was annoyed with them because they weren't consistent. Today I understand why they couldn't be consistent, and I'm no longer infuriated. I am better equipped to prepare far in advance and not be crushed by disappointments. My organic, vegetative conviction of the correctness of my views is the source of the strength that people admire in me. What occasionally made me *very* insecure was people's negative reactions. They always appeared to be saying I was wrong. They seemed more "rational," "clearer," more "realistic politically," and more "worldly-wise." I knew I was right but I couldn't stand alone forever; I needed people to help me. Until now I have really only had people or groups who were temporarily willing to help me over a certain period. The speed of my development was too fast for all of them. To date, not one has really followed me all the way. Whoever is able to stand by now, and dares to, must prove it! To strike out at human structure, including my own, means to be able to rout it, conquer it. I was incapable of doing this. Perhaps because I am not a politician, but perhaps also because the problem lies even deeper than I have recognized until now. I know that my cause can only be saved permanently through the strictest recording of facts. Today I am confronted with the question: *Can the real sexual-political task at hand be combined with my scientific work on a long-term basis?* It is obvious that my work is more important.

The Leunbach affair is the first test of what the organization can bear.

Two physicians, both hard-core Sexpol members, are locked up for doing nothing more than practicing medicine. One loses five years; the other, two. An essential part of my medical and scientific work involves being in conflict with the law. Leunbach and Philipson* are fighting as well as they can. But this shows that even these two trained men who are close to us were not in full command of the Sexpol arsenal and were unable to put it to use. That is why they lost. Then how can we expect or demand that other people do better? People are so willing to call themselves Sexpol members, but good intentions are simply not enough.

Sigurd Hoel did nothing. Nic Hoel went to Copenhagen and returned with valid criticism of the attempt to found a mass organization. Nevertheless, I sensed she was disappointed in the nature of the struggle (defensive rather than aggressive) and in the poor attendance at the meeting.

I went to Copenhagen fearing that L. and P. would exercise their

* Tage Philipson was accused of neglecting a sick patient.

right to appeal for clemency. I would not have reproached them for this, but it was good to hear that they hadn't even considered it and that they held themselves accountable, recognized their greatest mistakes, and knew that this trial was only a beginning. It was obvious that their lawyers were seriously hindering them. Moral: Don't use lawyers. Don't be passive or simply defensive. They could have saved themselves, and the cause as well, if they had used sex economy to its fullest extent and not taken a middle course between the World League for Sexual Reform and Sexpol.* But even all these mistakes give no one the right to trample on them or to accuse them or to be ashamed of them. They were the first members of Sexpol to stand before a court and fight. No one has yet proven he could, or would, do better. Our highest duty was absolute and unconditional solidarity.

But what *did* happen on that score—and what is happening? Again, an example to illustrate this: Lisa Jensen, with her 30,000 members, didn't lift a finger, merely sent a telegram expressing her sympathy and advising them to seek clemency.† Oeverland‡ didn't write. Nor did Sigurd, Nic, or Raknes. If Sexpol does indeed exist—with everyone from the communists to the fascists against it—and Leunbach is its exponent, struggling for it, then this attitude is out of the question.

Either we take the cause seriously or not. If we do, we ought to know what we're involved with; if not, then let's get off our high horse. I left with the threat that, if Leunbach received no help, Sexpol no longer existed.

There's constant discussion about not only practicing criticism but learning to accept it. At the moment I shall not withhold my criticism. We'll see who takes his own advice seriously.

Recently there has been a lot of talk that my visa will not be extended. People regularly ask me most solicitously, "Then where do you think you want to go?" Very friendly, very warmhearted! No, I will not entrust the cause to that kind. Nor will I entrust myself or the many people who are being ruined. No one is expected to be a fighter, but

* The World League for Sexual Reform, led at the time by Magnus Hirschfeld, maintained that sexual reform was apolitical and divorced from the social order.
† Lisa Jensen, a Swedish woman involved in the National Organization for Sexual Education.
‡ Arnulf Oeverland, poet laureate of Norway and a friend of Reich's.

then no one should lay claim to having set things in motion or to the right to make decisions.

Several very real aspects of the objective situation must also be considered:

The unrecognized Nazification of the world

The socialists' relation to the question of sex

The severity of people's irrational reactions (Elsa)

My inability to cope with everything at once

It is perfectly clear that Sexpol has the answer to National Socialism. This constitutes an obligation to decency, courage, and solidarity. Or perhaps correct knowledge still can't be converted into action. But then—no organizational nonsense!

26 December 1936

The temptation to put an end to all of this filthy politics is too great. But then what was the purpose of these fifteen years? If I renounce politics I run the risk of becoming inflexible. If I continue with politics I run the risk of overdiversifying and of sacrificing the full utilization of my scientific work.

1937

"I want something very simple: a woman who just says, 'Come, lover, let's make each other happy,' with no ulterior motives!"

1 January 1937
What was known before me?

The idea that life = sexuality (Freud, Hartmann)
The concept of orgasm
The concept of tradition—subjective factor
The reactionary role of the family
The relationship of religion—Oedipus complex, father
The concept of the stasis of sexual excitation
The idea of spontaneous generation
The idea of sexual reform, indeed world sexual reform: sexual politics
Pregenitality
Character as fact
Methodology of dialectical materialism
The idea that the "savage" has another kind of life
The concept of social freedom—external conditions of same
Strategy and tactics of revolutionary politics
Social democracy

What did I bring?

The experimental proof of "sex = life"
The unknown formula of sexuality
The definition of the orgasm concept
The knowledge of the *means* of the traditional effects of the family
Religion = sex with a negative sign
Church = sexual-political organization of the patriarchy
The experimental proof of spontaneous generation
The fundamentals of socialistic sexual politics
Unconscious = vegetative
Stasis = electrical tension
Character as dynamic-economic principle—armor

Functional identity of psychic and vegetative

Origin of the inner contradiction—dialectic law of development

Proof of the changeover from sex positive to sex negative in ethnology

Concretizing "freedom" as the capacity for sexual happiness, inner condition of this freedom

Restoring and making specific the concept of the masses—revolutionary politics = politics of need

Psychic fundamentals of social democracy, conditions of its failure

My faults and illusions

Little self-confidence despite absolute inner certainty, despite confirmation of hunches

Too short-term in my outlook

Requiring the other person to see things and act as I do

Demanding performance and recognition instead of conviction

Overlooking the effects of organizing = rigidification of movements (psychoanalysis and communism)

Not understanding why people flee from me—as fear of being disturbed

Too strongly bound to authorities

TO THE FRENCH ACADEMY
OF SCIENCE
8 January 1937

Under separate cover, I am sending you a preparation produced in the manner described in the provisional report attached hereto. Would you kindly let me know your opinion of the outcome of the investigation, and would you please, as well, file this report with the academy and publish it in the academy's official publication.

At present, my institute is producing a detailed film of the entire process. The film should be ready in a few months, and a copy will be sent to the academy. I would like to add, in particular, that the first cultures have been made from the preparation and they turned out positive. The boiling test described will be dealt with in detail in the near future, together with other biological experiments I have carried out over the course of the past year.

TO ALBERT FISCHER
9 January 1937

Dear Doctor,

I asked my two friends and colleagues Dr. Leunbach and Dr. Philipson to maintain contact with you after I gave a demonstration of the boiling experiment at your institute. Today I received a letter from Dr. Leunbach that greatly surprised me because what he told me about your present opinions would seem to stand in sharp contrast to the highly accommodating and understanding attitude you displayed on the day of the experiment. I have no intention of commenting on the remarks that, as Dr. Leunbach has reported, you made about me personally, because they have nothing to do with the factual assessment of me and my work.

All I wish to do is to take immediate steps to avert a particular kind of comment on factual matters that will no doubt occasionally, and possibly even frequently, crop up in the further course of my work and otherwise in the scientific world to which I must expound my research. Dr. Leunbach informs me that you accuse me of being uncritical and a fantast. I really cannot recall at what point in the demonstration I might have displayed such qualities. Before demonstrating my experiment I told you explicitly that the matter was so "laughably simple" that I was hesitant to demonstrate it at all. You encouraged me to proceed nevertheless and, after understandably hesitating for a while, I stopped vacillating and gave you a full report. It was not my intention to slight either you or your coworkers. I would like to stress that.

A different situation is created by your criticism that I asked for ridiculously large magnifications when, as you reportedly said, "whatever there was to be seen could have been seen at ordinary magnification." My assertions are based on observations that were made not at the usual magnifications of about $500 \times$ to $1,200 \times$ but instead at magnifications in excess of $2,000 \times$. It is a distinctive characteristic of my work that at magnifications of less than $2,000 \times$ the phenomena I am referring to can only be seen after long and intensive examination, whereas they show up clearly and unmistakably at the stated magnifications. I use a Leitz binocular microscope with angled binocular tubes that give about 50 percent stronger magnification than a straight single tube. At your institute I tried in vain to obtain an appropriate magnification. This remark is certainly not intended as a criticism, but I must ask you, please, to appreciate that I must protect my work from being misunderstood.

Furthermore, according to Dr. Leunbach's report, you assert that all the motion observed was merely movement of the liquid. I must counter this by pointing out that the preparations were all produced by you or your assistants, and the goal when so doing was to eliminate all fluid flow. In fact, none occurred; instead, you and your assistants were forced to admit that *instead of all the structures moving in one direction*, they were moving in relation to one another. The matter can be very easily resolved by producing a paraffinated, hermetically sealed preparation and observing it at magnifications of $2,000\times$ to $3,000\times$. Then the movements of all the structures can be clearly seen, namely locomotion, expansion, and contraction, as well as movement of the contents; this latter phenomenon occurs in individual structures. I am prepared to make this claim before any person or authority.

One of your assistants also carried out Giemsa staining and showed me the positive result of staining cocci- and rod-shaped bacterialike structures. I myself, in my own tests, did not get as far as staining. Similarly, I was astonished to learn that you refer to what you saw as "lecithin structures," whereas I demonstrated very precisely what a lecithin structure is, namely, an object that does not move from the spot but merely swells, as opposed to a structure that moves around in space in amoeboid fashion and, as stated, exhibits contraction and expansion movements when observed with sufficient magnification, i.e., between $2,000\times$ and $3,500\times$. I would like to stand by my opinion that the phenomena should be observed using the methods that permit this to be done.

I am not prepared at this point to discuss the question of whether these are simply old fairy tales dating from Pasteur's days; right now I am just interested in observations of facts that will—perhaps later— either confirm Pasteur's germ theory or give rise to a new interpretation. At the same time, I would like to assure you that I myself also firmly believe that rats and mice cannot be created by leaving a mixture of old rags, flour, and moisture to stand in the dark. But I do believe that there are a number of questions and problems in biology which cannot be solved by germ theory or by the old mystical theory of creation. It is part and parcel of the work we all perform to try to resolve such questions.

I would also like to set the record straight on another point. While at your institute, I never asserted that I had observed spindle fibers. What I did say was that at a binocular magnification of $3,000 \times$, and with good light conditions, i.e., dimmed so that the structures of the plasma stand out clearly, nuclear divisions can be observed, and at the same time phenomena that may resemble the spindle-shaped configuration are visible. I was very careful and explicitly stressed that, apart from the boiling tests, which have been explained, everything else is unclear. I would like to make sure that the demonstration I gave at your institute does not lead to false reports about my work reaching the biological world.

In conclusion, please allow me to make one more comment on your criticism of my mixture of biology and psychology. It has so far been my belief—based, at least, on the theoretical discussions in the literature on biology and psychology, and I am familiar with the principal works in these fields—that in epistemological terms scientific biology does not disallow the intermeshing of biological and psychological problems any more than scientific psychology would. I am very eager to make it clear right now that it was pure chance that led me from my work in the field of clinical psychotherapy to the experimental study of physiology and biology.

The purpose of the demonstration that I gave at your institute was to obtain technical advice from you on how I should best proceed. I would regret it very much indeed if I was not successful in making this clear.

18 January 1937

Wonderful! Egg yolk + KCl is "alive," just like streptococci. No Brownian movement—or is there?

The following possibilities exist:

1. Transitions from nonliving to living are fluid, developmental stages.

2. There are two fundamental spontaneous motions: chemical-physical (not culturable) and organic life (culturable).

3. Everything that moves spontaneously is "alive." Egg yolk in water, like milk, like leukocytes, like *Willi Reich*.

4. We eat and, by cooking meat, enable killed life to give rise to new life.

Control: Check tension-charge in dry and wet state.

25 January 1937

Radek,* Bukharin,† etc., will be corpses in a few days!! Stalin's a fascist! The dough is being kneaded by powers the revolution forgot to discover.‡ A catastrophe for the movement! Points of debate do exist but they are not within the grasp of the individuals upon whom it would depend.

The fact that humans are the only species not permitted to live according to natural law takes its toll, demands senseless sacrifices. Thus one revolutionary act follows the next through an unbroken succession of ossified imitators who never understood what the revolution really intended. And that's the way it will remain for a long time. Until the practice of human happiness has been grasped.

TO EVA REICH
27 January 1937

My dear Evchen,

Today I will keep my letter short. A few days ago I sent you 170 Norwegian kroner, which is the equivalent of about 210 schillings,

---

* Karl Radek, a Soviet propagandist and leading member of the presidium of the Communist International, was expelled from the party and tried in January 1937 on a trumped-up treason charge. He is presumed to have died in captivity.
† Nikolai Ivanovich Bukharin, Russian communist leader and active Marxist propagandist. In 1928, he opposed Stalin's policy of forced industrialization. Arrested in 1937, condemned to death, and shot.
‡ Reich refers to the prevailing character structure, to the human incapacity for freedom and happiness.

for February. Today, as you asked, I am sending an additional 70 NKr, approximately 90 Sch. Please write and let me know why you needed so much more money this month. Don't feel guilty, you should not begrudge yourself the cash. I was very happy to hear that you had a pleasant skiing vacation. But at the same time, I would like to make a brief comment on another matter: Motesiczky told me you said to him that I always want you to be together with boys and that you don't like this. I don't want to get into an argument with you over this, Eva, but I want to set matters straight. I have never asked you to spend time with boys. Only my enemies make such assertions. Where did you get this idea? Please be careful when making such remarks to other people, because if my own daughter makes such statements, then it must be true that I am a child seducer. I don't hold this against you, but I would ask you to remember that this never happened. Of course, this does not mean that I have changed my basic opinion that love between boys and girls is a natural human need. But I do not force anybody to indulge in it.

All the best for the future.

With much love.

1 *February 1937*
On the culture question

1. In the bion cultures *and* in the decomposed nutrient media there are numerous bions, but also *long, undulating, moving rods* (———) that are not present in the fresh bion preparation.

Question: Rot bacteria?

Answer: These bacteria are not found in rot preparations. They give a neutral reaction to electric current, unlike rot bacteria, which become paralyzed.

2. The long rods are not found in unboiled dust + H_2O. So, nothing came from the air!

3. Dust preparations contain relatively few bacteria—Pasteur??

Amazing problems—unsolved

1. Why do bions not precipitate out as a result of boiling, whereas cancer . . . ?

Two different substance states.

2. What does the movement in the yolk signify? Is the proto-embryo a vesicle that feeds on the yolklike bions?

4 February 1937
Doubts!!

Apart from bion strains I and II and one tube III, no more bions can be cultured. Possible explanations:

a. I, II, III were inoculated under nonsterile conditions.

b. Berle* is making some kind of mistake.

c. Other unknown conditions must be met.

On the other hand, boiled cultures yield further cultures of bions. Consolation: It is senseless to concentrate on cultures.

1. The others were also unable to culture *all* the bacteria.

2. The problem has shifted.

Formerly: Are bions living organisms?

Now: Since most of the boiled material is motile, at what point does metabolic activity commence? Where does the jump from physical movement to life occur?

3. I have never claimed that I created life, merely that I uncovered the life process.

Through experimentation, I reconstruct the life process and make it controllable. I revoke the ideology of finished life, without a beginning or an end. *There is a beginning and an end to life, evolution of species, stages in the development of life.*

Lifeless and living matter that moves.

Everything is confusing!

---

* A laboratory assistant.

TO PAUL NEERGAARD *
24 *February 1937*

Dear Dr. Neergaard,

As regards your connection with your firm, I would like to make the following comment, solely on my own behalf:

If it is absolutely certain that your firm does not, under any circumstances whatever, have any legal claim to any practical results of the work performed by you in the firm's laboratory, then there is in principle nothing to prevent us from working together. In that case, I will send you in the next few days, once we have agreed on the first experiments, a provisional contract that you and I should sign.

As for the experiments you have conducted, you committed two errors. First, you fell victim to the fetish term "Brownian movement." You are aware that scientific designations originally intended to summarize a set of facts change their function and act as a total block to any further scientific thought. So far it has not occurred to anybody to carry out truly concrete tests and to determine what Brownian movement really is and in what way it differs in principle from the movement of biological organisms. In addition, you committed the error of not allowing the earth to stand a few days before observing it. You would then have noticed certain changes in the structure of the crystals—namely, amoeboid movements and vesicular disintegration. To encourage you, I would like to tell you a little story. When I instructed my current assistant, Miss Berle, in the technique of performing the earth tests, I showed her among other things a contractile earth structure at approximately $3,000 \times$ magnification. She looked for no less than ten minutes without seeing the totally clear movement. I kept on asking her whether she could see something and she always replied, "No, I can't see a thing." After about ten minutes of uninterrupted observation she suddenly cried out, "Yes, it's moving"—that is, she suddenly saw something that had been taking place already although she had been unable to observe it. The same thing will also happen to you; it happened to me as well, and that's the way it is with all new discoveries. So, please allow the earth to swell up and be sure to carry out long and precise daily observations for at least eight days.

* Danish plant pathologist.

Not only look for the movement of the rods and vesicles, about whose biological nature one can argue, but focus your attention in particular on the vesicular disintegration of the crystals of earth and the motility that then sets in. For modern scientific ears this is naturally an unbelievable process. But it is absolutely true; it exists. I have filmed it and that is certainly an objective method. The organisms you saw in my laboratory were already motile amoeboids of earth and coal. Please repeat the experiment over and over again until you really see this. I believe that this is a prior condition for our cooperation, because everything else is based on that observation.

I am currently performing culturing tests with swollen earth. These tests were positive right away, but I have to carry out a large number of control tests in order to be absolutely certain. We have prepared a control specimen here in the laboratory using the earth that you autoclaved. You will hear from us on this matter in the near future.

The bion cultures can now be regarded as an absolutely definite phenomenon, and I will reveal them or send them to you at a later date. But please be patient and take your time.

28 February 1937

A vague something is pressing ahead. Am in the middle of it myself. I construct theories on life, but life doesn't depend on theories—it lives.

How petty and laughable man's strivings are, how lamentable even the greatest human endeavor, revolution.

Life must be affirmed: development, joy, pleasure, children, growth.

Union and separation—life lies in these antitheses. We allow ourselves this at midnight, only to forget during the following day's work.

Children who blossom, flowers that bud, breasts that swell, lips that kiss, arms that embrace, life, life.

Death—a most ridiculous absurdity.

People live to die, this is realpolitik. But the truth lies in rhythm, ecstasy, love. Basically, what everyone wants is physical contact.

TO FRANK BLAIR HANSEN AND
H. M. MILLER *
2 March 1937

After detailed talks with Professor Malinowski, in London, and with Mr. Kittredge, with whom I had a discussion a few days ago here in Oslo, I am now turning to the Rockefeller Foundation.

As is clear from the enclosed "Provisional Reports" to the French Academy and to Professor du Teil at the Centre Universitaire Méditerranéen in Nice, I have succeeded in producing and *culturing* sterile, colloidal, lifelike structures. There is every reason to believe, therefore, that this is a successful experiment that does not merely imitate living protists but also actually produces them. These experiments have been monitored and verified by Professor du Teil in Nice.

I have succeeded in procuring the necessary apparatus and in setting up a small laboratory using privately obtained funds. Up to now friends and I have invested about 30,000 Norwegian kroner. But the development of bion research and of the experimental setups is proceeding so quickly that it is no longer possible to manage with private means alone. I merely wish to indicate the direction in which things are going.

It has been discovered that when fresh bion mixtures are injected intravenously and peritoneally into animals, they do not elicit any harmful effects. Further animal experiments are required to confirm, limit, or disprove this initial finding. Some initial experiments conducted with staphylococci, streptococci, and cancer cells seem to indicate that if the bions are produced and cultured in a thorough and comprehensive manner, some hopeful prospects are opened up, particularly when the composition of the bions is varied. I would not like to say any more on this topic than I am personally willing to back up at the present time. However, the phenomena that have been observed indicate that every effort should be made to determine what effect the bions have on pathogenic states. The work should be focused essentially, in the first instance, on cancer research.

---

* Along with Tracy B. Kittredge (referred to in the first paragraph), representatives of the Rockefeller Foundation. The foundation was the principal source of funding for physical-biological research and to a great extent controlled its direction.

The following apparatus and staff are needed to carry out appropriately thorough and reliable experimental work with the bion cultures that have so far been obtained and that will be obtained in the future: a biology assistant to study the biological nature of the bions, an assistant in bacteriological techniques and animal experiments, an assistant for metabolic testing and for determining pH values, an assistant specifically trained in cancer-tissue techniques, an assistant specifically trained in filming microscopic preparations, an assistant for histopathological testing. In addition, a properly organized filing system and an office should be set up.

The work is being carried out provisionally on a small scale in an old rented house that is equipped temporarily as a working laboratory. I myself possess a complete bacteriological-biological laboratory with filming capability.

Please let me know whether, on the basis of the experimental results that have been achieved, there is any prospect of obtaining a grant from the Rockefeller Foundation. Leaving aside the cost of the apparatus, the monthly operating costs are already on the order of $300–$400, but it is quite clear that as the work progresses at a rapid pace, more and more money will be required. In the long term, there can be no doubt that housing the work in the old wood house, as we currently do, will not be appropriate for performing accurate research work.

I would ask you to get in touch with Professor du Teil on this matter because not only is he kept up to date on the ongoing experiments but he is fully familiar with the preliminary electrophysiological experiments conducted on the human body ("Experimental Results on the Electrical Function of Sexuality and Anxiety"). Professor du Teil was also good enough to translate this work into French.

I would like to add one more personal comment. I am not a biologist by profession, but I did receive good practical training in biology some years ago; in fact, I am a practicing psychotherapist with special knowledge of vegetative neural functions. I am employed here as a professor of character analysis at the Psychological Institute of the university under Professor Schjelderup. Over a period of about fifteen years of studying psychophysiological functions in the vegetative nervous systems of mentally ill people and neurotics, I have arrived at a formula describing the function of life that, to my own astonishment, has by chance led me to the present central area of biological research.

8 March 1937

Again I am in the midst of a great inner crisis. Breaking with the old is becoming a necessity! Must forget! Forge ahead. Yesterday Eva answered my letter telling her of the experiment with the cultures and du Teil's congratulations. She wrote, "I am very happy that there is *some truth to it.*" And how could I expect her to have faith if not out of her love for me, when even I myself waver and time and time again have doubts in spite of the facts, in spite of being proved correct in the end.

I have no one, literally no one. Sigurd could possibly hold out if he didn't have a "big name" complex. I am very cautious with him, don't get too close. I literally tremble for my work and for myself when I see the emotional reactions of my best coworkers.

And now what if I distrust Elsa deeply, if I sense intuitively feelings of animosity within her and dread a future with her? Judging by old experiences, I ought to sever the tie! But I love her, will probably have "to drink the cup to the dregs." Somehow I don't believe that, and precisely because of my disbelief, I may be ruining my chances. Probably the greater the circle of people, the lonelier I'll become.

This crisis once again demands breaking with the old, the useless. What a damn good nose I have for people—too good, this intuition of mine! If I could only use it to guide them better. That is my weak point. But the circumstances are just too insane! Above all, people's fervor for me and then their protests afterward! I am coming ever closer to the damnable situation where I cannot allow myself to make any major blunders. And how can one experience one's intelligence if not in the light of one's own mistakes?

I am betting with very dangerous odds!

No, this mess that calls itself socialism will have to go before the new world can be won. Cowardly diplomatic dogs! Courage, energy, internationalism are all on the fascists' side. Disgraceful! Woe to Spain. And Soviet Russia?!

Thjötta,* the Norwegian bacteriologist, received the cultures today. Did the Rockefeller people get them too?

Thjötta told Havrevold† that these things have been known all along. Said there were spores in all of them. But he couldn't explain why no growths developed from the individual substances.

First evening at the laboratory. Berle was afraid, so was Havrevold. They're all cowards in the face of authority. I spoke very frankly with them.

9 March 1937

For months I've been noticing an attitude of disapproval in Havrevold. He avoided all participation, lost touch with the experiments. But he did play the "supervisor," ran to the authorities. I could see his fear of being made a fool of through me. If *I* had my doubts, even after months of actually observing things, then how could *he* help being doubtful? But why play the supervisor? He was struggling to prove his maturity and independence—that is, until yesterday, when he told me he had caught himself in an act of sabotage against me.

Although I had sensed this, it was still a shock. How can such a decent, inoffensive person act that way?? When the hostility of the whole world has to be reckoned with, then one's coworkers ought to take a firm stand and not lie in ambush. I explained this to him and he understood, agreed with me, resolved to continue. But the problem does not end here. *The problem of the enslaved, emotionally humiliated human being who fears and avoids anyone stronger than he.*

15 March 1937

I never realized that people could obey so blindly, that they would simply, unknowingly slaughter one another. The political events in Madrid remain a complete mystery to me! France: the socialist Blum had the Spanish border closed. England is "policing" the situation. The Italians and the Germans are storming Madrid!

* Professor Theodor Thjötta, Rikshospitalet, Institute of Bacteriology. Unbeknownst to Reich, Thjötta had asked the Rockefeller Institute for annual support for his own institute. Thjötta had a long-standing connection with the Rockefeller Institute in New York City and his opinion would be significant for the Rockefeller Foundation.
† Odd Havrevold, Norwegian psychiatrist involved with Reich's work in Oslo.

Harald Sjelderup, Nic Hoel, and Wilhelm Reich, Lucerne, August 1934

REICH: *"Did you know anything?"*
SJELDERUP: *"No, I know nothing."*

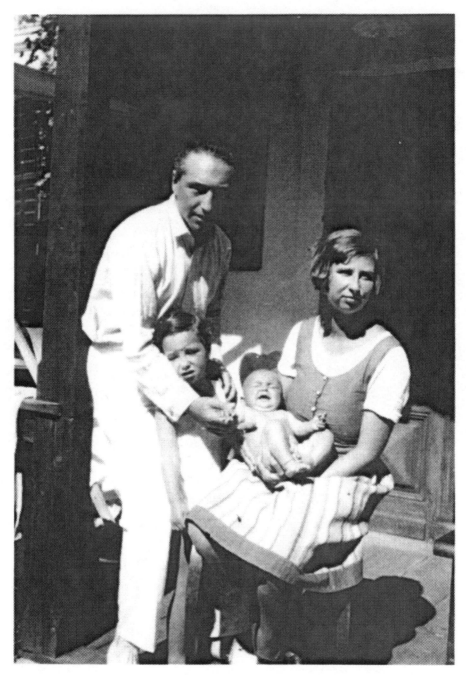

Reich and Annie with Eva and Lore, *c.* 1928

Reich and Elsa, 1934

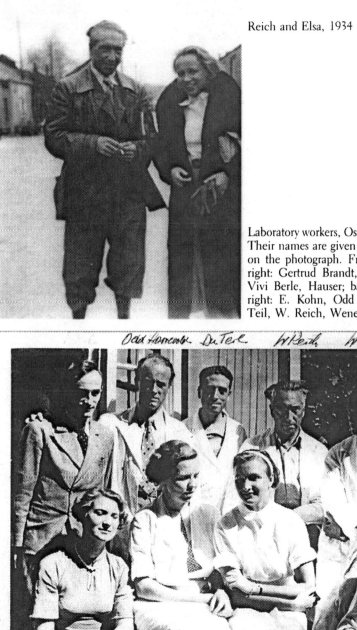

Laboratory workers, Oslo, August 1937. Their names are given in Reich's hand on the photograph. Front row, left to right: Gertrud Brandt, Kari Berggrav, Vivi Berle, Hauser; back row, left to right: E. Kohn, Odd Havrevold, Du Teil, W. Reich, Wenesland

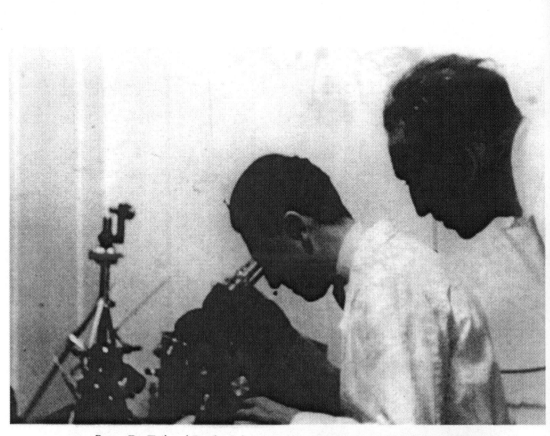

Roger Du Teil and Reich, Oslo,
August 1939

Reich's study in Oslo, 1935–39

VISTEMANNEN PÅ KAMPEN

Ypperstepresten Wilhelm Reich innvier menigheten i livets mysterier.

"WISE MAN FROM KAMPO: High priest Wilhelm Reich reveals the mysteries of life to his followers." Cartoon from Norwegian newspaper campaign, September 1937

"Meine Elsa," 1939

Wilhelm Reich, 1939

Reich's first home in the United States, 75-02 Kessel Street, Forest Hills, New York

16 March 1937

Havrevold declares that he is vacillating. He cannot break free from
the traditional theories. He tries to do my work by proceeding from
alien theories. That is impossible. I cannot adjust myself to the com-
pulsive manner of bacteriologists. I have to move forward to the cancer
problem. Will it all work out?

23 March 1937

Midnight. My fortieth birthday. Probably about two-thirds to three-
fifths of my life is over. A life full of struggle, pain, pleasure, and a
wealth of experience, including the discovery of the life process as my
most important birthday gift.

The summit has probably been reached but I am still not satisfied.
Removing unnecessary suffering from this world cannot be the task of
one man alone. However, the discovery of its most important causes
is *my* achievement. Is that enough? A new age is dawning, an age of
naturalness, no longer of yearning for but of reaching happiness itself.
In a hundred years people will understand our present times even less
than we understand the burning of heretics at the stake.

In completing the fortieth year of my life I think first of my two
children, Eva and Lore, who are so far away, so alienated from me
that they understand neither my motives nor my work. They considered
me insane because they were able to understand as little as I the
underlying reasons for my actions.

I have discovered life itself, true, but I paid for it with a part of my
own life—namely, the pleasure of watching my children grow up!!

  Well, then, my forty-first year! I am grateful to Elsa in spite of
everything. I think of my mother, who cared for me, loved and cherished me, as primitive and inconceivable as her ways might seem
today. Thank you, Mother. You gave me part of this burning desire
to be aware of life and to reach out for it, not mystically but in
truth.

As for myself, I might say that I have sought and also found part of
the truth. I've made an honest attempt to live the truth, though errors
and stupidity may cloud the picture.

I loved and still do love children. Life in flux.

I fought the fight for my work, for a better existence.

I felt the pulsing of the universe, the first step forward, perhaps. It may be. If not, I know, I desired it, struggled, suffered for it. Life cannot be extinguished!

What did they say? That I was a seducer of children, a psychopath, mentally ill, a charlatan, unreliable, and egotistic.

It's not true. I am simply a small, headstrong boy who is unable to comply with the stupid rules, that's all!

25 March 1937

Eureka! An inspired discovery! It is claimed that spores are killed off at 130° C. Good. We heat earth, coal, gelatin up to *180° C* in a dry sterilizer. Then we boil the earth and coal, which has been heated to 180° C, in KCl at 100° C. It breaks down, disintegrates into vesicles. Immediately there is amoeboid movement. If we prepare cultures, growth occurs from autoclaved coal.

26 March 1937
The germ problem is solved!

Germs are vesicles that form in matter as a result of gradual swelling and become living organisms on culture media. They can be "killed off" at 100°–180° C, i.e., they are dried out to such an extent that they do not swell back again in broth. Heating to 180° C and, recently, boiling at 100° C is merely a radical acceleration of the normal drying and reswelling process of the so-called spores.

The living arises from the nonliving!!

28 March 1937

Rockefeller Foundation in Paris declined politely.* They hope that I will be able to continue on a private basis! Thank you!

I'll probably have to face real difficulties. Hopefully du Teil will hold out.

6 April 1937.

Telegram from du Teil: Bion cultures successful in Nice.

---

* Documents in the Rockefeller Foundation archives have revealed that its representative, Tracy B. Kittredge, had reported that, in the opinion of geneticist O. L. Mohr, physiologist E. Langfeldt, and Langfeldt's assistant R. Nicolaysen, Reich was a "charlatan."

9 April 1937

Several sterile and "nonsterile" (e.g., esophagus) cancers exhibit the same picture: motile and nonmotile cancer cells, also bionlike rod-cocci and pseudo-amoebae in the liquid. Started to culture the cancer liquid this week.

The theory of "infected cancer tissue" appears false to me: The cocci and rods from the cancer tissues bear no resemblance to rot bacteria. In addition, putrid decomposition should occur in the presence of strepto- and pneumococci. Also, sterile cancer tissue yielded cultures with peculiarly motile structures (jerky lateral movements).

Assumption: The so-called postinfection in cancer is probably nothing other than cocci or rods that form from tissue, with decay and swelling occurring. According to this assumption, it was not the cancer cells at all but the bacterial autogenous structures that were the fatal agents. Autoinfection.

20 April 1937

Pasteur merely verified the effect of the air.

The theoreticians of spontaneous generation did not perform any experiments.

Nobody attempted to culture boiled material.

There are problems:

How can the specific association of protozoa with the parent material be *proved*? Why do amoebae not form from germs that are not on moss? Why does a tulip leaf give rise to no living organisms? Why do algae give rise to living organisms?

Fresh green grass and moss, juicy and moist, do not yield protozoa, perhaps just cocci.

On the other hand, in the fall protozoa are easily obtained—i.e., the structure must first break down and swell again. This is no doubt what happens in the case of cancer: first the tissue breaks down by losing tumescence, and then it swells up again.

22 April 1937

The assumption is inescapable that the disease of cancer is:

1. Self-vivification—protozoal disintegration of the organism
2. Autoinfection—bacteria from the decay of tissue
3. Bodies as incubators for bacteria

The formula: "cancer = not keeping sterile" = stupid. *Cancer is infection* (cf. autoinoculation of the nutrient medium)

20 May 1937

Thjötta states that he cannot give permission for animal tests to be carried out. He says that everything in that field has already been thoroughly studied. He asks Schjelderup whether I am an immigrant. ("Yes." "Therefore *Jewish!!*")

TO ROGER DU TEIL
24 May 1937

Dear friend and colleague,

I have gradually become more aware of my faculty colleagues' complete astonishment and even hostility, which is not based on any specialized knowledge. Again and again the objection has been raised that all we are dealing with are very well-known spores or development products of spores. It occurred to me that I could conduct an experiment with coal that would make it impossible to talk of the presence of spores. I am sending you a copy of some extracts from our records so that you can see the entries that we made here immediately after the experiment.

This experiment seems to me to completely refute the spore theory in the form in which it currently predominates, because nobody can assert that spores can survive such temperatures as those reached by incandescent heat. I do not deny the existence of spores as postulated by the old theory. All I claim is that the vesicular character of the material and the disintegration of swollen, heated, or boiled inorganic material into vesicles is the central point from which further research into the formation of viable microorganisms must proceed. The spores themselves must therefore be derived from matter—namely, by swelling. This appears to be an inevitable assumption.

You have not written to me for a long time and I do not know why. In view of the complicated and difficult nature of the work I am doing here, I can certainly understand that you are not having an easy time carrying out the control experiments, especially in the presence of prejudiced individuals. If you do not immediately end the friendship on receipt of this most recent report on the coal-heating tests, then I would be very glad to make the following suggestion to you. Would you be interested, say in August, in taking a trip to the beautiful northern part of this continent so that you could personally convince yourself of the scope, nature, and results of our work? I do not wish to put you under any kind of pressure, but I am prepared for an unbelievably difficult struggle with official opinion; the simpler and more self-evident the results of the work, the more gloomy and difficult that struggle will be.

Are you aware that Italian farmers prefer using lava rock to fertilize the soil? I would imagine that because of the glowing heat of the material, the cohesion between particles has broken down, and the electrical charges released are directly manifested in the growth of the plants. May I make another comment? The coal-heating experiment is only astonishing if one proceeds from the assumption that the living structures that are observed afterward, during the swelling process, were already contained in the coal in the form of spores, because then it is impossible to understand how spores can withstand such high temperatures. This theory, however, is false. The elements—let us call them bions—from which the motile structures are then formed are not previously contained in the coal but formed by the disintegration of the heated material. So, the spores to which people constantly refer must also once have formed and—please permit this hypothetical leap in reasoning—they must have formed when the earth was in an incandescent state. They must have developed when the previously incandescent material came in contact with water and swelling substances.

I needed to write and tell you this because, however things turn out, I believe that any progress I make, which never fails to astonish me, will only be made by struggling against counteropinions, but also with the support of understanding friends.

25 *May 1937*

The breakdown of matter into vesicles when heated to incandescence undoubtedly releases large amounts of electrical energy. The glowing heat must correspond to the emission of radiation by this energy.

Combustion = release of energy
Organization = binding of energy
Radiation tests are needed!

26 *May 1937*

No word from Eva for three weeks after her letter saying she looked forward to spending the summer with me. Today I received a letter calling it off. I have the feeling that they are working on her now.

Here in Oslo, Ellen told me that Annie, Rado, and Gerö held a discussion at the psychoanalytic congress in 1937.* Gerö was in tears for hours afterward. They had warned him about me, said that I was threatened by mental illness.

Those are the weapons they used against me!

20 *June 1937*

Du Teil working frantically in Paris—lecture at the French Academy in Paris. *Le Temps* is going to publish an article. And he is coming here!

21 *June 1937*

Summer solstice 1937! Actually, I have every reason to be *very* happy: work, love, knowledge. I miss the children. I must overcome the stigma that people like Stalin attach to revolutionary ideas and the concept of freedom.

Perhaps I shall succeed in laying a few foundations for freedom.

22 *July 1937*

Back from vacation. It felt good to do nothing for once. Five happy days with Elsa at the end! Once again she realized a lot. Will it work?

26 *July 1937*

Du Teil has arrived. I am still completely struck by Heiden's† account of Hitler's rise to power. Suddenly an old suspicion of mine has

---

* Reich probably refers to Ellen Siersted, a Danish woman who was interested in his work. Sandor Rado was a psychoanalyst with whom Reich was briefly in analysis in Berlin.
† Konrad Heiden wrote several books on Hitler.

been confirmed, namely that the separation of work and politics—in other words, the development of future politicians away from their life's work—is a major calamity. It is absolutely unbelievable to think of all that a clique of forlorn do-nothings was able to accomplish for the sole reason that the working population thinks politicking is some kind of work and has the greatest respect for it. *The overthrow of statesmanship will mark the beginning of the true flowering of work and love!*

Life must no longer be dominated by uprooted beings; it must seize its own social potential!

Love and work, the natural foundations of society, must be activated!

Program for the coming year's work:

1. Publication of biological research
2. Organization of a political-economic group

TO EVA REICH
7 August 1937

My dear Evchen,

Barcly an hour ago, du Tcil lcft for Paris, taking with him 700 meters of film, many preparations and cultures of animalcula, and a large microscope that I used here. In Paris a commission of scientists from various disciplines is awaiting him. On Monday, the ninth, he will give a detailed report of my work and present the films. These last two weeks of working with him have been the happiest period of my life. Du Teil is a biologist and a professor of natural philosophy at the University of Nice. Since February he has been performing my experiments and has partially confirmed them. Now, working here, he has learned precisely how to do the experiments, so that he can function in France in coordination with me. Evchen, this is a very big thing. My most important assumptions on the origin of life, which I discussed with you and Lotte Liebeck that time in Sletten, have now been irrefutably confirmed by experiment.

I should tell you that the experiments are very closely linked with my work on sick people. This is because the cornerstones of life, namely currents and electrical charges, are disrupted in modern people, and this makes them neurotic. I have confirmed by experiment Freud's thesis that the sexual drives are the vital drives, and from this I have derived the solution to a basic scientific problem that has existed for hundreds of years. We have been working like the devil here. Our heads are all buzzing after these two highly important weeks. We had to do everything very precisely because many people who will not look into the microscope will say that it is all crazy. And for this reason, du Teil's visit was extremely important.

You will now see why I have not been able to write to you for the past few weeks. I simply did not have any time.

With much love and kisses.

23 August 1937

Soot, ash, and charcoal can come alive! I have succeeded in that!

The great fame in store for me will cause my total isolation. People already feel honored to be in my company, but it is also a burden for them. I am an unwelcome guest in my own house. I disturb people's peace of mind. They're happy when I'm away for a couple of days. I have become an authority, so to speak. This has an "oppressive" effect—people want things to be uncomplicated, comfortable, care-free. They don't want their enjoyment of life disturbed by "heavy demands."

Two days ago a notice on both du Teil's visit and the bion experiments appeared in the *Arbejderbladet* and the *Dagbladet*.

Power increases; it's tempting to misuse it.

1 September 1937

Preliminary work on cancer. It is clear that the transformation of grass into protozoa is the model for the formation of cancer. Therefore prepare grass for a film.

11 September 1937

Things are going better with Elsa. I am hot on the trail of cancer.

15 September 1937

Mice diseased with tumor bacteria do not die when injected with bions.

Informed all coworkers at the laboratory this evening that we're after the cancer plague.

TO ROGER DU TEIL
23 September 1937

My dear friend,

I am enclosing the translation of some articles that recently appeared in the Scandinavian press, unfortunately somewhat prematurely, as if due to an oversight. I would like to give you some more details about this matter, because it could be important for planning our future tactics.

On Sunday, our *Journal for Political Psychology and Sex Economy* printed the article "Dialectical Materialism in Life Research." Barely had our friends received the issue when an extreme right-wing newspaper, acting with veiled malice, seized on the material and at first published a factual article on the subject. But at the same time the newspaper arranged for an inquiry by some highly reactionary university people who are not held in very high regard here by the scientific world. One of them is a physiologist and fascist, the other is a fascist and genetic scientist. They have committed a major blunder because they have commented on a matter about which they cannot possibly have any knowledge at all. They have not even read the article to which the newspaper referred. Their actions created a very bad impression with everybody here, from scientists to laymen. Their actions helped *us*.

Let me report a new experimental matter that I do not want to keep from you, because it provides enormous encouragement and confidence with regard to the earlier experiments. I recently telegraphed to inform you that the mice injected with the S-bacillus* either died after

---

* A bacillus Reich found first in a culture of sarcoma tissue. Much smaller than other bions and with an acid smell, it is lancet-shaped, gram-negative, and exhibits zigzag motion. Reich later referred to it as T-bacillus (Tod = death) and learned that it originates from degeneration and putrid disintegration of living and nonliving matter.

twenty-four hours or, if they did not die, after about ten days developed a very large infiltrating cancer tumor under the skin on their backs. The S-bacillus is thus in all probability one of the causative agents of cancer, or perhaps it is the only one. It is cultured from sarcoma liver metastasis. Now, the following thing happened. To carry out controls on the preparations, we injected my 3e incandescent-soot bions, and after ten days the mice had developed tumors. I do not understand this at all. I am waiting for the medical pathology examination to be performed and also for further experiments of the same kind to be carried out. But if it is correct, then it solves a major mystery connected with cancer.

I would now like to share the following thoughts with you in confidence:

1. When tar is applied to the skin, it leads to the development of cancer within about six months.

2. Pipe smokers are prone to cancer of the lips.

3. Soot bions cause cancer.

Conclusion: When an excess of carbon is supplied to the organism, it is a vehicle of cancer. But how? Cancer pathology has long established that cancer tissue exhibits an asphyxiation metabolism—i.e., an excess of CO_2.

This fits in perfectly with the producing of cancer by soot bions and tar and tobacco residues. If this is confirmed, then the possibilities it opens up are immense. Because of these recent observations, I got in touch with a Dr. Lejv Kreyberg, a cancer researcher here in Oslo, and he visited me the day before yesterday. I showed him the Preparation 6 film* and he reacted very decently. I then showed him the incandescent-soot test, which completely took his breath away. But he is behaving objectively and has promised me he will identify the 3e bions in his department at the university, will supply us with blood taken from cancer patients, and will help us determine the mouse tumors obtained. This is a great deal of help and I think we will make rapid progress.

That's all for today. I could tell you much more, but I don't want

* On the culturability of bions.

to overload you. We are delighted every time we receive a letter from you. Please go on delighting us as often as you can.

23 September 1937

Why do the 3e bions cause cancer?
1. 3e are living organisms of pure carbon.
2. Cancer tissue has a developmental metabolism.
3. 3e produces excess of C which cannot be combusted.
4. Tar $= C \rightarrow$ cancer
   Pipe smoke $= C \rightarrow$ cancer
   3e $= C \rightarrow$ cancer

Causes of cancer:
a. Poor respiration $=$ lack of oxygen in tissues.
b. Stimuli arising from excess C promote local formation.

The inhaled O combines with the bion C to form CO_2, which is exhaled.
When there is an excess of C or deficiency of O the tissues suffocate.
Cancer is a pathological attempt at regeneration.

TO LORE REICH
24 September 1937

My dear Lorchen,

The photos you sent gave me enormous pleasure. Many, many thanks. Let us agree that every three or four months you will send me a decent photograph of yourself. I was also happy to read of your wish to learn how to play the accordion. Of course you should have an instrument. Just write to me once you have asked a music teacher whether you can start with a proper, large accordion or whether you should first try a smaller, child-sized version. You should also ask whether it is better to learn to play an instrument with piano-style keys or to begin straightaway with one with buttons. The piano accordion is easier and also nicer, in my opinion. For the left hand it has buttons for the bass notes, like on a regular button accordion, and for the right hand there are keys like on a piano, only smaller and not as many. Altogether it covers two and a half octaves. I have such an instrument, which is much cheaper to buy here than elsewhere, but it is more expensive than the one you are thinking of. I am willing to let you have this instrument. I will give it to you as a present just because I am happy that you have developed an interest in music. Music is something wonderful. So make some exact inquiries, and write to me soon. You must also find a suitable teacher who can stimulate your imagination and not paralyze it. If you spend your holidays here next year, we can then both play together. How about it? From now on, I shall look forward to doing that.

Much love and many kisses.

TO ROGER DU TEIL
25 September 1937

My dear friend,

Today, just a few lines in reply to your letter. Kreyberg, the cancer researcher here in Oslo to whom I showed the three cultures of soot heated to incandescence and gave a sample for Gram staining purposes, sent me a short letter in which he states that, on the basis of this one staining experiment, he has diagnosed staphylococci. He also writes: "I believe that contamination from the air must have taken place." I do not understand how these colleagues are capable, first, of giving so little thought to the matter and, second, of assuming that I did not have the same idea myself long ago, at which time I established for sure that airborne contamination is not involved. In view of this experience, I have decided that from now on I will not casually reveal details to anybody, because it merely causes confusion, possibly creates enemies, and certainly does nothing to advance the cause. I believe the correct path to follow is to be willing, as before, to demonstrate the phenomena but to require that my colleagues either deal seriously and in detail with the matter or leave it entirely alone.

30 *September 1937*

I have found the bacillus that causes cancer!!!
T-bacillus as a degeneration.

4 October 1937

It is the death-bacillus.

My isolation seems inevitable. People are afraid to invite me to social gatherings because I am a "disturbing influence." Why? They feel resentful because I see through them. I, in turn, feel alienated because they are not forthright. They hide and remain superficial. Like insects, they are attracted to the flame of my knowledge while fearing it at the same time.

10 October 1937

Everything is changing. I find S in the blood of *healthy* young people! Either the entire S business is wrong or —— or ——

Unavoidable conclusion: It is possible everybody has S in them.

This would be the "cancer disposition"—that S can form spontaneously in blood, *but from what??*

14 October 1937

I am on the track of the matter.

1. Local oxygen deficiency due to poor respiration makes tissue decay.
2. S bacteria form.
3. The tissue regenerates itself as a tumor.
4. The S form the metastases.
5. Sarcoma S is more dangerous than carcinoma S.

T O   R O G E R   D U   T E I L
15 October 1937*

My dear friend,

I have just very carefully read the German translation of your letter of 8 October and I must tell you that I am quite unable to compete with you in the marvelous way you manage to approach scientists from other fields. What you have achieved with Bonnet, Martiny, and Reilly† on the first attempt is more than one could have dreamed of under the best of circumstances. If these colleagues truly keep their promises and carry out the experiments until they succeed, then we will certainly be home free as far as the first matter is concerned— namely, the production of bions. These remarks do not apply, or at least not yet, to the second matter—that is, the cancer question. I would like to state briefly that I am totally immersed in this subject and did not get into it by chance. In the same way that the bion experiments developed logically from my clinical orgasm formula, so the studies on cancer tissue and the experiments on animals are developing equally logically and consistently. I sometimes sit here completely dumbfounded and cannot believe that this logic is possible. I would like to stress that although I work with a great deal of intuition, this intuition is backed up by very solid clinical and experimental facts. I am helped in all this, last but not least, by the cognitive method I use. ‡

Because of the close contact that we have now, fortunately, established with the world of bacteriology, all of us have entered into an extremely dangerous phase. If the work that we now do is successful, then we will certainly triumph. If anything goes wrong at any point, however, the setback will be far greater than the disadvantage of having no contact with this particular scientific field would have been.

The bacteriologists with whom you are dealing in order to obtain confirmation of the bion experiments are highly specialized experts

---

* This letter was not sent.

† French bacteriologists for whom du Teil had demonstrated the formation of bions. He had reported to Reich that they had expressed interest and would give the matter serious consideration.

‡ See "The Dialectical-Materialistic Method of Thinking and Investigation" in *The Bion Experiments* (New York: Farrar, Straus and Giroux, 1979).

and I know that I could not engage in a discussion with any of these people in their particular fields. Although I am familiar from my medical studies with the fundamental aspects of bacteriology and its methods, the field of bacteriology has become much broader and deeper, and I would therefore not undertake to engage in any discussion of specific bacteriological problems. There can be no doubt that this is a correct assessment of the situation. On the other hand, it is equally certain and clearly established that the best modern experts in bacteriology cannot argue with me on the basic problems of my clinical experience and my specific experimental work. In this connection, I would like to express a feeling I have always had whenever my enemies, or people who review my work from afar, described me as a systematist, a philosopher, or a synthesist. I do not feel I am any of these three things. I am a scientist working in a field where I must use methods of research and thought developed entirely by myself that are not known in any of the existing specialized fields. I am referring to dialectical-materialistic sex research. Recently I had the opportunity to say to a cancer specialist who was very arrogant to me in the presence of several other physicians: "Dear colleague, I fully recognize your exclusive competence in the field of cancer research in its present form, but I would ask you to take note of the fact that I claim absolute authority in all questions of sexual functioning and its relation to vegetative life. I do not know about your cancer problems, but you are not knowledgeable about my field of expertise either. I hope that in the interest of the matter at hand we can arrive at an understanding." I have had this basic attitude for a number of years and I shall continue to cling to it.

We must demand from the experts criticism grounded in our work: to judge our work they must, if they are at all honest, temporarily abandon their own methods of thought and adjust themselves to our position and criticize us from the standpoint of *our* work. This does not mean that we would assume a superior air and declare that we know everything better and that the others are all fools. No, certainly not. Everything, absolutely everything, must be done or attempted to explain our material and methods to each and every specialist with whose field we come into contact. For example, you are absolutely right when you say that I must very soon employ a young bacteriologist who will try to situate our results in the overall bacteriological scheme of things. However, if this should sometimes prove impossible, then we would first of all have to check to see who is right—existing bacteriology or ourselves. (I am reminded again of the diagnosis of staphylococci that was made in the case of structures that beyond doubt are not staphylococci.) I will do everything possible to accelerate, and bring about, this linkup; of that you may be fully assured. But I cannot and must not adjust myself to the ways of thinking and the methods used by bacteriologists lest I lose the thread of my own study methods and thought processes.

You have now come up against a scientific world to which you must prove yourself a match in the capacity you have assumed. But I would like to be quite open with you. I have the feeling, and we have already talked about it here, that you are too optimistic in your assessment of the willingness of the scientific world to accept these matters today. Please permit me to retain my skeptical attitude until you succeed in convincing me that I am wrong in holding to it. I assure you that I will do nothing to hamper you in your attempts to convince the bacteriologists and biologists. On the contrary, I will make all the material and all the controls available to you so that you will be fully familiar with our work. I shall also be happy to learn of any objections, even awkward ones, you report to me. But you will not be able to make me surrender my skepticism about the willingness of the majority of scientists. I know all too well how the highly specialized worker is anchored in his own problems and ways of thought and I will not abandon myself to any dangerous illusions on that score. I accept the fact that I shall have to go on working for ten years and more, quietly but firmly convinced of what I am doing but without any means of arriving at a breakthrough. Please believe me that I do not want to play the role of martyr. I merely wish, using all the means available to me, to prevent you, a valuable and cherished coworker, from getting into difficulties by entertaining illusions about the possibilities of a quick breakthrough. Let us wait calmly and see what happens. We do not have to somehow raise ourselves up to participate on the same scientific plane as the current bacteriological or other disciplines. In our own specific fields, we are equally good scientific authorities. Yes, even better. Why should I hold back? A biologist or psychologist who does not quickly comprehend the basic function of life—orgasm and orgastic yearning, the orgastic convulsion of all living organisms and the relation to the charge processes in living matter—or who has never himself even come close to this fundamental fact cannot, at least in my opinion, be regarded as an absolute authority in the field of biology. That is not conceit on my part; on the contrary, I tend to be far too modest. But I say this in the absolute, scientific, clinically and experimentally obtained conviction that sexual aversion flourishes not only in religious dogmas but also in the mechanical, materialistic, and mechanistically specialized scientific disciplines. Over and over again, I have found that extremely personal character weaknesses have a damaging effect on many people's scientific work, which should be objective. Let me give you an example. Kreyberg is the only cancer researcher here in Oslo. When we obtained the first tumors in our mice, samples of the tumor tissue were set in paraffin in a scrupulously correct manner and sent to his institute for examination, with a request that he let us know his opinion. After a few days he convened a meeting at which he expounded his view in an extremely professorial manner, proclaiming that it was nonsense to speak of a carcinoma when all we were dealing with was inflammatory granulation tissue. He asked me whether I could diagnose a cancer cell under the microscope, to which I replied yes, because I really am capable of that. I then asked him whether he had ever seen a living cancer cell at magnifications of $2,000 \times$ or $3,000 \times$. It turned out that he had not. This cancer researcher is afraid that if I am allowed to examine his motives for even a moment, his status as a specialist will be questioned; but he has absolutely no reason to think that, because I very kindly and politely offered him the possibility of cooperating with us. Now he is trying to "finish me off." But the physicians who were present and who have to struggle with the practical work of treating patients were on my side. One elderly doctor said to him, after I had spoken: "Yes, why shouldn't there be any cancer cells in granulation tissue?" And that is also correct from the standpoint of current cancer research. It is absurd to strictly distinguish granulating and proliferating granulation tissue from cancerous tumor tissue when, in addition, it is known that cancer can develop very easily from granulation tissue. But this example shows quite clearly that we are exposed to great danger—namely, the danger of colliding with all the forces of conservatism in science. To escape destruction and, on the contrary, to make gradual headway, I have employed the following people in my laboratory: a specialist in chemistry and physics, a trained bacteriological laboratory assistant, and a trained film maker. And in Dr. Havrevold I have found an extremely well-trained expert on internal organs and, in particular, on internal secretion. As soon as financial circumstances permit, I will be very happy to follow your advice and employ a bacteriologist and a cancer specialist. As you correctly observe, in this way I will discover in advance what the objections might be and will be able to take part in discussions armed with the necessary counterarguments.

At the moment, unfortunately, I am struggling with colossal financial difficulties. It is not pleasant to have to tell you that, as things now look, it is very doubtful whether I will be able to continue operating on the present scale. There is not one official government source to back me up, in contrast to the many, many government-employed specialists who are provided with all the necessary means to conduct their research without having to assume this responsibility themselves. But this circumstance imposes two obligations on me. First, I must be extremely careful in the way I process my results, but at the same time, I am also firmly determined to defend them with all available means.

TO DR. LEJV KREYBERG
19 October 1937*

Dear Dr. Kreyberg,

I call upon you in your capacity as a cancer researcher to take the following steps in the interest of public hygiene:

1. Observe your cancer patients to determine their ability to breathe deeply and exhale fully. You will discover that this most primitive vegetative function is disturbed not only in your cancer patients but also in most people, whether they are old or young. The respiration of cancerous tissue is poor (asphyxiation metabolism).

2. Explain why the majority of women contract cancer specifically in the sexual organs, such as the genitals and breasts, so that, for example, in Germany 18,000 women a year die of genital cancer alone (according to statistical data).

---

* This letter was not sent.

3. You have asserted that it is not possible to diagnose living cancer cells. Again, in the interest of public hygiene, I call upon you to take a fresh, sterile preparation of cancer tissue, if possible from a deep-lying tumor or metastasis, and observe it carefully at a magnification of $3,000 \times$ to $4,000 \times$, using direct water immersion and a $0.1n$ KCl + methylene blue solution. You cannot fail to detect the cancer cells, because they stand out so clearly from all the other structures.

4. Take some grass and moss tissue from last fall (it can still be found), immerse it in nonsterile water, and examine it daily for two weeks. You cannot fail to notice the vesicular disintegration of the tissue, the formation of a margin, and the organization of the matter into protozoa. The cancer cells form as protists in the body in the same way. Observe the edges of fresh cancer tissue as described above *without killing it*. You will find vesicular disintegration, the formation of margins, and organization.

5. Take blood from a vein in the arm under sterile conditions; spread it in a sterile petri dish and place it in the temperature-controlled cabinet. After twenty-four hours, once it has dried and fibrin has formed, sprinkle over it a thin layer of blood charcoal that has been heated to incandescence. Allow it to stand for another twenty-four or forty-eight hours at room temperature. Then pour autoclaved $0.1n$ KCl solution over the preparation, taking care to observe sterile conditions. Immediately examine a control sample under the microscope. At a magnification of $3,000 \times$ you will immediately observe that the substances have mutually penetrated each other. After another twenty-four hours, inoculate sterile egg media. You will obtain a bacterial culture. This is the cancer model test. It shows how the carbon particles that, as is known, contribute specifically to the formation of cancer, act together with blood to form bacteria.

6. Autoclave human blood for half an hour in broth + KCl after you have shaken the mixture thoroughly. Heat the human blood charcoal to incandescence in a gas flame, add it to KCl + broth and shake thoroughly. Mix the two solutions in as sterile a way as possible. Score sterile egg media and pour the blood bion solution over them. Then observe the small growths that occur at the score marks in the egg media and go on observing this tissue. At a magnification of $3,000 \times$ you will be able to observe directly the formation of nucleated round cells. This is the model test for the known effect of highly distilled tar, or other substances containing carbon particles, on tissue. I will

send you two cultures of cells that I obtained in this way. Please identify them, but if possible at 3,000 × .

7. At the same magnification—while the cells are alive, not stained—examine fresh blood from all patients suspected of having cancer. You will immediately note the presence of extremely small, fast-moving rods and the blue blood bions cultured by me. The signs of self-destruction in the body can be seen before the tumor becomes visible to the pathologist or surgeon.

8. Place the fresh cancer tissue, after it has been cut up into small fragments, into an easily observable live preparation containing a bion culture, which I will make available to you. You will be able to observe directly the destruction of the cancer cells by the bions. I mentioned this to you when I explained why I need cancer tissue and blood from cancer patients to continue my studies. I believe that if the blood picture of a person suspected of having cancer is thoroughly analyzed, using bions cultured from the blood, it is possible not only to diagnose the cancer at an early stage but to treat it. Not to do this would be a crime.

I am prepared to give you further information on the results I have so far obtained in my work. I am equally willing to demonstrate all the above-mentioned experiments on the cancer problem. I did not seek out this problem; it arose by itself in the course of my work.

On the basis of my experience in dealing with sexual problems as a physician, as well as of the experimental results I have achieved so far, I seriously believe that cancer is essentially a complicated sequela of dysfunctional sexual energy from which almost all people suffer. Poor respiration, intended to suppress affects, leads to the disturbance of respiration in the tissues. Similarly, poor electrical charge conditions are created. The tissue whose vital functions are impaired in this way begins to break down vesicularly. Protists of various kinds, including the cancer cells, develop from the disintegrating tissues just as in the decaying moss samples. The process then continues to develop in the known manner, leading to the formation of tumors, metastases, ulcerous breakdown, etc. The human body undermines itself. It dies while still alive.

19 October 1937

I regret that I am creating trouble in public. I have made an enormous effort for two years to cooperate with various agencies in solving the problem to the point where a practical therapy could be guaranteed. This is now being made impossible. I am no longer able to obtain cancer tissue for examination, and Kreyberg has declined to let me have any blood from cancer patients. People are becoming uneasy. But it is clear that I cannot and may not abandon one iota of the conviction I have developed, certainly not in my capacity as a physician. I am fully competent to judge the role of sexual disturbances in the formation of cancer. So far, cancer research has not been able to provide any explanation for the origins of cancer because no thought has ever been given to the possibility that immobile matter can organize itself into mobile matter, that the nonliving can turn into the living. The sexual relationships of human beings in all their aspects, including the physical, have also been the subject of very little study. I myself am just at the beginning, but it is the beginning of a process of development backed up by experimental results.

27 October 1937

Ingjald Nissen writing in the *Arbejderbladet* against psychoanalytic quackery: "The Hour of Truth for Psychoanalysis in Our Country." Characterizes vegetotherapy as a type of quasi-medical relaxation analysis, the sole purpose of which is to stir up the patients sexually. Compared with this method, the old methods of rhythmic gymnastics, dancing, and massage were better. Furthermore, managing sexual problems is not the specific responsibility of a psychoanalyst. Sexual problems have long been studied—for example, by artists such as Grünewald in the Middle Ages.

28 October 1937

Dagbladet: "Campaign Against the Swindlers Practicing Analysis." Quackery. Linking of vegetotherapy with the problem of quackery.

5 November 1937

Start of the campaign in the Psychiatric Society, five doctors, mass meetings.

6 November 1937

At the moment the situation looks *very* nasty.

What is in my favor?

1. My cause. It's really alive!
2. Mankind's yearning. It's everywhere, on *all* levels.
3. My intelligence and capability, experience and strength.
4. Human decency.

Against me:

1. The machine guns of the fascists and communists.
2. Mankind's fear of pleasure.
3. Politics and the lack of awareness.
4. The world order.

8 November 1937

Saw a movie on Beethoven today. Kitsch, but on a grand scale nevertheless. That is, not the production but Beethoven. A movie on Beethoven can't be bad!

And yet people smirk at everything, even at Beethoven's fate.

They are titillated by the misery of great men. They honor them after they have died in misery so that they themselves can continue their own paltry lives, so that they can transform the humiliation of great individuals into profit. Down with this filth!

A man like Beethoven *has* to be unrestrainable. But if he is wild as a youth the living dead scream at him, "Behave yourself! Don't rock the boat!" Swine!

Still, they are all humans—haywire electrical machines.

T O   T A G E   P H I L I P S O N
8 November 1937

Dear Philip:

I have just received your telegram and I want to reply as quickly as possible. Please inform Leunbach and Ellen of the contents of this letter.

We are now being forced from outside (against my will and my instincts) to officially organize the group of sex-economic therapists and teachers. The fact of the matter is that people seem to have more respect for a stamp or seal than for good solid work without such a stamp. We must make allowance for this fact. We are being attacked viciously from all sides. The personal link with the IPA, which still exists—for example, through Raknes, Nic Hoel, and Lotte Liebeck—is proving terribly bothersome. Since I am usually attacked here under the general title of "psychoanalyst," for which of course the poor psychoanalysts are in no way responsible, we are forced to adopt a course of action that will permit us to go on the counterattack together with the psychoanalysts. Unfortunately, this means renewing our links with them and this can only be harmful. That is what we wanted to discuss next Thursday. In principle, it would be most desirable to sever the personal links between sex economy and psychoanalysis. However, we must pay for the sins of the past and therefore it is necessary to proceed carefully and cautiously. The fact is that the local psychoanalysts have become very strongly influenced by us. This does not yet mean that they are willing to support the entire theory of sex economy. They merely wish to acquire the technique of character analysis for professional reasons. I am afraid that if major errors are made, the meeting could lead to several people quitting, despite their personal friendship. On Thursday, the only questions that will be dealt with are those mentioned in the letter. We will not yet discuss the "how" of the technical organization. At any rate, it would be very useful and desirable if you, as the representative of the Copenhagen group, could be there, if only to reinforce the numbers in the face of those who are vacillating. It is not absolutely necessary; it would just be very advantageous.

Now a few words about the general situation. All at once a large number of people have started to run amok, although there is no reason yet for them to react or to adopt a critical position. In cooperation with the socialists and the bourgeoisie, a semiofficial committee has been formed here with the task of "refuting" my work. The physiologist Langfeldt, the biologist Mohr, the eugenicist and socialist Scharffenberg,* and a few other people are members of this committee.

---

* Johan Scharffenberg, a Norwegian psychiatrist with a particular interest in genetics. He took part in public debates on all kinds of political and cultural issues and supported

I have been assured that they will not succeed, but I am not so certain. A great deal depends on when the results of the work in Paris will become known and what impact they will have. Naturally, it will be catastrophic if the academy in Paris does not find the necessary patience and objectivity to truly see what there is to see and issues a negative appraisal. If that happens, my work will be in bad trouble, but naturally only for a short time. It would be very good to talk all these matters over. Please let me know whether you can come. Of course, the ideological and financial welfare of our friends in Copenhagen is also involved. But I do not want to create any panic by saying so. The situation is serious, but it would certainly be advantageous to hang on. Nic has a particularly important role to play in this connection because she is called upon from all corners of the country to expound on our topic in election speeches and to young people.

Hearty greetings to you, Leunbach, and Ellen, and please write to me.

15 November 1937

Soltre, a psychiatrist, told Christian Lange that I would soon be deported because I have slept with all my female patients and also charge too much.

I will mobilize everyone against this outrage.

Decided to threaten to publish an account of all the dirty dealings I know of if they do not stop.

Being defensive now would spell ruin. Attack the impotent bastards!

28 November 1937

Today, in the Continental Hotel, I was attacked by an engineer: "We don't need any psychologists!" I wanted to punch him in the nose but friends restrained me.

6 December 1937

Yesterday Elsa was unfaithful to me with her pianist, Ragnerud. Her working at the National Theater (through my influence with

---

a law for the compulsory sterilization of vagrants and their children, "habitual criminals," and similar groups. As late as 1951, he advocated sterilization of the insane and feebleminded.

Gerda Ring) set everything in motion, although she is not conscious of this fact. The National Theater put a pianist at her disposal. Gerda told me that R. thought Elsa was delightful and Elsa told me that she thought R. was different from other Norwegians in that he was refreshing and lively. The facts are as follows:

1. Over the last two weeks Elsa has shut herself off from me sexually, as she did once before. She has avoided me, affected a cold expression, rejected me.

2. When I asked her what she would do if I had to leave the country she replied that this time she would not go with me. Said she would stay here. I understood this and agreed.

3. The week before she had made two dates with me for 7:30. Both times she arrived at 9:30 and gave me excuses. Once I met her unexpectedly in front of the theater café—walking quickly. She was somewhat taken aback but covered it cleverly.

4. She is still keeping her "secret." She has never been frank with me about sexual matters. She claims that nothing ever happened in all the six years. I have always had the feeling that this was impossible.

5. Several times she decided that this life was too difficult for her and that she wanted to live her life in a happy, carefree fashion. Yesterday morning she remarked that I was "so tiresome." I realized that it was true.

6. She loved me but she developed appalling attitudes. I became a mother whom she spited, a brother whose advances she resisted. She did not see me as her lover except occasionally. *With me she was blocked orgastically.*

7. Yesterday I heard her speaking with Theille. She was interested, unaffected, and human. With me she could only speak self-importantly. She was constantly compensating for inferiority feelings, always forced to prove through her dancing that she too was "somebody."

8. A while ago I found a slip of paper on my desk on which she had written "Ragnerud, Wengelandsvei" and two telephone numbers. One of them was his home number, I found out through information yesterday. The situation is obvious!

9. The day before yesterday she innocently informed me that she would not be able to go skiing with me on Sunday, said she had a rehearsal at the National Theater (Sunday!). Then she said the re-

hearsal only began at 5 p.m. When I came home from skiing at 4 o'clock she was on the phone with Gerda Ring and discussing very loudly and clearly what she planned to practice with Ragnerud. At 4:30 she rushed off with a look on her face that spoke for itself. I had a visitor and thought no more of it. Supposedly, the rehearsal was at the National Theater. On a Sunday! And alone with Ragnerud, who was putting himself at her disposal out of professional interest! At ten to nine I had a feeling I ought to phone Gerda. She said that E. had gone "to dinner" with R. and would be back any minute. Now E. had not told me anything about that. But since she did tell me about the evening with Ragn., wouldn't she naturally also have told me that they were going to have "dinner" together? If it was innocent then why didn't she tell me about it? If it wasn't innocent then she deceived me. It's obvious. At about 11 o'clock I called Gerda again. E. came to the phone in a state of complete confusion. "But it's twelve o'clock, not eleven." "Were you at the movies? What did you see?" Completely incoherent.

She had taken her diaphragm along! Therefore she had spent at least four hours with Ragn. Surely not a four-hour rehearsal!

All at once everything became so clear to me, and I understood Elsa. From her point of view she was right. Her neurosis had destroyed our relationship. Until yesterday I desired her, tolerated her rejection of me because it was based on her anxieties. She wanted love, as everyone does, but without inconvenience. I only sought other women when I was hungry and not able to have E. But she could always have me. For six years I never rejected her. Only once or twice was I not quite all there! She unconsciously developed a sly way of making herself comfortable and secure with me. Her disappointment began when she wanted to marry me and I refused. She wanted to secure her life. When I suggested having a child last fall she did not want to. Just as she dreamed of her dancing and has only now gotten down to work, she also dreamed of a child as a toy to play with. But I wanted to have children with her under *decent* conditions, with an independent woman. Without being destroyed in the process. Still, I honestly wanted to live with Elsa, in spite of all the difficulties! For love of Elsa I went without Gerd last summer. For love of Elsa I went to other women in order not to distress her with my desire.

But now I am through with it. I am quiet and composed, a new chapter can begin! I committed great blunders. People don't want to be given that much. While they strive for happiness and fly into the flame, they still remain their trivial selves. It is not my fault that I must act differently, nor are others at fault that they must act the way they do.

Last night I had a girl, a working girl, who told me, "You have such good eyes. You are different from the others. I understand you." She had only seen me in a restaurant. She trembled and loved me, simply, making no demands. That's decency! My theory is correct! Sex must be free and unencumbered.

Poor Elsa! She loves me but is all mixed up. She can't go on any longer, goodwill notwithstanding. That's the way it goes. I am not angry at her and I am not offended.

However, I have to get hold of myself. The begging was unbearable. After all, most women are happy when I love them.

I have made some very foolish mistakes. My self-sacrifice has been a hindrance. I must limit myself to political work without laying claim to leadership, must remain a simple human being and worker. I want to keep my friends, not lose them because of poor pupil-teacher relations. My cause will be victorious. I do not want to rush anymore, would like to live a little bit.

Why should I sacrifice myself for someone like Lotte Liebeck, who tells me—just when I am in the midst of a terrible mess—that she finds my path revolting! Why work for Schjelderup? The world doesn't want to be saved. I will cease wanting to save it, while still continuing to work on my own part of the truth.

In the newsletter I will explain why I am rejecting the role of the leader. I am not a power-oriented person.

My life is full. Yesterday my bions devoured a mass of tbc-bacilli.*

13 December 1937

I think my research on the difference between bions and S from cancer blood is on the track of the problem of life and death.†

This is the way things stand at present: while I am pursuing the life problem, while the Norwegians are defending me and my views, I myself am running around in the streets looking for love. I am looking

---

* Tuberculosis bacilli.
† November 1938: Correct! [W.R.]

for love; it's very simple, just plain love. A woman, a female with thighs, who gives love and takes it with no silly antics. But this doesn't exist in today's world. They want to be married or they want to be loved—that is, taken care of for the rest of time. But *I* want pleasure, just very simple, natural pleasure.

What liars these women are! They want pleasure just as I do, but at the same time they want no responsibility. Who will love *me?* Who will take *me?*

I yearn for uncomplicated, simple sex. Is that sooo horrible? It's perfectly natural, isn't it?

I want something very simple: a woman who just says, "Come, lover, let's make each other happy," with no ulterior motives!

TO ROGER DU TEIL
18 December 1937

My dear friend,

I am writing to you today on an extremely important matter that will undoubtedly have a quite decisive influence on our work. I must ask for maximum discretion. From the reports that I have sent you on the production of the S-bions and the blood charcoal bions you will probably have seen that, as was anticipated one and a half years ago, the work has progressed quite logically. Much more progress and much more complicated events have taken place here than I informed you about. The first cancer-therapy tests have been initiated with the terminal female patient about whom I have already written to you. For the time being, things are going well, but it is not possible to say anything definite yet. I assure you, without having to fear that you will regard me as someone who acts and thinks precipitously, that I now have 100 percent control over the methods of determining the disposition to cancer long before it manifests itself in the form of a tumor. To carry out the experiments on the therapeutic side, I would now need at least 200,000 Norwegian kroner and well-trained medical personnel.

A short while ago, my friend Sigurd Hoel drew my attention to the enormous danger that looms from the various trusts set up to manufacture and sell radium for the treatment of cancer. I do not know to what extent you are aware of the practices and the brutal determination of the representatives of these trusts and of the people who profit from them. After vigorous and detailed discussions of this matter with our friends here, we realize that if my method of cancer prognosis and possibly also my method of cancer treatment were to succeed, it would completely pull the rug out from under the cancer radium industry. Everyone who lives off that industry, and there are tens of thousands of people all around the world who do, would turn against me. Not because they are bad people but simply because they would fight quite unconsciously for their existence and against the need to undergo difficult retraining. The most dangerous reaction of all would come from those people whose vast earnings would be jeopardized. (That was not my idea, it came from a very smart and foresighted person.) In addition, I learned yesterday that some years ago a journal article critical of the Belgian Radium Trust appeared. The article claimed that prices for radium were kept extremely high by the trusts and that profits of up to 1,000 percent were being earned. I cannot check these matters, but to the extent that I know "business," they are probably correct. Unfortunately, I did not have an opportunity to discuss this side of our work while you were here—namely, how much scientific research is hampered by the profits derived from its incompleteness. Think, for example, merely of Davos,* which exists only because tuberculosis cannot be cured. It would make me happy if you fully understood what I am trying to say. It is not an ideological anticapitalist or an ex-communist speaking in me but a physician who, under all circumstances, clings to his function and does not wish to be destroyed in the process. Because I am usually very naive and these facts had to be pointed out to me, it would be wrong to claim that my behavior is paranoid. To put it briefly, I ask that you observe the utmost caution in whatever reports you make to anybody about my ongoing cancer work. You got to know Sigurd Hoel here and I am sure you were persuaded of his absolute intellectual honesty. He believes that the simultaneous existence in Belgium of a league against cancer and of a radium trust cannot be a mere coincidence. Only recently have I understood the reaction of local radium therapists to the initial rumors about my cancer work, although they were unaware of their own

* Reich refers to the tuberculosis sanitarium in Davos, Switzerland.

motives. My friends here and I still do not see how we will cope with this problem. I would appreciate it very much indeed if you could write and let me know your opinion, without making me wait too long for a reply.

In the deep conviction that you will not misunderstand this letter and that you will assist me with your advice, I remain

Yours most sincerely.

22 December 1937

The academic council held a meeting. Mohr is moving decisively for refusal of my residency permit. Schreiner, the dean of medicine, has a positive outlook and is objective.

1938

"My experiments show that there are developmental stages on the way from lifeless, immobile matter to life, that in nature the emergence of life from inorganic matter proceeds presumably by the hour, by the minute."

4 January 1938

I am once again confronted with the problem of where to go from here.

Yesterday August Lange* remarked correctly that with people as they are today one will only meet with defeat.

12 January 1938

An article by Gabriel Langfeldt in *Aftenposten,* "Guilt Feelings, Morality, Neurosis, and the Education of Children," argues the absolute necessity of having education instill feelings of guilt in children.

23 January 1938

Agitation about psychoanalysis, a mass meeting at the Students' Association. Schjelderup and Nic Hoel defend character analysis. *Dagbladet:* "The meeting degenerated into broad propaganda for the Reich movement." Schjelderup distances himself from this remark. The *Dagbladet* asks whether the professor is too afraid to participate.

25 January 1938

Overwhelming victory at the Students' Association.

But they're still so timid and are clinging to the word "psychoanalysis," even Nic.

The physiological institute of the Paris academy, through Professor Lapique, confirmed the shipment of bions dated 8 January 1937. First, a deep silence—and now, a year later, they reply. Scientists!

The Bions† will be published next week.

How infinitely difficult it is to succeed with something that will be a matter of course and entirely commonplace twenty to forty years from now. Then no one will have any idea of the bruising difficulties encountered every hour of every day. Someday those who are now standing aside waiting will be red in the face with embarrassment because they were not willing to help when fate tried to strike me down.

---

* Norwegian sociologist.
† Published later in English as *The Bion Experiments.*

15 February 1938

In his letter of 8 January 1938, Lapique of the French academy is attempting to downplay the cultures and pass them off as Brownian movement.

The director of medicine in Oslo is afraid of the three idiots who want to get me out. He's afraid of me too; during our talk today he practically put into my mouth the words necessary for me to survive.

9 March 1938

Oslo is so confining. I'm suffocating. I want to teach, to instruct scores of pupils.

Elsa is very loving or is trying to be, although she can't bear these "heights," this aloneness. What am I supposed to do? For a short while now she has been giving herself completely. What was going on before—or with whom?

Today the German ambassador told her she would not receive a passport, said she didn't need one anyway because the Norwegians wanted *so much* to keep me in the country.

11 March 1938

Hitler is getting closer to Austria without any resistance.

Reasons for this:

1. Apathy of the masses.

2. The "politics" and "weaknesses" of the parties.

3. The not entirely abandoned faith in [the intervention of] "foreign countries."

4. The fact that life has not been understood.

In the world within the compass of his power, Hitler has all the moral arguments on his side, as well as solidarity, courage, and strength.

His opponents do not have all this. Only when one sees things through Hitler's eyes can one understand that he has smoothed the road for us. He has made the nation capable of bearing arms against the capitalists. He has united the country and thus saved us the task. He has unleashed life's sexual yearnings (in a mystical sense, but nevertheless).

He has exposed the deficiencies in socialism. He has shattered age-old conventional ideologies. *But since he has no practical goal he is destined to fall in the end.*

The representatives of economic production will eventually refuse to work solely for destruction!

And yet the enthusiasm of the masses is genuine (see the reception in Linz) and decisively important.

TO ROGER DU TEIL
16 March 1938

Dear friend,

We have just learned that Freud has been arrested in Vienna by the National Socialists. Not only does this dastardly act mean enormous personal suffering, but it is a crime of fundamental significance. I ask you most urgently, in the name of all those who still believe that something can be done and who wish to fight for it, to undertake everything in your power to organize a massive protest in the French scientific world against this attack on Freud by stupid barbarians. Please write by return mail to let me know what you can do along these lines. We are organizing here in Scandinavia.

TO ROGER DU TEIL
25 March 1938

Dear friend,

Thank you very much for your efforts and for your sympathy with regard to the Austrian tragedy. We are all completely bewildered by this turn of events and for the time being we can do nothing but concentrate on how to rescue our work for posterity from the mystical flood. For this reason, and I say it quite openly, it would be very advantageous to force the pace of the work. In the long run, this madness will not continue. All that matters now is to survive the coming period.

TO ODD HAVREVOLD

29 March 1938

Dr. Nic Hoel showed me the two letters Dr. Scharffenberg wrote to you about me.

I have no idea at all what official function Dr. Scharffenberg is performing in the matter of my work and residency permits. Nevertheless, the last letter, which tells of the application for my expulsion, requires that I set certain matters straight.

If I have so far not responded to the endless rumors, statements, and assertions, it has simply been because of lack of time. I would get very little serious work done if I replied to everything that is asserted and said. I shall limit myself to some of the principal questions:

Dr. Kreyberg is reported to have claimed that he checked my bion experiments and found them incorrect. I have never asked Dr. Kreyberg to verify my bion experiments, nor has he ever applied to me to do so.

According to Dr. Scharffenberg, he was informed by Dr. Jessing that in Dikemark I had requested that sexual intercourse be arranged between mental patients. Without at this point going into the dynamics that lead to the telling of such fantastic tales, I would like to set things straight.

With the approval of Dr. Jessing, my oscillograph was moved to the mental hospital in Dikemark, where my assistant at the time, Dr. Löwenbach, was to measure skin potentials on catatonics. Naturally, the potentials of the erogenous zones were also supposed to be measured, but in fact this was never done. In the course of a visit with Dr. Jessing, we talked a lot about Freud, psychoanalysis, sexual stasis and its role in mental illness, and I expressed some thoughts on a possible connection between the nitrogen studies being performed by Dr. Jessing and sexual-physiological dysfunction in catatonic patients. It is possible that in this connection I mentioned the advanced treatment of the mentally ill in Burghölzli and stressed how much sexual stasis probably encourages the development of the schizophrenic process. I never made a request of the kind referred to above and it would never occur to me to do so. But I do not hesitate to assert that totally ignoring the sexuality of schizophrenic individuals is one of the main reasons we are unable to obtain a clear picture of the problem of schizophrenia.

Dr. Jessing was very interested in my sexual-physiological electrical experiments; he ordered the illustrations from my report for himself and never made any negative comments to me.

I am including a copy of the letter to Dr. Kreyberg, copies of the letters from Dr. Scharffenberg to Dr. Nic Hoel, and some other letters for your information and guidance.

TO ROGER DU TEIL
30 March 1938

My dear friend,

The extremely stupid smear campaign conducted against the experiments here has taken on serious proportions. Among other things, Lars Christensen, who was our financial sponsor, is being severely criticized from Copenhagen on the grounds that at the time I did not have a residency or work permit. Now, under pressure from our friends, Christensen has inquired through the Norwegian embassy in Paris how the experiments are proceeding. All this is just for your information. I must stress once more that it is crucial to our work and our existence that we learn of any positive result that is obtained in France. We will be able to survive the immediate future only if we can counter this abyss of envy and infamy by responding with clear, factual answers based on experiments.

You will be pleased to hear that the S-mice keep on producing tumors. Yesterday I obtained a subcutaneous tissue tumor that penetrated into the skin and infiltrated along the blood vessels; the kidney and liver were totally invaded by metastases. You can see how upsetting the situation is when such facts are obtained in the face of this smear campaign. I will keep you informed of developments.

TO WALTER BRIEHL
30 March 1938

Dear Dr. Briehl,

I am writing this same letter to Professor English.* You are undoubtedly sufficiently informed about the situation in Europe to understand the following question. Would you please let me know what opportunities currently exist in New York or Philadelphia for me to carry out my work there? You are aware that a major shift has taken place not only in my psychological and therapeutic studies but also in my scientific work. From my most recent writings on vegetotherapy and character analysis you will certainly have noticed that I have moved entirely into the physiological realm, without losing sight of the psychic sphere; on the contrary, the latter has come even more clearly to the fore. But increasingly my work involves biological experiments, not to mention my clinical activities.

Conditions in Europe have become so catastrophic that, quite apart from their general impact, they are also beginning to specifically affect my own work. You know that I hold fast to the sexual theory, but in the current climate doing so involves enormous difficulties and risks. I would be very grateful if you could let me know, just in general terms for the time being, under what conditions I could consider moving to America with my entire laboratory. I would also appreciate hearing what American colleagues think of the bion experiments. The work is proceeding extremely well here, especially in France.

---

* American psychiatrists Walter Briehl and O. Spurgeon English had studied with Reich in Vienna.

3 April 1938

Once again I am completely alone in outer space. Man is a miserable mass of protoplasm. It makes no difference if one part or the other is destroyed. People protect their existence at the cost of love. All ideology is trash compared to the one great rhythm of life! I love loving! I love my ability to suffer without running away. Does it matter? It's a great achievement to have discovered life. And yet how natural and simple. How we lie to ourselves! One pays dearly for a small fragment of truth. What a capacity for love I have—but women want security! I must not demand of others what they demand of me. Must hold out. Hang on. Not die a living death. Music—the stream of unity with the incomprehensible! I am so utterly alone.

TO ELSA LINDENBERG
4 April 1938

Elsa,

Please take some time to think over and accept the following proposals.

This is the first time since we met that *I* do not wish to be bothered by *you*. This accords well with your plans to rent a room for yourself. The matter can be easily resolved, because I have already rented a room for a period of six months. I took it originally in order to have my own treatment room, which I urgently needed at the time. Why don't you take this room? I will move your furniture over on Monday. The room can't be occupied before then. In this way you can get away from me and my atmosphere, something you have wanted, justifiably, for a long time now. I do not want to see you or talk to you for the time being. If you want to pick up your clothes on Sunday or Monday, then please make absolutely sure to call first so that I can stay out of the way. You must now, please, show some consideration for me and not create any difficulties. I am only doing what you yourself want. The room has been paid for until 1 June and it is very nice. I will then renew the rental for another three months. So you can be sure of having somewhere to live for at least six months. The room is rented in my name. Either you can go on renting it for yourself or I will cancel the lease on 24 June or continue to rent it. There is plenty of time to decide.

I fully understand your motives and I am not angry or insulted. But this time I am no longer willing to give in. There is no sense in that and neither of us would get out of our difficult situation.

Please give back the keys for Drammensvejen. Also please do not make any attempts to see me or speak to me. I cannot do any more and I must now prepare myself in peace and quiet for the difficult work I have to perform in the summer months.

I cannot give you anything more than the room at present. We will send you enough students for you to make a living. And you already have a good start.

In order to head off gossip, which is inevitable, I will send an explanation of what has happened to all my friends who, like myself, are responsible for the movement. I shall tell the truth—namely, that the objective situation, and not personal attitudes, is to blame. They will understand.

So I hope everything goes as well as possible for you. You had the correct feeling about your situation. You must get away from me for your own good. It makes no difference whether I now go to pieces— in which case you would certainly be right—or if I succeed. You would not be able to stand this life, but that does not make you a bad person. I have long agreed with you on that point. It is sad but true.

Farewell.

TO   ROGER   DU   TEIL
9 April 1938

My dear friend,

Thank you very much for the opportunities you offer for carrying out experiments on the cancer studies. But, as I have always done in the past, I would like to speak to you quite openly on this occasion. You are sufficiently familiar with my situation that I do not have to explain in detail to you why I am forced to take maximum precautions.

The cancer therapy, which in principle I now have "in the bag," so to speak, represents the high point of two decades of scientific work conducted under extremely arduous circumstances and in the face of major risks. I have come to see people—that includes academics—in a very dark light, and you will understand that I do not wish to let something like this slip from my hands. However, from a purely objective standpoint, it would be crucial for all concerned, and particularly of course for people suffering from cancer, to have an opportunity to clarify the question quickly. I am not trying to ignore that fact. I have available the results of a large number of experiments, conducted with animals and under the microscope, which have provided me with a more or less satisfactory picture of the way in which cancer cells form and how the bions act on the cancer cells. I would be very happy to make these data available, provided that I received from the experimenter or clinician in question the assurances of his strictest discretion, and provided also that he kept me informed in detail of the results. I urge you not to regard this as exaggerated mistrust on my part. If anything, I tend to be all too lacking in caution. But this time I am dealing with what is, in effect, the main part of my life's work. I would therefore recommend that, if possible, you draw up with the head of the clinic in Marseilles or some other clinic a written agreement that animal experiments performed there would be carried out on terminal cancer patients using the bion cultures from this laboratory. The agreement should also guarantee that I have priority in the use of any practical therapy that may be developed. Please consider whether such a request can be made to the clinics. The work would involve applying to human beings the results of the observations I have made here under the microscope, in vitro, and also on animals. Naturally, I would prefer if I could personally take part. It is extremely important to have a good understanding of the idiosyncrasies of the bion problem in order to arrange the tests in such a way that they yield positive and not negative results. The bions are in effect special organisms that one has to have studied continuously for years to take full advantage of any potential they offer. The details obtained from assessing the effects of the various bions are too complicated to explain in an understandable manner in a brief report. Furthermore, I have carried out a number of experiments with pneumococci, tubercle bacilli, streptococci, etc., which are all extremely promising, but only in conjunction with certain types of bion cultures that I am carefully maintaining and propagating.

For about two months, I have been working on a model experiment for cancer cells that provides very satisfactory insight into the process by which the cancer cells organize themselves. As soon as I have completed this experiment, and cooperation with the clinic in Marseilles or in Paris, or with both clinics, has been settled to everyone's satisfaction, I shall make available to you the details of this very interesting procedure, which I believe is also of critical importance to cancer research. Among other things, it confirms your statement that the essential thing about all our bion experiments is not so much the media themselves as the effect achieved on the media and the changes that occur in them. That is also part of the cancer problem.

TO ROGER DU TEIL
19 *April 1938*

My dear friend,

You will probably remember that when you were here I warned you about specialists. At the time, I had the impression that you took this a little amiss and later interpreted it as an expression of my quarrelsome nature. I can assure you that about eighteen years ago, in the battle over Freud, I experienced to the limit all the dreadful sides of human nature that are now manifesting themselves, even though at the time it was not my own cause that was involved. I have always had the feeling that you are too optimistic, that you believed it would be an easy matter to convince the authorities as long as one had something good to show them. I often expressed my doubts to you on that score. In the meantime, we have discovered that partially disclosing individual experiments or dealing with fragments of the whole involves an enormous risk, namely severe disappointment, which then does more harm than the good that might have been obtained. We have no doubt at all here that bion research cannot be understood, and therefore the practical details of the work cannot be mastered, without one's taking into account *all aspects* of sex-economic theory and the dialectical-materialistic method. The way I have set things up here with my assistants is that they must carry out accurately and independently the entire set of experiments, starting from the very beginning, before I demonstrate the more advanced, complicated experiments to them. Therefore, it is also impossible to understand the cancer experiment and to carry it out in practice unless, for example, one is firmly convinced from personal observation that (1) the protozoa really are seen to develop from disintegrating grass tissues and (2) in principle precisely the same process is involved in cancer tissue.

If I were to announce today the hitherto unreported cancer experiments that have been going on for the last one and a half years, it would be the coup de grace for everything. The work is comprehensive and follows a logical path down which one must laboriously and diligently proceed, beginning with the preliminary experiments with grass and earth. I would therefore like to make the following proposal to you, if you wish to include third parties in our cancer research.

I am trying as far as possible to devise simple test procedures that are achieved gradually, without any initial relation to the cancer problem, and that thus will automatically open one's eyes to the cancer question. Please let me know whether you are in agreement. I would then arrange the experiments in a logical manner and finally lead up to the cancer experiments. Choosing any other route appears too hazardous to me. I will therefore wait to send you the cancer reports until you have given me your approval or made some other suggestion. The first proposal that I would like to make today is that these experiments should above all focus on continuous and extremely accurate observation of how protozoa form from decaying moss and grass tissue; this phenomenon should be studied and confirmed. The processes can be directly observed under the microscope. Then some model tests with egg nutrient media and charcoal heated to incandescence could be introduced, and finally we would come to the work on cancer tissue itself.

I would like to give you the reasons for my extreme caution, so that you do not decide that I am inordinately apprehensive. My opponents here have submitted various inquiries to Bonnet, Martiny, etc., which is of course quite inappropriate, because they did so without my knowledge and without my approval. An article written by Scharffenberg, who is a psychiatrist here in Oslo, casts doubt in an extremely insulting way on your competence to deal with scientific matters. I am including a translation of this passage. Please let me know what has happened to Bonnet, Martiny, and the others, so I can see to quashing any rumors that arise. It is better to be aware of an unpleasant truth than to live in a world of illusion. Finally, I must ask you, if possible, to enjoin those colleagues who are seriously working on the matter to take whatever steps they can to ensure that we are granted the necessary peace and quiet to continue here. It would be sufficient for one or the other of them merely to confirm that the experiments are being carried out and that it will take a long time to complete them. That's all for today. I hope that these comments will to some extent have made it easier for you to accomplish your own very difficult work.

21 April 1938

Thjötta in the *Aftenposten*: "In the first set of experiments that I carried out, dust bacteria grew on our media when they were inoculated with Reich's cultures. It must be added that one of these bacteria is able to withstand temperatures of 120° Celsius without suffering any damage under steam pressure. A boiling aqueous solution cannot, of course, get any hotter than 100° C. After that, the usual Reich culture was heated in autoclaves to 115° C. It then stood for half an hour, and when we took it out of the autoclave and prepared new cultures, we found that they were sterile." At the same time Kreyberg stated that what he saw were "ordinary staphylococci."

Headline in the *Tidens Tegn*: "Genius, Dilettante, or Psychopath?" The results of Thjötta's and Kreyberg's statements. Pasteur proved over seventy years ago that life can come only from life, so it is absurd to think that life could emerge again from dead matter. At the end there is a comment on the financial donations made to Reich.

ABC (fascist): Lead article says: "Proof That Reich Is a Fraud."

TO ROGER DU TEIL
21 April 1938

Dear friend,

Over Easter, a fantastic smear campaign broke out here, but we have launched a successful counterattack. All I have done is to draw up an explanation of the fundamental principles involved. I am sending you a copy with the request that, if you think it is correct to do so, you should distribute it to the press in France. It is hard to believe how fantastic and childish people's reactions are to the issue of the origin of life. Obviously, forces and fantasies of which we are totally unaware are behind all this. We are holding our own very well, not just here but throughout Scandinavia. But this smear campaign might make it impossible for me to go on living here. If that happens you will hear about it. That's all for today, but please write soon to let me know how your talk with the cancer researchers in Marseilles turned out.

22 April 1938

Tidens Tegn: Fascist Laban. Recommendation that Reich be sent to a concentration camp.

Nissen makes accusation to Schjelderup that the university is dominated by the Reich movement. Kreyberg threatens to sue Havrevold. Havrevold writes a detailed article on the meeting between Reich and Kreyberg.

On the basis of a comment made by Havrevold in his article, Professor Schreiner reports Reich to the social affairs department for having injected experimental animals.

23 April 1938

Fritt Folk: Reich is the slimiest kind of pornographer and he was driven out of Germany. This is a scandal for Norwegian science.

Morgenbladet: Jörgen Quisling writes: "When Dr. Reich claims that his so-called bions are a type of spontaneously emerging cell, he shows not only that he is trapped in biological prejudice but also that his experiments are proceeding along entirely the wrong track because—

true to his prejudice—he is trying to produce *directly* a development that in reality is extremely *indirect* in nature. In addition, Dr. Reich apparently has no philosophical understanding of the fact that life is based on abstract transformation centers, which are metaphysical in nature, like the so-called ether, and which therefore, like the ether, exert the same abstract or biogenetic pressure on created life. This in turn means that life, like such pressure, has by now penetrated so far into the original lifeless energy and matter that it is just as hopeless to attempt an experimental demonstration of proto-life as it is to entice human beings to emerge from modern-day apes."

26 April 1938

Statement by Schjelderup's student Rasmussen. He affirmed that Schjelderup never mentioned Reich's ideas in his lectures at the university.

Link between the bion question and the residency question.

Tidens Tegn: Schjelderup is trying to distance himself from sex-economic theory, my naiveté, and orgasm theory.

27 April 1938

New campaigns by Scharffenberg: "Is Dr. Reich an Honest Scientist?" The *Arbejderbladet* gave special advance notice of this article. The article claims it is impossible to verify the bions. It is nonsense to claim that one must be familiar with the prerequisite requirements of the experiments. And if a biologist who patiently sits down at the microscope to see how plant cells turn into unicellular organisms (amoebae) does not experience this miracle, the objection is raised that a negative result of this kind does not provide any contradictory proof because Dr. Reich saw what he saw. (So one does not even have to look into the microscope in the first place.)

Lay people believe that magnifications between $2,000 \times$ and $4,000 \times$ guarantee careful analyses. In fact the reverse is true and the image becomes less sharply focused. To study amoebae, such high magnifications are unnecessary.

Dagbladet and *Arbejderbladet* publish signatures in support of Reich's being allowed to remain in Norway. They also publish Reich's proposal for a public verification of the bion experiments.

Dagbladet: "Science and Truth," Nic Hoel's reply to Scharffenberg. Inquiries made by the Aliens Office.

Scharffenberg doubts Reich's status as a doctor of medicine. Reich submits documents.

Scharffenberg continues to doubt.

28 April 1938

"Psychoanalysis as Suppressed Christianity" published in *Tidens Tegn*.

T O   R O G E R   D U   T E I L
28 April 1938

My dear friend,

After spending a few fantastic and so far extremely fruitful days engaged in the battle against the most narrow-minded and corrupt of personal attacks, launched under the guise of a scientific critique of the "bions," I now find some time to report the salient results to you.

Yesterday my proposal that we put an end to the senseless debate in the press by demonstrating the experiments in public before an investigatory commission was published in the local newspapers. The medical faculty at the university here has already publicly accepted the proposal in principle. The proposal itself was made by a plant pathologist from Copenhagen, Dr. Paul Neergaard, who, as you know, is working together with a bacteriologist to analyze bion cultures. Now we actually have to get this public commission together and conduct the experiments in public. This has enormous advantages and consequences that will also affect all the rest of our work. As you can see from the press clippings that I sent to you, the background to the campaign against the bions was nonscientific in nature. Now we have to address ourselves to the task as follows.

1. The members of the commission should not be drawn solely from Norway. Instead the makeup of the commission must be international.

2. A preliminary working group must put together precisely the test

and verification procedures to be used. In the coming week we will
hold a meeting here to work out the initial proposals. I would like you
to participate in this preliminary group and to make suggestions based
on your experience.

3. The matter must be very thoroughly prepared. The demonstration cannot take place before August or September.

4. The commission will probably have to be paid for from private
sources and we are initiating the work required to raise the funds.
Please give your opinion on this as well.

5. Please let me have your suggestions on who could serve on the
commission from France. I would imagine that the most suitable
members of the commission would be people who have not rejected
the bion book but instead have adopted a wait-and-see attitude. Also
suitable are those people who are carrying out the identifications.
Above all, it is necessary to avoid the many traps which our opponents
will set for us. Principally, these will be of a tactical and bureaucratic
kind. We must try to demonstrate our best test procedures.

The university here in Oslo has requested that our opponents Kreyberg and Thjötta be allowed to sit on the commission. But Kreyberg
is absolutely out of the question because the commission must be
objective, which Kreyberg was not.

I have just received your letter of 26 April. Many thanks for your
willingness to participate. We will now certainly succeed in getting
our views across and will spare ourselves twenty or thirty years of being
hushed up and put down. People will have to accept the facts. At any
rate, the first success scored was that the machinations aimed at having
me deported miscarried, and for the time being I shall remain here.
You will therefore receive from us an accurate list of proposals on how
the tests should be performed.

The day before yesterday, a representative from an international
press agency who happened to be in Oslo paid me a visit and I brought
him up to date on the matter. He is going to write a long report for
the American papers and for the rest of the European press. I will be
allowed to see the report before it is published and have an opportunity
to make corrections. In the near future I will send you an article I
have written in a simple style for the local press entitled "How I Came
to Study the Bion and Cancer Problem." This article is intended not
to report the results that are already available on cancer research but

merely to acquaint the public with the conditions that lead from sex research to cancer research.

I am sending you a copy of a film about amoebae, shot for the most part in time-lapse mode, for possible demonstration purposes.

CORRECTION OF THE STATEMENT MADE
BY PROFESSOR THJÖTTA ON 28 APRIL 1938
REGARDING THE BIONS

. . . I have never asserted that I am "creating new life." Is it correct to say that artificial life is being created? Vanity tempts me to say yes, but the correct answer is no! If life were to occupy its own metaphysical region, completely separate from nonlife, then I would have the right to say that I am creating "artificial life." But my experiments show that there are developmental stages on the way from lifeless, immobile matter to life, that in nature the emergence of life from inorganic matter proceeds presumably by the hour, by the minute . . . All that I have been able to uncover experimentally is the developmental process of life. Perhaps in that process a new type of organism was artificially produced.

30 April 1938

Sigurd Hoel against Scharffenberg. Proof that the fascist newspapers obtained all their arguments from Scharffenberg.

Scharffenberg doubts du Teil's effectiveness as a teacher. Du Teil submits documents.

In May, lay people will become involved in the discussion on the bions.

10 May 1938

There was a break-in at Arbejderfoto. Over one hundred of my microphotographs were stolen.

13 May 1938

Scharffenberg calls for a legal investigation of Reich's financial affairs. Newspapers splash this news across their pages. Scharffenberg claims that Reich is receiving 100 kroner an hour from an English woman. The woman in question corrects this statement. The matter will be turned over to a lawyer.

TO ROGER DU TEIL
16 May 1938

My dear friend,

On Friday I gave a lecture on the bion problem to several hundred Norwegian physicians who had been invited by the executive body of the local medical association. Bacteriologists were also present, including my opponents Kreyberg, Scharffenberg, and many others. I think I can say that it was an enormous success. Using eighty photographs and 250 meters of film, I was able to demonstrate that the work is deadly serious. We all agreed that at least 80 to 90 percent of those present understood what was involved. Our opponents kept quiet. I shall publish the text of this lecture together with the associated photographs.

Everything is going well here and we have learned a major lesson: for us, authorities cannot be regarded as authorities.

TO ROGER DU TEIL, EMIL WALTER, *
AND PAUL NEERGAARD
26 May 1938

This is to let you know that I am accepting a very sensible proposal made by Dr. Paul Neergaard of Copenhagen. He wrote to me on 23

---

* Professor of chemistry and physics at the Zurich Trade School.

May 1938 to express his opinion that it would be much better if the public demonstration of the bion experiments scheduled for the summer was not performed by me but by some other person or persons. I would therefore ask you to consider whether it would be possible for you to write to the local university, perhaps jointly, and arrange the organization of a public demonstration of the experiments. The medical faculty here already stated several weeks ago in a daily newspaper that this type of public verification should take place, but that it must be paid for by the supporters of the bion cause. Please let me know as soon as possible whether you would be willing to negotiate in my place with the local university.

TO EMIL WALTER
1 June 1938

Dear Dr. Walter,

I am aware of the fact that it is difficult for you to get in touch directly with the local medical faculty. The matter will be dealt with here by Dr. Havrevold, who will convey your approval.

With regard to the virus question: When I made the first observations of the vesicular nature of boiled matter and matter that had been heated to incandescence, I of course also immediately thought of the relationship to the virus question. I am forced to conclude from my experiments that the virus is nothing more than a vesicle, probably very much smaller, that is produced under certain conditions in the course of the complicated physiological processes taking place in the body. When I first cultured organisms resembling staphylococci from autoclaved blood, I had no choice but to assume that *the organism was self-destructing* and, at the same time, producing living or lifelike organisms. I hope to be able to show you each and every one of these things here. If the local university should refuse, for philosophical reasons, to perform the control experiments, I would propose that you come nevertheless. We could carry out a private demonstration and verification with some other friends, acting perhaps as a kind of preparatory working group for a later commission. In such a case we would pay your travel expenses.

T O　R O G E R　D U　T E I L
8 June 1938

My dear friend,

I will try to reply as calmly and as factually as possible to your deeply distressing letter of 5 June.*

I would like to assure you personally, on behalf of myself and also a number of very important friends, that we are entirely at your disposal and you may count on us in all respects, if necessary even for financial support. It is vital for us to maintain solidarity in such a battle. But the situation requires that I speak very openly to you, drawing on all the battle experience and severe disappointments of the past eighteen and more years. Right from the start I asked and warned you not to rely too much on universities and authorities. My error in the matter that now affects you so badly is that I failed to prevent one of our coworkers here from seeking assurances from Paris to allay his own lack of certainty. Unfortunately you have not kept me fully and openly informed from the start, because if you had I would not have persisted in the view that decent work is being performed in Paris. But there is nothing that can be done about that now. You write that nothing should be undertaken from here. We will not do anything that you do not wish us to do, but in view of these very painful experiences I must ask you again to have a little more trust in my method of going about things. If I managed, by myself, to survive for twelve whole years simply on the basis of honest and open publication of the facts, despite going through some extremely bad periods, then a group of people of various types and widely differing backgrounds should now be able to stand fast, but only under one condition: we must hold true

---

* Du Teil had informed Reich that he had been suspended from his post at the university because, it was claimed, his work with Reich, done privately, had involved the university's name in a public polemic.

to and never deviate from the line of openly declaring our scientific facts, and we should above all abandon any belief in the goodwill of academic authorities. There is only one way for us to go, and many people are saying this: we must arouse the conscience of public opinion against all the behind-the-scenes maneuvering and dishonesty of a few people in high places who are particularly adept at this kind of behavior.

The arguments with which you were dismissed are fully in keeping with the dreadful methods that such cliques use against any kind of serious work. There is no sense describing to you in detail how I felt when I heard the news and how deeply touched I was by your almost superhuman decency in trying to show consideration for me in this situation. Please direct this consideration elsewhere, in the interest of our cause. There are many decent truth-seeking persons in the world who know nothing about us. They can only give us their support if the waves created this time by all the nastiness finally reach them and bring us to their attention. I am firmly convinced that we would be putting ourselves in serious danger if we stood by quietly and considerately, merely observing what was happening and leaving the field entirely clear for the meaner elements to do their dirty work. Please keep me fully up to date on what actions you are considering at your end and what impact the matter has had on your friends and on people in general.

For the time being I will not undertake any official action until I have convinced you that open battle is the best way and until I have received from you all the material that will enable me to make the correct moves. This material includes, above all, the letter you received from Bonnet on 23 October 1937.

I urge you to accept my invitation and come to Norway as my guest as soon as you can get away. You do not have to have any fears on my account. As things stand at present, my enemies are seeking ways to force me out of the country, but they will not be successful.

P.S. When official agencies repudiate our work, that is all right. But when other official agencies confirm our work, that is wrong! Objective science.

TO ANNAEUS SCHJÖDT *
16 June 1938

Dear Dr. Schjödt,

With reference to our last conversation, the following is a summary of my general report on the affair that is still pending. In August 1937 Dr. Roger du Teil, professor at the Centre Universitaire Méditerranéen in Nice, worked for fourteen days in my laboratory in Oslo, performing some experimental procedures, and he took back with him to France a number of preparations, films, and descriptions. According to the reports he sent me in his letters, the films and the preparations were demonstrated in Pontigny and in Paris. It was his impression that the presentations were received in a positive, wait-and-see manner. Control experiments were to be carried out at several laboratories, including the laboratory of the Medical Faculty, which is headed by a Professor Debré. His assistant is Dr. Bonnet. Sometime around 4 October, du Teil was staying in Paris with Bonnet, who had promised to look into the matter. In response to a specific request from me, du Teil informed me that the work in Paris was still going on and had yielded contradictory results. I waited several months without making any further inquiries. In November 1937 the first campaign against my work started in Oslo with five meetings at the Psychiatric Society led by Professor Vogt. † One of the financial backers of the institute was bombarded with rumors about me from an unknown source in Denmark. Dr. Havrevold asked me to name the laboratories in France at which the control studies were being conducted. After some hesitation, I told him the laboratories and gave him Dr. Bonnet's name. A certain Roald Dysthe, as I later found out, then traveled to Paris and to Nice. Bonnet supposedly told him (this is what he reported in a meeting attended by Professor Schreiner, Dr. Gording, and Dr. Havrevold) that Debré knew nothing of the bion work and that he, Dr. Bonnet, ought to know, because everything for Professor Debré passed through his hands. This took me completely by surprise because du Teil had written to me from Nice that Professor Debré had (and I quote) "ordered more" bion cultures. In addition, Dysthe had reported that, at his urging, du Teil had shown him a letter from Bonnet dated 23 October

---

* A lawyer.
† Ragnar Vogt, prominent Norwegian psychiatrist.

1937, i.e., about three weeks after du Teil had visited Bonnet. According to Dysthe, this letter contained confirmatory information about the work in Paris. But Dysthe had the impression the letter was a fake. He deduced this from the differences in the signatures: the letter from Bonnet to du Teil had a signature in tiny letters while a letter from Bonnet to Dr. Gording in which he states that he had obtained "only negative" results was signed with a larger signature. The accusation that such a decisive letter was a forgery is a matter of great consequence.

The attack by the psychiatrists failed. In March the first provisional publication on the bions appeared. It was around then that the second campaign got under way, although this time it was based not on my psychotherapeutic work but on my biological research. It was in this connection that the articles known to you appeared and the attacks by Dr. Kreyberg were published. The article published by Dr. Havrevold in *Dagbladet* and *Arbejderbladet* contains the most important facts needed to refute Dr. Kreyberg's assertions.

At a meeting of the Socialist Physicians Association, Dr. Kreyberg stated that he had been in Paris, had talked to Bonnet in the presence of Debré, and Debré had merely laughed at the whole business. I do not know what Kreyberg said when he was with Bonnet, but quite a bit can be deduced from his behavior here. I immediately wrote to du Teil that he should try to clear up the Debré affair for me. I then received two handwritten letters from the president of the psychobiological department at the Sorbonne that show clearly that Professor Debré not only was interested in the matter but had expressly ordered more bion cultures and in fact had made very precise inquiries about the nutrient media, etc. I later answered these queries through du Teil. Once I had this proof of the accuracy of du Teil's statements in my hands I wrote a letter to du Teil asking him to send me all the material, in particular the letter from Bonnet to him. So far I have not received a reply. An objective analysis of the facts permits only three possible conclusions. (1) I am a swindler, as Scharffenberg and Kreyberg claim. I am willing to submit all the documents to a court and also to carry out the bion experiments in public. (2) Du Teil is a swindler and a forger of letters who claims to have received positive reports from Bonnet, although this was not true. (3) Bonnet first wrote a partially confirmatory letter to du Teil and then a totally negative letter to Dr. Gording.

Bonnet should himself have made an exact record of the experiments, but he did not do that. Nor has he so far replied to my query.

Nonscientists, again for reasons unknown to me, have intervened in a scientific matter and created confusion. This is particularly true as far as Dysthe's slanderous attack on du Teil is concerned. It is possible, at least judging by what has already happened here in Oslo, that Dr. Kreyberg, by virtue of his official authority in Paris, has without basis created a situation I do not understand but one that poses difficulties and dangers to our work. I believe I am right in assuming that these actions are the reason Dr. Roger du Teil was suspended without pay, as he recently wrote and informed me.

These, in brief, are the facts. I would ask you to use all legal means at your disposal to seek clarification of this matter, which is assuming a criminal character.

17 June 1938

It is quite clear, according to everything that I read, that I am on the right path. Kreyberg is a swine. I shall just press on steadily. One experiment after another. Kreyberg rages because he is against the bacterial etiology of cancer.

19 June 1938

The sum total of eighteen years of difficult scientific work—after twenty-five years of homelessness and transience.

1. I am without a home or a passport.
2. Am an émigré Jewish sexologist, scientist, socialist.
3. Have lost my children.
4. Lack the support of a scientific organization.
5. Have been ostracized as a charlatan, swindler, and con man.
6. Have been deserted by the second woman I loved.
7. Deserted by dozens of pupils.
8. Thrown out of two large organizations.
9. Must appear in court to prove my integrity.
10. Am penniless.
11. Have no hope for success during my lifetime—or for children.

But still: The bions were my discovery!

Every opportunity is at hand. It is no longer a question of whether I am ruined or not. The stakes are high! Shame on me if I yield now for the sake of "decency" or "love." Unthinkable! There will always be women for me—and friends as well.

What's the use? I have discovered life! Am I supposed to make myself dependent on Ring, Lotte, or Schjelderup? My road leads beyond them.

TO ROGER DU TEIL, EMIL WALTER, AND PAUL NEERGAARD
20 June 1938

On 24 April 1938 the Medical Faculty in Oslo announced publicly in the *Dagbladet* that it would be a very good idea to investigate the bions. Dr. Neergaard proposed that instead of a private commission, which would have little effect, an official agency should be appointed to carry out the verification. In consultation with Dr. Walter, Professor du Teil, and Dr. Neergaard, Dr. Havrevold and Dr. Nic Hoel wrote a letter to the Medical Faculty in Oslo on behalf of the Institute for Sex-Economic Research. We have now received a reply which says that at a meeting of the faculty the following decision was made: "The Medical Faculty is not convinced that the experiments which are to be verified exist in such a form that they can receive serious scientific consideration. The faculty therefore sees no reason to appoint a member to a control commission."

TO EMIL WALTER
25 June 1938

Dear Dr. Walter,

Now that the Medical Faculty in Oslo has refused to appoint a representative to the control commission it is not possible to carry out the verification procedures this summer. Whether or not the preparatory commission can meet depends not only on the agreement of the participants (apart from yours no other notification of acceptance has been received) but also on the financial circumstances.

Because of the friendly ties between us, I can tell you openly that I accept the reason you give for your participation in the preparatory commission. You write that the task of the preparatory commission should be to "carry out the bion experiments in such a way that publication in strictly scientific form" is possible. I have been carrying out scientific research and producing scientific results for the last eighteen years and, as you will probably admit, my work contains some truths and is not without consequence. So far, I have managed to get by without the so-called strictly scientific form, if by this you mean a certain type of convention in publishing scientific papers. Look at any yearbook of official experimental psychology or of standard biology, as I have often done, and you will have to agree with me that at least 90 percent of all the papers could easily have remained unpublished. To me, "strictly scientific" means describing as accurately as possible, and in accordance with the truth, things one has seen. You have unfortunately failed to understand that the Medical Faculty's excuse that my work lacks proper form is nothing more than that—an excuse. My experiments with incandescent matter and the autoclavation tests have been described in such detail that any chemist or bacteriologist could imitate them within five minutes. Instead of doing this, people are now hiding behind the objection that the publication of the results is not scientific enough. I must reject any such statement. I was the one who discovered the vesicular nature of boiled matter and of matter heated to incandescence. It should also be the duty of so-called highly official, authoritarian science to concern itself not only with the proper form of publication, which in any case is a dreadful procedure, but also with the truth. I can wait, and I am still prepared to show these things to anyone who is really willing to see.

26 June 1938

Fascism is not a new phenomenon, merely an intensified mode of making even the oldest issues seem fresh, young, and desirable. It is everywhere in daily life: in mankind's fear of pleasure, which turns into romantic impotence; in his helplessness and irresponsibility; in the polluting of life with irrationalism; in the art of lying, deception, and taking advantage of others. Fascism is the abomination of this world taken to a revolutionary extreme. A compromise between most sacred desire and disgusting human reaction. The petty bourgeois socialist does not understand this paradox. Fascist mentality lurks in psychiatric stupidity just as it does in the cowardice of a person like Schjelderup or in formal correctness, in Nic Hoel's dependence on authority just as in Sigurd's feeble skepticism, in the excellence of the Jewish character just as in its disgusting aspects. Fascism is the desire not to have any problems. A desire for nature dressed in crinoline, sensuality doing the goose step, life's will in the trenches. It means the courage to die a cowardly death, straightforwardness based on dishonesty, unrelenting consistency in exploiting human helplessness.

TO ROGER DU TEIL*
30 June 1938

My dear friend,

I am extremely happy that you have succeeded so quickly in setting your situation straight. We can deduce from this the moral that nothing is ever as bad as it seems. It is a major benefit that the whole business was not hushed up and that the hullabaloo that arose without any prompting on our part drew the attention of quite a few good people to my work and to the successful control experiments you have carried out.

But now I must correct a few comments you make in your letter. You seem to believe that I was the one who unleashed the press campaign and kept on fanning the flames. That is not true. Apart from

---

* This letter was not sent.

one basic statement to the press, in which I asked for calm, I have not responded to a single line or a single objection or reproach from my enemies. They have also ridden themselves totally into the ground and exposed themselves to the world. The press campaign is still continuing because some Norwegian scientists and physicians simply could no longer tolerate the disgraceful behavior exhibited by, in particular, a psychopathological, querulous person like Kreyberg. They are now struggling to eradicate the shame that two—no more than that—private persons have inflicted on Norwegian science. I cannot prevent my friends and the others from doing this, nor do I want to. This is how Debré, Bonnet, and others were brought into the discussion, and they are not entirely blameless. Let me just make the following clear.

1. Bonnet was not in the least entitled to write a private letter to Dr. Gording stating that negative results had been obtained.

2. Bonnet had even less right—unless he was thinking of publishing and justifying his results—to write a letter to Kreyberg in which he repeated what he had said to Gording and also to receive Kreyberg in Paris and report to him on this matter. Kreyberg published Bonnet's letter here in the press.

You still seem to be of the opinion that I get into these difficulties for some political reason. I have already written to you once that this is not true. I am not involved in any political activity, I do not belong to any party, and I have always been attacked solely because of my scientific work. But one point must be cleared up because it affects our cooperation (and I thank you for also being open with me). The bion experiments have a long history, and you have not been involved in all the events in that history. Without my studies in the fields of social sciences and orgasmo therapy, there would have been no bion theory and no bion experiments and therefore no successful control tests in your laboratory. I understand very well that people focus on that part of the work which is of particular concern to them. But in the interest of this tremendously important work, you must concede that I cannot now abandon the orgasm theory merely because someone like Kreyberg or some aged psychiatrist does not like it. Nor can I concentrate my activities solely on the bions, which, incidentally, those people hate most of all. Anyone who wishes to espouse the noble bion cause must of necessity also bear the burdens arising from its history —namely, in the field of scientific and experimental sex research. And the word *sexuality* as well as the scientific work in this field will long remain a stumbling block. We have to reckon with that. I have no illusions that a psychiatrist like Scharffenberg, a pathologist like Kreyberg, or a bacteriologist like Bonnet will very soon declare themselves willing to consider the bion experiments in their total context and to verify them using the methods that derive from my sexual theories.

I fully share your opinion that we can only make headway step by step; but thunderclaps like those which we have just experienced cannot be avoided, although we must do everything we can not to provoke them. When they are instigated by enemies, however, we have to strike back forcefully and courageously, making no allowances. I fully understand your wish to show consideration for your French academic colleagues, but when I am fighting for my scientific, material, and intellectual existence, I cannot tolerate such consideration.

There is another point that requires clarification. So far I have sent you a series of preparations, mainly for identification purposes. These are preparations that nobody else has been given in this form and in this manner to work on in his laboratory. I have every right to know precisely what has happened to these preparations. May I remind you of an S-culture, three types of cell cultures, etc. Please let me know what became of them. If Debré ever had any cultures in his hands that I produced, literally by the sweat of my brow and under the enormous pressure of my financial and social situation, then I don't care how well respected he is as an academic, I have the right to demand from Debré that he tell me what has happened to these cultures. And I am sure you understand not only that this claim is justified but also that it must be put into practice.

When you write that the French scientists have done you a great honor in showing interest in the matter, I for my part would like to claim the honor of having sent the French scientists, for the first time in the history of biology, experimentally produced spherical cells for their examination and identification. Under no circumstances can I place my work lower than that of some academic teacher, precisely because I do not enjoy financial assistance from the government and I do not have major laboratory facilities. Instead, I personally have to find the funds for each bit of difficult research. In addition, all this has to be accomplished in a world situation I did not create and am not responsible for. I have become its victim although I have done nothing bad. I must therefore ask you, my dear friend, to keep me informed of every step affecting my cultures, my reports, and my work, because in the final analysis it is I who am responsible for what happens in my laboratory.

Our cooperation has yielded such excellent fruit that I have been so bold as to reply to your openness with equal candor. I am certain that you will not hold that against me but on the contrary will regard it as an expression of the absolute trust I have in you.

TO ANNAEUS SCHJÖDT
July 1938

Dear Mr. Schjödt,

Yesterday at 10 a.m. I was at the Aliens Registration Office. Mr. Konstad had requested in writing that I be "interrogated" to determine whether and when, and for what reasons, I had been in France. I started out by protesting that I was to be interrogated as if I were an accused person. In addition, I stated that I was willing to provide whatever information was desired, although I would have to conduct the negotiations and make my statements through my lawyer. The reasons I gave for doing so were that a group of private individuals, acting out of hostility toward my scientific work, is maneuvering behind the scenes to obtain my deportation from the country. Since I have no legal training, I am afraid that by answering questions whose purpose I did not understand, I might fall into a trap.

The foregoing was noted. Apart from this written statement, I made another statement to the officers that, for the time being, I did not want to have recorded in writing. I gave them another reason for wanting to know the purpose behind the questions. It is well known in Norway that Konstad is a confirmed fascist. * I have heard this from various quarters.

Now, there is a logical connection between the campaign of per-

* 12 May 1949. After Hitler's downfall this same Konstad was shot for treason. [W.R.'s note]

secution pursued by my scientific opponents, all of whom believe firmly in the genetic causation of most diseases, and fascist racial theory. Thus it would not be a purely legal matter. The officers told me that if it were ever to come to court they would have to give evidence as witnesses. I told them that I would of course have nothing against that. I am telling you this so that you know what was discussed.

When I return from my vacation, I will request a meeting with you and on that occasion I will give you exact details regarding my French connections and my stay in France. However, I must ask you not to pass these on automatically to Konstad. I continue to maintain that I have not committed any crime, I am not accused of anything, and therefore I have the right to know the purpose behind any question put to me.

30 July 1938

My diaries, documents, and papers have all been removed for four months because I was afraid my house would be searched. How they would have misinterpreted my private life.

Today I returned from vacation. Spent four weeks in a tent.

21 August 1938

Haven't made any entries for a long time although a lot has happened:

The whole filthy press campaign.

Had time to reread Svante Arrhenius,* understood it this time.

My experiments with lava and iron explain the origin of the spores.

The process involved in a spinning wave seems to illustrate Einstein's $E = mc^2$ formula, like throwing barbells with unequal sides o———O. Details later.

Things went well with Elsa.

I am beginning to realize that no one other than myself will accept or advocate my cause. It will take time, a long time.

The thought of a "school" repulses me. That would only confuse

---

* Swedish physical chemist; first to present the theory of ionization.

my work and bring it to a halt. Pupils want to earn money, they don't want the risks.

I still have time before I submit to the law of retrogression.

Rough draft of "The Natural Organization of Work" finished.

More leisure, more quiet, less concern for others. Would like to have a child.

Still haven't received a residency permit.

Cancer research: maturing slowly—will take my time, experiment by experiment.

Much clinical material.

Excerpts published from "Basic Problems of Sex Economy."

Get free of the socialists.

1 September 1938

My spinning-wave hypothesis* seems to solve a multitude of contradictions in physics.

How to elaborate this?

5 September 1938

I am so alone. Will I give up—and when? That will be the beginning of the end. I'll sense it, feel it deep within my body—the beginning of death.

I am still resisting it. And always there is music inside me! If I could only grasp it, write it down.

Music and pleasure always and forever, eternally young, beyond all generations. I feel Beethoven as I feel my own being, simple and true! He died miserably and if I don't yield I shall die miserably as well. The thoughts that have crossed my mind since I began to think could stop the earth in its orbit.

Pity they are not all available at once.

In a few thousand years the human mind will comprehend itself, get hold of itself. Incredible!

Time, duration, the eternal human being in the void—nothing but revolving energy.

---

* Reich's spinning-wave theory represented his evolving thought on the relation of mass and energy.

Alone. Today Norway, yesterday Germany, the day before Austria, tomorrow perhaps Australia. At home everywhere and yet nowhere.

I am growing wise, am learning to give up raging against the senselessness and to stop surrendering myself to other people's ideas.

I am struggling with the problem of life and death, and no one is even aware of it. A great burden, this knowledge.

12 September 1938

Heard Hitler's speech today.* How correct the man is within the context of this filthy mess! There are no reasonable arguments against him!

At present the spirit of rational thought and truth is at odds with the spirit of the masses. Tomorrow and in the future they will coincide. Today humanity will follow any Hitler like a flock of sick sheep.

But tomorrow—alas, a deep chasm yawns between today and tomorrow. A gap in our knowledge of man's deepest, undreamed-of secrets! Today and tomorrow—problems with the Sudeten Germans and pulsating energy.

13 September 1938

When will the new fool with an inflated crop crow that the orgasm does indeed equal life itself, but "only theoretically"!

While in practice there is only politicking and greasing the right palm.

To hell with the whole pack.

I want to dance with a sweet girl in my arms and still conquer the vesicular nature of the atoms.

TO ROGER DU TEIL
16 September 1938

My dear friend,

Quite honestly I do not understand your silence. There are a number of still unanswered questions to which I requested your reply. Now I have another question or request for you that is of decisive importance

---

* Reich refers to Hitler's speech at the party convention in Nuremberg.

for our work. Since my existence as an émigré citizen of the German Reich would be extremely endangered in the event of a war, I must take steps to ensure that the approximately ten types of bion cultures that exist and that are the sole tangible proof of the accuracy of the bion theory survive the war. I am therefore writing to Stockholm, to England, and to the French academy in Paris, as well as to you, to find out whether and how it might be possible to hand over a series of each of the cultures available here to a biological or bacteriological institute for safekeeping. Each of the bion cultures requires a special type of treatment that I would describe in detail. Please let me know by return mail whether you could perform this act of kindness for me and find out who in Marseilles, Nice, or Paris would be willing to accept a series of bion cultures.

19 September 1938

German refugees from the Sudetenland are filling Dresden. The assembled Freikorps is on the march. War!!

21 September 1938

No, not just war but a combination of war and disgrace. Hitler, who is a psychopath, is the right Führer and dictator for all other psychopaths.

The collective neurosis carried to the extreme.

I have a choice between withdrawing to the laboratory and performing research for the rest of my life or complete political activity—that is, laying claim to leadership.

What an insane decision. My science has no place in this world. Political leadership? I have no desire for that and probably no talent either. Although even a talent like mine would be equal to Chamberlain's!

1 October 1938

Czechoslovakia has been sacrificed. The Western democracies are groveling before Hitler.

TO THE FRENCH ACADEMY OF SCIENCE
1 October 1938

Dear Sirs!

I confirm with thanks receipt of your letter dated 27 September 1938 in which you inform me that, for technical reasons, it would be impossible for you to accept the cultures. However, you suggest that I publish the results I have achieved so far in the academy's journal. I will gladly follow your advice. In the course of the next few days I will write a brief report on the existing bion cultures and their origin and will send you a copy of this report together with photographs for publication. I will also enclose some culture tubes containing bion cultures consisting of small cells that so far have not been identified.

I would like to add that, since my first report to you on 1 January 1937, a great deal has happened here. The report I sent at that time has long been superseded. I must ask you, therefore, please to be patient and to await the arrival of my mailing to you.

16 October 1938

I am human but have been removed from the daily debasement of sexual existence because I have grasped its nature and significance, in other words, I became a "famous person." I may not speak to a girl on the street, may not flirt with a waitress—in short, I have been "elevated." How do they intend to solve the problem of youth loitering in the streets, bored to death, hungry, craving, desiring? How will they solve the question of prostitution? No distinguished "leader of the people" will dare to touch this problem, because he is "elevated," isolated, may not take such steps "because of his position," may not smile at girls anymore: it is incompatible with the dignity of a responsible man.

Filth! Lies! Disgusting! To hell with the dignitary's dignity. I want to be allowed to smile at pretty girls despite the fact that I have solved the life problem.

How could I ever have solved it if I had been dignified and conscious of my responsibilities in that sense of the word!

T O　B R O N I S L A W　M A L I N O W S K I *
18 October 1938

My dear Bronislaw,

Many thanks for your good letter and my best wishes for the recreation in the USA.

Of course, there are reasons enough to doubt the value of today's science. But I don't believe that humanity can *live* without science, and where life is concerned, their right instincts cannot fail in the long run. Maybe that humanity will have to suffer and to learn from misery and chaos until rational thinking will get to power.

I am in full prepared to secure the possibility to live and work in the USA. There are two possibilities for me: either to make use of the German immigration and to go as homeless, pitied, and in the end a bit despised emigrant. Or to keep through until I shall be called, a quite different start! If my publication of the achieved results in the bion investigation comes through in the French academy, then many doors may open themselves. My psychotherapeutic work is quite well known and regarded in specialist circles in the States. It's only miserable that one likes very much to get one's health through my so-called radical ideas and work but does not dare to stand for them and to take risks. That's it!!

When I start to think about the poor devils in Czechoslovakia, who are defenseless and sacrificed just now, I have to become less arrogant about scientific work. Can you imagine what being homeless, without passport and money, means?

Neill† wrote me just now that England is starting to become fascistic. Is that true?

Let me hear from you please!!! What's with your health?

---

* This letter was written in English.
† A. S. Neill, founder of the Summerhill School in Leiston, England.

29 October 1938

Somehow a new life without plan or pressure is beginning.

My illusions concerning general human capability and willingness to keep up with me have vanished.

I realize that I must continue giving, just as before, knowing full well that the recipients will disappoint me in the future.

The pseudonarcissism is crumbling.

The synthetic reproduction of cancer cells is assured.

I am extremely lonely—but I am regaining my old inner independence.

31 October 1938

I cannot stop thinking about Eva. She is constantly on my mind. Ever since she has been in New York my mental picture of the ocean that separates us has changed. She is on the other side of the earth. I'd have to travel all the way around to get to her. It's all so senseless.

TO THE AMERICAN CONSULATE, OSLO*
7 November 1938

I inclose two petitions for visa to the USA, one for myself and one for my assistant Mrs. Gertrud Gaasland [Brandt]. The aim of my journey is to visit my children who immigrated to the States last summer. I intend also to take up personal connection again with some pupils of mine, American citizens who studied with me many years ago in Vienna psychiatry and psychology. I refer here only to Dr. Walter Briehl, 745 5th Avenue, New York. I am German citizen now, previous Austrian, and have to place my connection of scientific research work now in the States, as those to Germany are not possible anymore. Living in Norway since October 1934 I intend sometime to immigrate to the USA. The journey for which I beg you to give the visa is merely or should merely be a visit to see my children and for orientation. Affidavits for the case of definite immigration will be sent

* This letter was written in English.

very soon by American citizens. It is not sure yet if the German authorities will be willing to prolong my passport, which is valuable until 1941 (Austrian), and replace it by a German one. If not I shall have to get a Norwegian stranger passport. I am writing all this only to inform about some peculiar circumstances caused by the last political events. I would beg you to let me know under which conditions the visa for my case would be filled out. It may be important to notice that I have Viennese citizenship and am born in a village which belonged to the old Austria in the east of it. Now the village is either Rumania or Poland.

Expecting your kind information,

P.S. Laboratory-outfit, worth about $10,000. Instruments for biological research work would follow me. The custom officer in the German consulate in Berlin stated already that this personal working tool could pass without payment of duties. There are many instruments of American origin.

TO W. F. BON *
7 November 1938

Dear colleague!

Yesterday I received your letter dated 2 November via the publishers. The question you raise, namely, whether the world is ready for my discovery, puts me too dangerously in the position of appearing arrogant to be seriously considered, but I am afraid that you are right. At least, the reactions exhibited so far by the world of responsible official science indicate that this discovery will only lead to misery for the time being.

I am fully aware that my vegetative formula of tension-charge-discharge-relaxation requires a strictly physical basis, but it has so far proved its worth as a guiding principle in my experimental work to such an extent that I no longer doubt its scientific correctness. It has led me right to the heart of the cancer problem.

* Dutch physicist who had contacted Reich after reading *The Bions.*

I would not dare to assert that radiation is emitted when the bions are formed, as you have written in your letter, but there are phenomena that can only be interpreted in this way. For example, striated or vesicular substances that I have made swell and have exposed to electrical voltage pulses supplied from outside begin to glow vigorously with blue light rather like the brightly glowing nuclei of some protozoa. In general, in the tests, the electrical energy is not supplied from outside but is derived from the breakdown of matter in the incandescent heat.

I have asked the publisher to send you each new publication.

With many thanks for your interest and best wishes.

11 November 1938

I love my life—what satisfying work!

The most beautiful and effective revenge for Hitler's atrocities will be my victory over cancer.

Yesterday they set all the synagogues in Germany afire, plundered the Jewish shops. *That* would suffice to turn me into a chauvinist.

TO BRONISLAW MALINOWSKI*
17 November 1938

My dear Bronislaw!

I hope that I don't disturb your quiet and need of rest by writing this letter. If that should be the case, then write please frankly. The matter is the following: The Norwegian authorities did not seem to dare, as they wanted, to simply throw me out. But they are willing to continue the allowance for me to stay and to work under rather checking conditions. My electrophysiological experiments about the electrical nature of sex and anxiety may not continue, even if such experiments are not submitted to penalty. (Very soon they will be, I

* This letter was written in English.

am afraid!) Further I am allowed to teach people in psychology only if they are physicians or psychologists with at least four years' psychological training in an official university institute. My work has to be controlled by Norwegian authorities and so on. All this because an old and knowing nothing psychiatrist did not like my clinical work. Well, I told them that they may control as much they want, because I have nothing to hide, but I refused to limit my experimental work of investigation or to give it up. I don't know yet what they will do. Probably they will try not to make noise about it and will give the permit. But the situation is intolerable. No money, no sufficient assistants, animosity all around, and a lot of mice with tumors in the cellar, kept illegally there. There exists namely a "Tierschutzverein" here, which would cut me completely down if they knew anything about the mice. I had to kill about 400 of them a few weeks ago, because the owner of my home did not like the smell of the cages. So I have simply to do and to try what is possible, to get the freedom to work without such obstacles. There will remain enough troubles with the problem itself and the discussions about it.

It may be or sound incompatible with the tremendous mishap in the world to be so egotistic about my own matter. My excuse can be that perhaps a success of this experimental work could help a bit to regain faith in the future and to counteract to a small extent the robberies of crazy idiots who spoiled the reputation of a whole well-brained and hardworking nation, apart from the help it may once perhaps mean to the real problem of the endemic of cancer.

We are always having in mind your visit in Oslo. You have got very good friends here. We are all hoping that you will recover soon and that we shall meet again soon.

I shall be glad to hear from you about everything.

TO WALTER BRIEHL*
19 November 1938

Dear Dr. Briehl!

Now I think the moment has become acute to transfer my work to the USA. And I am asking you frankly if you are still willing and able to help my immigration on the easiest possible way. You are, so far as I know, well enough informed about my special kind of work that I don't need to explain much. My interests are at the time being concentrated upon the psychosomatic field of research work as well as therapy ("Vegetotherapie"). I have a completely established laboratory for biological and physiological as well as bacteriological work. These instruments shall also be transferred. I have just written to the Custom House in NY City to get clear if I can get them in without paying duties as my personal working tool. As I am known well enough in the specialist circles in the USA I shall be able to make my living easily. I may add that my work would not mean competition with anybody. I am using a technique which I have developed in the course of the last years out of the psychoanalytic and later character-analytic principles. I know there are needed official affidavits. The only ones who could stand up for my name and work are my previous pupils. May I beg you to confer with Kaufmann or others who know my work and are not being influenced by my enemies, who would give the *formal* guarantee for me. My papers have been also referred to in the psychological abstracts. The psychoanalytic review had also referred to my papers and books.

As not having any passport anymore I have to get a Norwegian stranger passport. I have a few thousand dollars which would help me around the first corner in the first months. My children are since summer in New York. One New York psychiatrist and psychoanalyst is now working here with me studying psychosomatic problems and technique. I would beg you to be cautious with asking psychoanalysts. They mostly are afraid to get in touch with me, bad conscience and not knowing where to put me. My laboratory is worth about 10,000 dollars. It was build up by Norwegian psychoanalysts and other friends who appreciated my work. A couple of letters to the American embassy

* This letter was written in English.

in Norway about the value of my scientific work and my ability to make my living easily without harming anybody would I think be enough to get the visa. Write please as soon as possible, how much you can do for me. I am preparing the immigration to the USA for some time in the course of the following winter or spring. I have to add that a war would put me under the damage through Hitler or other rot which is spreading itself now throughout Europe. My political past is not making it better. Now there is no hope for effectuation of sincere problems in the social field.

23 November 1938

Cancer preparations sent to Malinowski in America, Neill in London, Hoel in Bergen, Bon in Amsterdam, French academy. What will come of it?

23 November 1938

It's no use. I am waiting for a person who will commit himself for the sake of the cause and work the way I do. That person will never appear. Also had some illusions about Gertrud. Yes, she would go to America with me, but only in order to get a nice free trip, not in order to help me.

The world of mankind is a miserable dung heap. They dream of atoms and light-years in outer space but not of the electrical vibrations in their own bodies. They don't want to think about that. That would be idealism. Wrong; they are not *allowed* to think about that.

Today I discovered the first indication of death on my right cheek, a cankerously hypertrophied piece of epithelial tissue. Added calcium chloride to a piece of it. Within five minutes blisters and ca cells developed. All I need for cancer now is sexual stasis.

I will inject myself with bions and keep a detailed daily account.

With death in my body I shall fight death as best I can. Continual verification of T-bacilli. They developed from my scales* within five minutes.

---

* Reich probably refers to scales of his skin. He had psoriasis.

I must persevere in the human sense.

Would like to have a child, two children.

Will suggest to Eva that she become my assistant.

According to one beautiful theory of astronomy, the universe is expanding, everything is expanding. Uncanny, this logic. I am beginning to understand why human beings cling together like a flock of sheep. Minute fleas in an expanding universe are *of necessity* afraid of being alone. They warm each other with their illusions, their motherliness. To be alone is to be suspended in outer space. It means feeling the infinite and making the acquaintance of God. Music is pure vibration, unity with the original source. This is not metaphysics. The spokesmen for the poor call it hostile metaphysics because the poor are unable to share this feeling—they can't even afford to go to the cinema.

I have only one desire—namely, for the strength to persevere mentally and physically until I can bring my work at least to partial completion.

My work which with the tears of toil unites electrical oscillation, bions, sexuality, spirit, and nature.

24 November 1938

I protest the fact that I am not permitted to voice an opinion on my right to live as I please, just because I am stronger, offer protection, prepare people for a profession, and play the role of a mother, father, and physician. I protest that I am not allowed to give of myself, or be myself, or go to a party and flirt with a woman when I feel like it. I'm not even allowed to make a mistake or be mean.

I've had enough. I'm too young to be a straitlaced authority figure.

And yet, it appears that I will have to be a rigid authority in the interest of the cause. Too many vivid experiences have shown me that people cannot stand to be treated without restraint.

T O   O D D   H A V R E V O L D
24 November 1938

Dear Odd,

Here is an overview of the protocols for the mouse experiments; naturally they are available for specific inspection.

In the course of one and a half years, up to June 1938, 526 mice and 2 guinea pigs were used in the animal experiments. The purpose of the experiments was always the same—to determine whether the bion cultures are harmful in their effect. No vivisections occurred. Unless they died spontaneously, any mice which were no longer usable were killed with ether and their bodies burned. The animals were only given subcutaneous injections. Among the 526 mice we can distinguish four major groups:

1. Mice that were painted with tar in the early experiments.

2. Mice that were injected with bion cultures made from sterilized materials. This group revealed that the Pa-type of bion* is harmless.

3. A group of mice that were injected with T-bacilli, resulting from the degeneration of rod-shaped cultures. A great many mice in this group died and postmortem examination revealed infiltrating and destructive cell growths.

4. The fourth group contains mice injected with the "bluko" cells† (ca model experiment). Here, too, the experiment revealed infiltrating and destructive cell growths in various kinds of tissue.

T O   W A L T E R   B R I E H L‡
28 November 1938

Dear Dr. Briehl:

New York is far away, and therefore letters cross often without reference to each other. In accordance with our previous correspon-

---

* Pa bions are blue, orgone-charged energy vesicles.
† Cells obtained from a bion culture of blood and charcoal—*Blut* and *Kohle*.
‡ This letter was written in English.

dence I have to inform you about the latest events. It is sociologically interesting, but not pleasant, to follow the entire consequences of the big events in the European world upon the small human affairs. Our chief of the department of strangers named Konstad is a well-known fascist. Lately there had to come here about hundred refugees from Czechoslovakia. The minister of justice, the chief of Konstad, Lie, is a socialist. There was a great fight about those people, who to be taken care of. Now the fascists in Norway succeeded as much that Konstad himself leaves for Czechoslovakia to elect the people he likes to be allowed to come to Norway! Nobody can do anything about it. In Sudetengebiet, which was occupied by Hitler, socialists, democrats, and Jews had been shot, where they had been found without trial or even the farce of it, which before was performed. It is not believable. Prominent Norwegian authors, physicians, etc., begin to prepare emigration. Fascism is sitting here in the far edge of Europe under the nose of the socialist government like a cat waiting for victims, mostly workers and high-standing intellectuals. We are fighting here as well we can against the stream. Estimation for psychology of irrationalism grows, but so does the fight against it. Please understand why I wrote to you a few times that I wait as long I can. It is dangerous but important and interesting. More and more people are coming to learn psychology from our group psychology to understand the crazy happenings. A weak beginning, but something new. People are sent from one side of the border to the other. Many simply to Germany. Everything can happen anytime and anywhere with anybody. My friends here are trying to fight through a permit for me for another year. The success is doubtful. The Germans don't answer applications for passports, the Konstads don't want to give stranger passports without statements of the German authorities. I conferred with the vice consul of the American consulate. They asked me already to submit evidence of my economic state. I am going there tomorrow to ask about the passport question. I told them too that affidavits had been promised from NY. Our group suggests that it would be best to have all documents in order, but not to leave unless nothing else can be done. But also not to jump into the trap, which threatens each of us. You understand how problematic our situation is. We are not political men. Don't belong to any party. But they fight us as if we would be going to overthrow them here. They fight simply truth anywhere. By the dirtiest tricks. I wish I would get time and quiet to write all that down, what we experience now here, not only politics but also human reactions, craziness, anxiety, run-off into complete self-armoring. The same is going on in England, as friends are writing us. Still forces seem to move on where they can. Nearly I would like to say that I would regret if I had really to leave by force.

I beg you to give me some information about the following. I had intended already to make a trip over to NY to investigate the situation concerning it: I have to take care of about ten types of bion cultures, which represent an enormous value. They are types got from sterilized material as human blood, which could not be identified yet as known. Some of them produce cancer in mice, as I wrote you already. They have to be inoculated again and again to remain fresh. I understand that when I shall have to establish in NY there will pass by weeks, perhaps months, until the laboratory work will be reestablished. Which possibility would be found there to continue the work of inoculation twice a week and the preparing of the necessary substrata until we could do it ourselves? It may sound like comical or crazy to think now about such things, when people are killed thousands and thousands. Still it is tremendously important. The matter should itself be not only a pure matter of strange scientific work. Somehow it belongs to the fight against those devils. Perhaps because if the bions are true then must the racial "theory" be a failure. Otherwise the hatred of the fascists [for my work] cannot be understood. They started the fight against it and wrote about it in papers. Of course presenting me as a Jewish faker and betrayer. Friends in England are trying, too, to help settle this question. It would be sufficient if I or my assistant could get the possibility in a bacteriological laboratory to come twice a week to do the absolutely necessary work.

I am very sorry to have to trouble you so much. And I hope we understand each other even on this long distance and on this new problem which is strange to you. I wanted also to beg you to be cautious showing my books to people. It may arise harm as well as sympathy for the matter.

We keep on giving each other informations, don't we?

29 November 1938

It is not just events that shock me again and again but rather people. They destroy the splendid qualities within themselves, are ashamed, and even feel indecently exposed because of them. Take the letter from Eva! This child, or the person she once was—the memory alone devastates me, as do my feelings about people in general and my feelings about myself as I could be *if*, alas, if!

Things are not going well with me, not the way I would like them to go. Can almost feel the transition to old age. Apparently it has all been a little too much for me.

I am neither a "fanatic" nor a "madman." Simply happen to be involved in work that is destroying me slowly but surely. People do love me, want to help, but they also want to live their own lives, separate from mine. And rightly so! This is true for other people as well, for everyone! But my case is exceptional in the sense that I cannot derive any gratification from the illusions of marriage, family, or anything else. At least they have their own "postures," their "armor," their money, and their cunning.

My deep intuitiveness of other people will someday be my undoing.

If there isn't some glimmer of success or the possibility of results in the near future, I have reason to be afraid. It is really dreadful to be this alone, to have to hold out so completely on my own. Everyone wants love from me. And I have to give it to them!

3 December 1938

My love for Elsa is unbounded—this proletarian Aryan girl. She has beauty and that is a rare quality. I wanted to have a child, two children, with her.

But she's too weak, ruined by the plague. First she deserted me in the midst of my struggle and now she is trying to prove that she is my equal. She is out of touch with my situation. My conflict: to remain human and still exercise the necessary authority.

And so I am losing something I loved dearly, something I was proud of. She wants to stay here, not come to America with me.

TO ANNAEUS SCHJÖDT
9 December 1938

Dear Mr. Schjödt,

I would like to inform you that the local American embassy is willing to issue me an immigration visa for the States; there are no problems. All the formalities have been completed. All that is missing are a few documents and I would be very grateful if you would help me obtain them as quickly and efficiently as possible. They are:

A valid passport. The German embassy promised to reply within a short while, but it often tends to allow such inquiries to drag on for a long time. In order to prevent that, I would propose that we wait for a while and then perhaps go there together and if necessary force them to give me a formal refusal in writing. Then it would be possible to have a Norwegian alien's passport issued.

In addition to a police certificate of good conduct from the Norwegian authorities, the Americans also require similar certificates from Berlin and Vienna. Fortunately, as we know, such police certificates are filed with the other documents at the Aliens Registration Office. Would it be possible to obtain copies in English (three copies of each) of these already existing certificates for the embassy?

Please have the enclosed birth certificate translated into English (two copies).

I have received your letter to the central passport office and I find it excellent. Now that we are assured not only of an American immigration visa but also of American citizenship, it will be very much easier to accomplish things at this end.

My departure for the States will probably take place about one year from now because I have to slowly wind everything up here.

10 December 1938

Such an awful lot has been achieved, but I tremble when I wonder whether it will ever be recognized. Why isn't it simpler!

11 December 1938

Read Silone's *The School for Dictators* today.

Apparently this is what has happened. Until now life has fared miserably within mankind, it has been ashamed of its own existence, called itself by other names, ventured forth only under cover of darkness. It is just beginning to discover itself, and to take a very cautious look around. It does not wish to be mistaken for what it was previously forced to be or to appear. It cannot choose "membership" in some "party" to "represent its interests," cannot vote or "nominate a proxy." It has never heard of "pupils" any more than a mouse teaches its young to walk. For the time being life will simply dawdle along. Then it will begin, first in one place, then in another, to move independently. It will recognize its identity within itself, will gain courage to be itself, and finally conquer everything that is unnatural. Nothing will stand in the way of life's final victory. There will be little said. Life will simply prevail.

18 December 1938

Today Gertrud invited me over. It was her husband Willy's* twenty-fifth birthday. Several other people from the old parties were also invited. It was *ghastly*. One of them had "centers" in all countries bordering on Germany. The other was giving a New Year's party with "commissions," "statutes," etc. A third told me that being a member of the German Communist Party had been impossible because it was "too small" (and therefore, if he had been allowed, he would have joined Hitler immediately because he has the biggest party). Willy is a child who smokes his pipe with dignity.

I only went for Gertrud's sake. I am worried about her holding out. Despite her clear insight she still hangs on to this riffraff because of Willy. I do not want to make the same old mistakes of not being demanding enough or of demanding too much, too late. But this will not do! Whoever wants to fight with me must have a feeling for life —and these people are corpses!

24 December 1938

It is not true that I do not care about individuals and only see the goal they can help me reach. I love people but I must leave them behind if they are incapable.

---

* Willy Brandt, future chancellor of Germany.

1939

"Bearing in mind the origin of its discovery,
I have called this radiation 'orgone.'"

4 January 1939

4 January 1939

I must become my old self again! Strong, inconsiderate, dynamic.

The loss of my children almost killed me through guilt feelings. Disgraceful!

The path before me is clearly indicated.

I'm too weak for this path and yet immensely strong.

This life is incredible. Can identify with Beethoven's Seventh or with Mozart. It's like hearing myself: clear, plain, *life*. Life *is* understandable. It swells from a thousand vibrant sources, it surrenders to all who grasp it, refuses to be expressed in tedious phrases, recognizes only clear deeds, true words, the pleasure of love, but these are the flaming banners of the social revolution.

May clear thinking discern life's modes of existence, may strong desire provide the impetus and the energy for life to find itself in the fervor of wholesome sensuality!

TO THE FRENCH ACADEMY OF SCIENCE
19 January 1939

Dear Sirs,

In response to your requests of 27 September and 5 October 1938 to publish all the results of the bion experiments that have been achieved to date, I sent you a brief report on 18 October 1938 together with two copies of my book *The Bions*. Subsequent to that, I sent you some eosin-hemotoxylin tissue sections obtained from mouse experiments. In my last letter to you, on 20 December 1938, I requested you to confirm receipt of the preparations, but so far I have not received any reply. In the meantime, the bion experiments are continuing to evolve and the results need to be published from time to time. So that I can prepare myself, I need to know whether and when you intend

[187

to publish the report I sent you three months ago. Please let me have a reply as soon as possible.

22 January 1939

I don't feel comfortable anywhere except in my room. Here I am still the old Willi Reich. Outside, in "real life," in cafés, or at the cinema, I am "that peculiar man," "the foreigner." "Of course, there are decent Jews too."

Win or be destroyed: that's the question.

16 February 1939

SAPA bions!* Radiation! A completely new world! I'm so lonely!

T O W. F. B O N
18 February 1939

Dear Dr. Bon,

I am writing to you today with an urgent request. A few weeks ago bion cultures were obtained that exhibited beyond any doubt radium-active radiation phenomena (penetration of a cardboard cover and black paper producing exposure of the plates inside, reddening of the skin through glass, etc.). At the moment I am completely unable to carry out the necessary physical studies here. Would you be willing yourself to undertake the investigations or could you have somebody else do the work? The matter must be handled with the utmost discretion.

---

* SAnd PAcket bions derived from a culture of ocean sand.

TO   TAGE   PHILIPSON
18 February 1939

Dear Philip,

Today I am writing just briefly on the following two matters.

1. Would you please get in touch immediately with Niels Bohr. The bions that were produced here from sand in your presence on 15 January radiate like a radium-active substance. I noticed this just a few days ago when my eyes began to hurt. Some reliable evidence of the phenomenon exists—reddening of the skin through quartz glass, light effects produced on photosensitive plates through covering material in darkness, etc. Please only ask Bohr whether he might be interested in carrying out the necessary physical investigations, which I am unfortunately unable to perform. We would send him a small sample of bion cultures that, as far as we can roughly determine here, have exhibited radium-active radiation phenomena. *

2. Please try to find out which eye specialist in Copenhagen possesses enough specialized knowledge to be able to tell you what danger exists for the retina when it is exposed to radiation from radium-active substances. I have been examining these bions under the microscope for several hours a day at magnifications up to $4,000\times$, also in dark field, for about four weeks. I have a general feeling of pressure and something that I can only describe as heaviness in my eyes. The bulb of the eye is very slightly sensitive to pressure, but there are no other signs of sensitivity in the eyes. I can only examine the bions in question for a very short time before my eyes begin to hurt. Havrevold, who was using the microscope yesterday, also complained of eye pain.

* Philipson subsequently advised Reich that Niels Bohr was in America at that time but that an assistant who was "very skeptical" would investigate it to the extent possible.

TO THE FRENCH ACADEMY OF SCIENCE
20 *February 1939*

I have received your letter of 15 February 1939, in which you again propose publication of my first report on the bions, dated 9 January 1937, together with the verification obtained at that time. I would like to remind you of the reason I asked you not to publish that communication. The essential information contained in my first report, in addition to the production of the bions, was the fact that all the bions can be cultured. According to the letter from Professor Lapique, the fact that the bion preparation produces *cultures* will not be published, and the report will be followed by an interpretation that explains the observed results as a physical phenomenon, namely "Brownian movement." Now, the essential aspect of the bion experiments is that the culturing experiment has shown the concept of "Brownian movement" to be an inadequate explanation for the sterile-produced bions and their *cultures*. Since the culturing experiment is the decisive factor, I can only accept your proposal to publish the report if, at the same time, the culturability of the bions is made known. I would therefore like to make the following suggestion.

Among the bion cultures prepared in the last six weeks, there is one which is extremely interesting. I would be glad to send you a sample of this culture together with a brief description of its origin and properties for your verification. Then my first, already verified report could appear with this new one. In that way the essential character of the bion experiments would be expressed. Please let me know whether you accept this proposal. I will then send off the culture together with the report.

TO TAGE PHILIPSON
23 *February 1939*

Dear Philip,

Thank you very much for your effort.

The pains in my eyes are unquestionably due to the bions, because yesterday I again photographed for two hours using one eye, and that eye started to hurt. You may rest assured that I am monitoring the situation closely.

Before I send samples to the physics institute, I must be absolutely sure that the people there will really perform accurate investigations —that is, do what I cannot do here—and that their work is truly useful and significant.

I have carried out the simple tests here using film, etc. In the enclosure I am sending you an X-ray film that was covered for twenty hours with a one-kroner coin on which a microscopic slide coated with culture was placed. I will, of course, give you precise details. You must understand that this film was never opened. I obtained four such samples simultaneously and I possess more images of that kind. You will hear further about this matter once I am ready.

T O W. F. B O N
27 February 1939

Dear Dr. Bon,

I am very grateful that you have agreed to help me determine the radiation. I would like to give you as a preliminary guide some of the main observations that have been made since my first letter to you.

1. The cultures fill the room in which they are located with a strange something that, after approximately ten to forty minutes, depending on the individual, is experienced as a curious heaviness.

2. They penetrate the packaging of X-ray films, cardboard covers, thin wooden boards.

3. The most remarkable thing is that the unknown factor X travels around corners—that is, passes through cracks to reach the films wrapped in lead. Probably it does not pass through the lead itself. Animals such as mice and guinea pigs react with obvious restlessness after a few minutes in the presence of whatever it is.

4. In an extremely mysterious way, my oscillograph ceased to function, and some batteries standing in the same room lost more of their charge than is usual under normal circumstances. The negative pole

lost more charge than the positive. Some phenomena observed at the oscillograph led me to assume that a positively charged emanation is involved (I know that this is not the correct terminology). Inside a Faraday cage, X-ray films did not react as well or did not react at all compared with the same films in a nonscreened laboratory.

5. Persons with strong body electricity, particularly at the palms of their hands, unmistakably detect something like an electric aura when the hand is held approximately 1–2 cm away from the copper wire wall of the Faraday cage.

6. The damage caused to the eyes when using the microscope has been confirmed. A few days ago, I worked for two hours using a single-tube microscope, attempting to photograph the visible radiations. Only the right eye, with which I was looking into the microscope, hurt afterward and felt strained.

7. There is no doubt that the radiation can be seen under the microscope. I distinguished it from light reflexes by removing the reflex mirror as well as the iris diaphragm. The radiation maintained its directionality and moved with the rhythm of the bion movement. I observed this at a magnification of 2,000× to 3,000× with dark-field illumination.

8. There has been repeated confirmation of the prickling on the skin and erythema.

There is now no doubt about the fact that radiation *does* exist. I myself cannot determine or measure the type of radiation. This is a matter for physical radiation institutes to deal with, but I am extremely worried that, since conventional scientific theory makes a sharp distinction between life and nonlife, the fact that living organisms were obtained from lifeless minerals and that these living organisms are radioactive will be thought shocking. I do not know how to get around this problem. I do not wish for a second time to become the target of another highly upsetting campaign against my work of the kind that raged for a whole year in Norway after the publication of my bion book. If you could help me solve these questions, I would be extremely grateful to you.

6 March 1939

Have just spoken on the phone with Dr. Bon in Amersfoort. *Because I'm radiating*—at the hands, palms, and fingertips, at the penis. Bon said it could be very dangerous, "not yet too late." Madame Curie may have died of it. I must not go to pieces. *But I'm radiating.*

T O W. F. B O N
14 March 1939

Dear Dr. Bon,

Thank you for your welcome report that the cultures have arrived safely. I was a little concerned.

Please do not allow the cultures to lie in the vicinity of metals in such a way that they are exposed to reflected radiation from the metals. I have now discovered that the bions themselves may be destroyed by this. The rods that occur are not due to contamination from the air.

When you have a chance, would you please write and let me know whether you think it possible that irradiated photographic plates could themselves emit the radiation. I think I have detected this phenomenon when developing both X-ray plates and normal light-sensitive plates, but I am not certain.

If you fix some crystals in the original solution, you will see very beautiful light effects in some of these cases, especially if you use the polarizer, and in some instances what looks like a bundle of flames (not the correct expression) breaks out at certain points.

I am slowly beginning to understand the phenomena involving the electroscope. The leaves fall together very slowly if they are exposed for a long time to air that has been influenced by the preparations. In addition, if strong preparations are brought close to the receiving plate of the electroscope, this obviously produces a discharge; removing the culture, provided that no contact was made between it and the electroscope, permits the original charge to return. This does not happen in the case of empty test tubes. The same phenomenon can, however, be observed when the palms of *strongly charged* hands are brought close to the electroscope.

Since I do not wish to abandon the true subject of my work, the cancer experiments, I would be extremely grateful if you could devote some attention for me to these phenomena, which are of concern more to the physicist than to a medical doctor and biologist. I hope you do not feel pressured by this request.

T O W. F. B O N
17 March 1939

Dear Dr. Bon,

Today I am writing just briefly to let you know that the strange and contradictory phenomena at the static (leaf) electroscope are gradually starting to become understandable. Our mysterious "something" does not appear to be ordinary electricity or ordinary magnetism. But it influences matter in such a way that phenomena resembling magnetism and electricity manifest themselves at the electroscope. Let me give you some verified observations.

1. Metals that have been influenced by the "something" (let us provisionally call it "orgonicity") attract the north pole of very sensitive magnetic needles.

2. Materials that are otherwise used to provide electrical insulation, such as rubber (gloves), hard rubber, glass, etc., are influenced in such a way that the leaves of the electroscope move even when the objects are held far away from them, and in certain positions this material *attracts* the leaves.

3. Using orgonized rubber, it is possible to charge the electroscope by slowly moving the rubber close to and then away from the instrument (repeating this procedure frequently).

4. In the presence of the orgone effect, an electrically charged electroscope slowly loses its charge. The arrangement is as follows: electroscope plate I—SAPA culture dish—electroscope plate II, which has first been rubbed. Once the electrical charge has become discharged, the charge deflection caused by the orgone is apparent when plate II is removed.

5. The electroscope can be alternately charged with electricity and orgonicity. O. weakens the electrical charge and vice versa.

17 March 1939
A Measuring Apparatus, an Orgonometer,
Is Needed

Principle: Materials with high dielectric strength used for measuring purposes. Glass and hard rubber.
Suitable for charging alternately with electricity and orgone.
For testing of cultures and orgone charge in bodies.
Reasoning: Insulators take up orgone.
Metals radiate it, probably amplified.

TO W. F. BON
18 March 1939

Dear Dr. Bon,

You won't, I think, object to my proposing that we inform each other, from time to time, of any striking observations we make. That could perhaps help speed up the results. So far, there is absolutely no doubt that some type of radiation exists. It can best be observed when the preparation is allowed to act on the lens system of a microscope, and a good matte screen, possibly reinforced with a fluorescent agent, is held continuously at the focal point of the ocular. I am at present struggling with a static electroscope to carry out qualitative testing. Although I am very familiar with the biological properties of the bions and the preparations from which they originate, I am nonetheless rather weak in the field of physical experimentation. I believe, however, that I have observed some rather peculiar things. So far, at least, it does not seem possible to charge the electroscope using the preparation itself. On the other hand, materials that normally screen electricity, insulators such as rubber and glass, appear to be influenced in a strange way by our SAPA bions; in fact, they appear to act in a manner contrary to the phenomena of normal electrical charge. I do not know whether I am making a fundamental error here, but there is no doubt that when, for example, a pair of thick rubber gloves that have been exposed for a long time to the preparation are brought up to the protective glass cover surrounding the leaf electroscope, the same effect is produced as if one had placed an electrically charged condenser plate in the vicinity. The leaf of the electroscope is rapidly attracted to the side of the glass wall and remains stuck there. A similar effect is produced when a rubber glove is brought close to the electroscope from above. Horizontal and vertical movements can be produced in the electroscope from a distance of approximately 20–30 cm, using rubber and glass, which somehow appear to be impregnated. All the phenomena are completely new and unknown to me. I have no idea if they are known to anybody else. But I think it possible that the radiation emitted by the SAPA bions, which does not directly influence the electroscope, might have something to do with the dielectric of poor conductors. The whole business is shrouded in darkness and for the time being is somewhat mystical. If a culture plate covered with glass is placed between two charged condenser plates, the previously charged electroscope discharges very rapidly. If the upper plate, for example, is removed, then the electroscope deflects once more.

I do not wish to report any more today. If you like, I can send you a detailed test protocol, but I thought I should advise you about these phenomena. The strangest phenomenon of all, which seems to contradict all the previously known laws of radiation, is that the optical lens system appears to deflect the radiation in the same way that it deflects visible light rays. Recently I achieved fogging of a plate after indirect exposure. Bearing in mind the origin of its discovery,* I have called this radiation "orgone."

---

* Reich refers to his investigation of the orgasm and formulation of the orgasm, or tension-charge, formula, which was central to the development of his work.

18 March 1939

Had a dream: I was an express train rushing over wide plains night and day. Stars above me, thundering earth beneath me. Occasionally I stopped at stations. Passengers got off, others got on. Some traveled for a long distance, some took only short trips. Again and again the train stopped, people got on, others got off. Many of them were motion-sick because of the terrific speed. I came from far away and rushed headlong into the unknown, through the world, with no certain destination.

19 March 1939

The radiating bions have revealed unheard-of perspectives: bioelec-tricity; energy production from material heated to incandescence; the discovery of life as a certain fact; cancer therapy; the charging of the organism (the problem of death); the answer to the dielectric ques-tion—opposites.

T O W. F. B O N
22 March 1939

Dear Dr. Bon,

Your telegram just arrived. The cultures are being sent off today. Here are some further comments.

1. SAPA I (Evin) bions are SAPA cultures through which 15-volt pulses have been passed for one hour. The individual structures are larger than those in the previous cultures.

2. SAPA II (Lorin)* contains some remarkable new structures that apparently emit strong radiation. They can be recognized from the vesicular vibrating "sheaths" around the SAPA bions.

3. In the meantime, it has been established that insulating materials such as porcelain, wool, rubber, and glass have an extraordinary affinity for the radiation.

4. Metals, copper, iron, etc., reemit the radiation in greater inten-

---

* Reich named the two species of SAPA bions for his daughters.

sity. As I have already written to tell you, the self-destruction of the bion cultures is most likely a form of reflected radiation from the surrounding metals. The problem of screening has still not been solved.

5. Please be very careful. A test conducted on mice has resulted in the death of one animal with precancerous neoplasms in the liver and a change in the blood that very strongly indicates carbon monoxide hemoglobin. This has not yet been verified. (Admittedly, a very large injection was given, corresponding to 10 liters in the case of a human being.)

6. I am working intensively on the problem of screening, using a newly constructed apparatus.

24 March 1939

My forty-second birthday. The children did not write.

SAPA bions open an entirely new realm for me. Astronomy! I have simply liberated solar energy!

27 March 1939

I yearn for a beautiful woman with no sexual anxieties who will just take me! Have inhaled too much orgone radiation.

Actually, I should be happy that I have absolutely rejected all the offers of political leadership I was encouraged to assume.

My life is my only and my greatest pleasure. It expands constantly.

In ten days a large microphotography machine will arrive—2,500 kroner. The orgonoscope is almost finished, the third piece of equipment I have constructed myself.

Shall I live to see the day when people believe my claims that:

1. Life equals sexuality.

2. Life sprang from solar energy that had solidified into stone.

3. The nebulae—unexplained to date—are probably orgone energy!

28 *March* 1939
Courage and caution!
Dangerous conclusion:

Orgone is a type of energy that is the opposite of electricity; it is the specific form of biological energy. In keeping with the orgasm theory, which equates the sexual and the vegetative, it must at the same time be the specific sexual energy, orgasm energy.

Concepts: "Orgone," "orgonicity" as a state, "orgonotic" as an adjective.

TO W. F. BON
30 *March* 1939

Dear Dr. Bon,

I am sending you the protocol of a series of tests carried out on the electroscope for the purpose of partially answering the question of what orgone radiation is. Based on the observations to this point, I have constructed a small apparatus that very conveniently permits all the manipulations required to determine the data. The tests described are extremely easy to perform, and with a little practice one can carry them out convincingly. It has been confirmed that the orgone is something other than ordinary electricity, even though it produces the same phenomena at the electroscope.

I would like to say a few words on an extremely important point that has so far played a very decisive role in my twenty years of scientific activity. I have hesitated for a long time to write to you about it because I did not know how much knowledge you have of my work. I was afraid for the promising scientific relationship between us, but on the advice of a scientific friend here in Oslo I have decided to talk about the matter. My work has a major shortcoming. Its results seem simple and obvious, and they are very attractive to people of various professions. But the world as it is constituted today places extraordinary dangers, in particular of a personal kind, in the way of this work. From defamation through sabotage all the way to direct personal threats, these dangers come in all shapes and sizes. Over and over again it happens that a scientific worker embraces these questions with enthusiasm, totally unaware of the threat posed by the forces of mysticism. When the danger becomes acute and has to be faced, most people tend to fail, not because they are indecent, but simply because they have no practice in such matters and because as a rule scientific work does not have to be performed in such a dangerous environment. I must therefore warn you of this. Sooner or later there will be trouble from one side or another. There is enormous irrational fear about discovering the origin of life; therefore it would be a good idea to consider at this stage whether, in view of the dangers, you would prefer for the time being to carry out the work privately and not have to be ready to convince somebody now or in the very near future, because our enemies do not make rational decisions. You know that I very much need your scientific assistance. Please write and tell me honestly where you stand.

1 April 1939

I do not know whether it is breathing in orgone that has changed me so greatly. I feel as strong as a bear. There are great decisions and changes to be made.

1. A two- to three-month vacation from work.
2. Go underground.
3. Journal *Das Lebendige* [*The Living*].
4. Compilation of all experiments to date.

3 April 1939

Just met—and left—a sweet woman. I must immerse myself in this life again—entirely. Can't live any other way. There is so much variety and joy in spite of the misery. I want to live. Now *I* want to live and I *can*.

T O W. F. B O N
4 April 1939

Dear Dr. Bon,

Just a few lines to inform you briefly of an experiment I would like you to check. When I replied to your observation that perhaps it was merely visible light that was involved, I wrote that we should consider the possibility that solar energy, which at some time became trapped, was being released again. I was struggling then with the thought of how this could be proved. Finally I made an inspired discovery: in the same way that the orgone can best be detected by using soft or hard rubber, one could also check whether direct sunlight produces the same phenomena as SAPA orgone when transferred to the electroscope by rubber. I have been unable to repeat the test since last week because the sky is always clouded over, but I am too impatient. When exposed to fresh air under a cloudy sky, rubber reacts in the known manner, i.e., it emits orgone and therefore does not produce any deflection of the electroscope. On the other hand, a rubber glove or a hard rubber rod that has definitely discharged all its SAPA orgone but has been exposed for fifteen minutes or more to bright sunshine produces a deflection on the electroscope. A control glove placed in the shade produces no such deflection. If the position of the two gloves is exchanged, then the glove that was previously in the shade but now has been exposed to the sun produces a deflection, and the glove previously in the sun and now in the shade produces no deflection. I was a little giddy when I noticed this reaction occurring several times one after the other, but I will repeat it as often as possible so that even the remotest doubt is eliminated. I was not yet able to verify whether the "solar orgone" behaves like SAPA orgone in relation to friction electricity. You will understand that I immediately connected the phenomenon with my earlier experiments on the human body, in particular the erogenous zones. I will write to you about that on another occasion. I am very curious to learn how the experiments with the bions are proceeding at your end. In the meantime, I failed in my attempt to produce a third sand bion solution, but the fourth one was successful and contained some slightly smaller but radiating structures. I assume that you will be happy to hear this. But please be very careful.

8 April 1939

While I was dozing the essence of life occurred to me in the form of a tangible image. It was like fire! Can we regulate flames, direct them, tell them how and when to leap up, combine, separate? No!

But we can build them a large stove or a fireplace with a chimney and a beautiful mantelpiece, where they may frolic without restraint. The metaphor is incomplete although it does illustrate the fact that there *cannot* be norms for sexual vitality! There can only be optimal conditions for satisfaction.

TO W. F. BON
12 April 1939

Dear Dr. Bon,

I was extremely pleased in all respects by your letter of 2 April because you are obviously closely following the line of my bion research and vegetotheory, because you yourself are now experiencing the same reaction from bacteriologists that I have experienced so severely, and finally because you were able to confirm my electroscope experiments.

We will no doubt very soon reach agreement on the question of whether the radiation is a kind of negative electricity or in fact, as I believe, a new kind of energy. The experiments will probably make clear which is the case.

As far as I know, the glass electricity was found to be positive and the resin electricity negative. Now, on reading your letter, I realized that glass is an inorganic material whereas resin is basically an organic material. It might in fact be that negative electricity exists along with a form of energy that has something important to do with the function of life. All this is very uncertain, but for the time being I do not wish to abandon my hypothesis (at least not until it has been proved totally unusable and false) that a specific biological energy exists that is similar to electrical energy. Interpreted in this way, it would not initially contradict the existence of negative electricity. So, if you are in agreement, each of us should continue to work with our own theories and we will let the experiments decide.

In the meantime, the list of peculiar phenomena is increasing at quite a pace. In the enclosure I am sending you some photographic plates. One of them, which is a uniform dark gray, was exposed for ten minutes in bright sunshine as a control plate. The second one, on which you will see straight black parallel streaks, was also exposed for ten minutes to the bright sun but had been covered over by a horseshoe-shaped magnet. According to common photochemical knowledge, the part of the plate that had been covered by the horseshoe-shaped magnet should have been significantly *lighter* in the negative than the remaining noncovered part, and in the positive it should have been darker in contrast to the bright field that corresponds to the part exposed to the strong sunlight. To my astonishment the reverse effect was obtained. The area on the plate that was covered with the magnet is *darker*. This contradicts photochemical experience, but it corresponds entirely to the experience I have had with the orgone—namely, that the radiation has a particular affinity to metals and rubber. A parallel test conducted with rubber yielded exactly the same result as that obtained with the magnet. I must therefore assume that rubber and the magnet both take up solar orgone radiation and pass it on in amplified form to the photographic plate. I am very curious to hear what you think about all this. Please undertake this experiment, which is very easy to perform, and give me your opinion. The experiment was repeated for me today by someone who has had photographic training, and exactly the same results were obtained. The following phenomenon also completely escapes my understanding: I concentrated the sunlight through a strong lens onto the plate. Instead of being blacker than the surrounding area, this point was lighter. Again, I would like you to verify this experiment please.

My experiments with rubber electrodes applied to the erogenous zones of vegetatively highly sensitive individuals are continuing and I will let you know the result as soon as it is reasonably certain. For the time being, the work is proceeding along the lines of the previous experiments and assumptions.

TO THEODORE WOLFE*

13 April 1939

Dear Dr. Wolfe:

I am making haste to get away from here, not only because my work is being completely suffocated but also because of the risk to my apparatus and my own person. However, if I do not obtain a preference quota number—that is, if you do not send for me—I might remain stuck here because my regular number is not likely to come up until after 1 July. Once I know more or less for sure that I will be permitted to travel to the States and not have to stay here, Gertrud will go ahead of me, taking with her the most important documents, and look for a suitable site for a laboratory. Please do whatever you can to help her when the occasion arises. In an emergency, I will pack up my apparatus and send it to you personally at your address. Perhaps it can then remain in customs until I arrive, unless someone can come up with enough money to have it released. Once I am there, the apparatus can enter the country duty-free. I am looking forward greatly to the calm and fruitful work environment I hope to find in America.

It is simply fantastic how the SAPA bions are radiating. In collaboration with the Dutch radiation institute, we are in the process of discovering what type of radiation it is. According to the data gathered so far, it is solar energy pure and simple, because sand is solar energy that at one stage solidified. But please keep these things to yourself; otherwise people will suspect that I am mad and the thought of that might actually drive me mad. But it was really stupid for people to imagine that you too might be crazy. Obviously they thought so because you came to work with me.

---

*A New York psychiatrist who had written to Reich in the winter of 1937 to request training and had spent time with Reich in Oslo the next summer.

TO ELSA LINDENBERG
18 April 1939

Dear Elsa,

I fully respect your wish, which until recently coincided with mine, that we should not see each other. But I will be leaving Oslo very soon and there are a few important things that have to be settled. Also, I do not want to leave you in this manner after the seven years we spent together. Please try, therefore, to find it in yourself to talk to me once more on a completely new basis, because our friendship should not be destroyed and you probably also want to keep in touch with our work. Naturally, if it has to be, then I would respect any decision on your part that we should separate as things stand now. But I do not think that would be good for either of us.

I sincerely wish you every success in your life. These flowers are intended to convey the message that I will never forget, not for one moment, the happiness that we had together. And I will never permit you to be belittled in any way whatever, or by anyone at all, because of any misunderstanding concerning how and why our ways parted.

Please let me know when and whether you are willing. I will also let you know when I have a firm date for my departure. I have suffered greatly!

21 April 1939

Elsa came back to Drammensvejen again. If I give in to that woman this time she will have to sweat blood. I've suffered enough. If I go to a prostitute she will tell me that her boyfriend is a dentist, that she has so and so many clients. I know with whom I am dealing. I can give of myself whenever I choose. I can give myself whenever and to whomever I choose! Marriage—and every relationship that speculates with personal security—stands far below prostitution. There is nothing more evil than lies.

This is an extraordinary case. On the one hand we must gain understanding and immerse ourselves completely in the filth. We may not float nobly among the clouds and merely allow ourselves to be splashed with filth, knowing that no one is really to blame for his base actions.

On the other hand we must not allow ourselves to drown in the muck. We must remain outside it, above it, must love and yet not admit disappointment.

I will take any girl at all, will give her the love I can give. I will gain enormous strength if I do not yield this time. I must not, for the sake of my cause. This situation is perverted.

30 April 1939

Read a book on Galileo. Could only read it very slowly. Was afraid of coming to the end.

I have just experienced Galileo's death—almost physically. This is the way the great have died, are dying now, will always die. And the clergy will rule the world as long as human consciousness does not tear unarmored life away from the clutches of the church. Somewhere I once wrote: "The church thrives on the life it destroys." It will die when life awakens, but this requires experimental control of the process of consciousness. The church will not die before that happens. The discovery of the orgone, life-giving solar radiation, was the first step in that direction. From now on I will keep my discoveries secret. I will set down in a comprehensive scientific document everything that perception and suffering wrenched away from the realm of darkness. But I do not, do not want to die like Galileo. I will be cautious. If I succeed in solving the problem of prolonging life, then . . . I am not far from it. All I need is peace, a little money, and some sort of a life.

A practical formulation of the spinning-wave theory will constitute the second step. For that I'll have to study mathematics.

The invention of an orgone accumulator is my third task; a final solution to the cancer problem is at hand.

Galileo Galilei! Through space and time the fire of scientific cognition is ignited within the great fighters for truth and knowledge, regardless of race, time, or place. I thank my destiny that it has included me in the ranks of these great fighters, that for a time I have had the privilege of nourishing the truly sanctified fire of knowledge! I experience this fate in deepest reverence and devotion to life, which embraces everything that has ever—in the past, the present, or the future—kindled men's hearts and nerves.

TO THEODORE WOLFE
2 May 1939

Dear Wolfe,

Your letter of 25 April has just arrived, but it had already been preceded by the telegrams sent last week. So, the consul saw no problem in promising me a nonquota visa on the basis of the request for me to do research work at Columbia, and I am simply waiting now for the alien's passport to be issued. It is still very uncertain whether I will leave on 20 May as intended or not until 17 June; my departure depends essentially on how quickly the paperwork can be settled and second on whether I still have to earn money for another month.

When I read through your letter, I became a little afraid of New York. I know that the conditions are very difficult, and I do not need much for my own personal existence, but, as you are aware, the absolutely essential laboratory work swallows enormous sums of cash.

Gertrud must come with me because without her the work could not continue. I assume that by doing, let us say, about four hours of vegetotherapeutic work each day, I will be able to earn enough to carry the costs of the laboratory. At the present time my aspirations are concentrated solely on concluding the cancer work and the radiation work.

With regard to your query about the laboratory:

The laboratory must naturally also contain mice. It is not really possible from here to determine how we will house them. But I must have them close by. Ideally I would like to set up the laboratory in my home. I would need a room in which I can work and live because I do the laboratory work by myself, usually in the evenings, and the office would not be a very suitable place for this activity. As I told you in one of my earlier letters, I absolutely must have a garden, no matter how tiny, because I have to work with sun and earth. An acquaintance of mine, a Norwegian lady living in New York, advised me to look for something on Long Island, a small house with four or five rooms in which I can set up my apparatus and my workroom, as well as a room for Gertrud. Again, from here it is not possible to decide how all this can be combined with earning money, that is, having students working with me. For the time being, it would be financially impossible for me to simultaneously maintain an office in the city.

I assume that the laboratory work can be resumed immediately after the laboratory has been set up. I will maintain the cultures during the journey. I will not transport any mice but will dissect those that I have here and resume the tests once I am in New York.

You and Briehl could do our work an enormous service, and I would be tremendously indebted to you as well, if you would see about the availability of a small house with a garden, not too expensive, either in the city or, even better, on the outskirts of the city. I do not know what the circumstances are and I have no idea how difficult it is to find or procure such accommodation.

I would like to know whether the research position is a pure formality or whether I will actually have access to university institutes and clinical material. It does not matter, or not too much, if the former is the case, because I am strong and experienced enough to gain the confidence of new circles of people through the work I perform. I would also like to know the attitude of your psychiatric colleagues and your superior regarding the problems and facts of sex economy and vegeto-therapy, but we can talk about that in detail once I get there.

When I arrive, I would like to set up the laboratory as quickly as possible and then go camping somewhere with a tent for four weeks in order to rest. I am quite worn out. In any case, work could not start before September.

Please do not worry about the money you owe me. I am convinced that the work we will perform together will compensate greatly for all the efforts we will no doubt have to make in the initial period.

TO MINISTER OF JUSTICE LIE
4 May 1939

My dear Sir:

The following matter is extremely urgent, difficult, and embarrassing to me. I have therefore taken the liberty of addressing this request for advice and assistance to you personally.

As a consequence of last year's campaign against my scientific work, I have not received an extension of my residency and work permit for the past year and a half. I now have an appointment to do research at Columbia University and require a traveling document in order to emigrate. In accordance with instructions from Mr. Konstad, I duly approached the German embassy in Oslo. Mr. Annaeus Schjödt, a lawyer, and Mrs. Constance Tracey* can both testify to the fact that the German embassy issued a passport to me under the name of Wilhelm *Israel* Reich and bearing the stamp "Jew." The above name does not correspond with my other documents and I refused to accept a passport in which my name had been changed without my request. My letter to the German embassy will attest to this. Mr. Schjödt then approached Mr. Konstad in order to obtain a Norwegian alien's passport such as is customarily issued. In response to this request Mr. Konstad replied that I was neither a Norwegian nor a stateless person and therefore not entitled to a Norwegian alien's passport. However, he was willing to issue me an identity paper bearing my photograph for the passage.

Mr. Schjödt then brought the matter to the Political Board and from there was referred to Mr. Konstad. Yesterday, at 1:30 p.m., I went to Mr. Konstad's office to pick up the identity paper. A lady there informed me that Mr. Konstad was unable to see me and that I should address a request to the Political Board if I wished to receive identity papers. My lawyer had just taken those steps and had been referred to Mr. Konstad by the Political Board.

This matter would be of no importance had I not already booked a passage for 20 May. I fear that a delay in the issuance of the papers will not only render my passage on the scheduled date impossible but also cause me great extra expense.

I therefore urgently request that you, esteemed Sir, take the necessary steps so that a Norwegian alien's passport can be issued to me by the beginning of next week. Since I shall be employed by Columbia University in New York, the American consul in Oslo has promised me a nonquota visa.

---

* An English woman interested in Reich's work.

6 *May 1939*

Important thoughts on the orgone:

The slow undulating movement of the orgone corresponds completely to vegetative movement, which in turn is nothing but energy displacement.

8 *May 1939*

Minister of Justice Lie (a socialist) promised to "handle everything." I received a filthy sheet of paper. Cannot make the crossing to America with it. Konstad, the fascist, was victorious over his boss, the socialist Lie.

TO THEODORE WOLFE *
9 *May 1939*

Private letter to consul insufficient. Official Columbia research contract necessary. Money for research secured. Telegraphic paying out New York possible. Journey delayed. Consul will write to you.

9 *May 1939*

I am like a moneylender who invested millions on some speculation that backfired and now has nothing left but a few old, worthless articles and knows that there are no more profits to be had. Yet he still hopes. Time and time again he looks back to see whether he can't turn it to his advantage after all. It is impossible for a cause to be so lost. I lack the youthful vigor to admit that a lost cause is really lost.

And so here I sit with a large laboratory and amazing problems and wait for my sixth emigration, without a passport, admired, mistrusted, and feared. My situation is not an enviable one. Something inside me has broken.

* Telegram written in English.

10 May 1939

Tomorrow the packers are coming. At first, only my belongings are going to New York, with Gertrud Brandt. Will I follow them?

The weakness of my friends and pupils, the hatred of my enemies, the helplessness of my admirers, and the dirty dealings of the bureaucrats are forcing me to cross the ocean.

TO W. F. BON

17 May 1939

Dear Dr. Bon,

You can imagine how much your letter troubled me and how happy I was to learn that you did not lose your confidence. * Didn't your coworkers also verify the positive effect bions have on rubber? That fact alone should have given them something to think about! It has confirmed once again that people who approach the problems with predetermined opinions, people who are under the influence of bacteriological terminology and are filled with harmful doubts, cannot be used for this kind of work. They do not possess the gentle patience and care, coupled with conviction, that are absolutely essential. What I would now like to know is how often the experiments were repeated and under what conditions they were carried out. With regard to the three points you raise:

1. I had many negative results with the plate tests. Contrary to what I originally assumed, I now do not believe that the fogging is caused by radiation penetrating the outer covering of the plates but think instead that the cardboard and paper covers absorb the radiation and then pass it on to the plate. Plates kept in metal cases did not react at all or reacted only very little.

2. Apart from a few individual cases (poor vegetative skin charge) the skin reaction was almost always positive here. The best reactions are obtained from persons with lively vasomotor systems. Did you use the quartz glass?

---

* Dr. Bon had reported negative results from observations made in his laboratory on a SAPA culture sent to him by Reich.

3. The visibility of the rays has been firmly established here. May I ask you to write and let me know how long you stayed in the dark and how often? It can happen that test persons fail to perceive the radiation for a long time until suddenly the phenomenon becomes evident. Once it has been seen, it can never be overlooked. I have noticed here with some individuals that there is something that makes them hesitate to perceive the phenomena, which occur after one has spent half an hour allowing one's eyes to grow accustomed to the complete darkness. When the person in question is assured that after half an hour he should not be able to see anything except complete darkness, and therefore anything that he still sees must be radiation phenomena, the descriptions of what is seen are always the same. At this point, in order possibly also to clarify point 1, I would like to add that my Faraday cage is filled with several dozen culture vessels and culture plates, i.e., all the inoculated cultures are placed in the cage. Today I removed about eighty culture containers. The large amount of radiation material may perhaps play an important role.

May I ask you to give me the most accurate possible description of the details of the test? I have by no means given all the facts and certainly not described all the conditions that existed here. Was the cage grounded? What kind of material was placed in the cage? Did you check the magnetic effect? As the months went by, the walls in my cage became very warm. *Are the cultures still intact?* Did you discard the old cultures or did you leave them in the room where the experiments were being conducted? How many cultures were used in the test? It just occurs to me that my workroom was filled for many weeks with material before I started on the detailed tests. Unfortunately, I do not have any opportunity at the moment to cooperate experimentally in solving the outstanding questions, because my laboratory was disassembled this week and is being sent to New York. For this reason I did not reply to your letter immediately. Instead of asking you a lot of questions or going into great detail, I want to tell you, in no particular order, what has happened here in the meantime. This account will give you some idea—apart from the rubber-electroscope reaction—of what role the radiation is playing in our clinical work. I place all my students and patients inside the cage for about ten to thirty minutes almost daily. After a while, some of them react, without knowing why, by exhibiting such symptoms as giddiness, sensations of electrical tension, headaches. In most of them, and in my case, too, the skin was tanned and became smooth, just as if we had been exposed to a great deal of sunshine. One patient developed a bad case of conjunctivitis. A person who was delivering a new instrument used to investigate the radiation sat in the darkroom while I was working and spontaneously declared that his eyes were hurting, as if he had "looked into the sun." His eyelids were severely reddened.

My assistant, Dr. Havrevold, took charge of a series of cultures. His patients asked him what was in the room, because the air was so heavy, and some people experienced headaches. Havrevold discovered that rubber that is charged with orgone discharges immediately when immersed in water. This fact can be verified with the electroscope.

When I noticed that some people can see the rays while others cannot, which is in itself an interesting biological phenomenon, I set about creating a device that makes the radiation stand out so clearly that it can no longer be missed. For this purpose I had a matte screen, impregnated with fluorescent material, built for me in Vienna. A brief test carried out today in the Faraday cage (which will remain here) revealed that the screen exhibits a square light-colored spot. If the north pole of a strong magnet is brought up close to the screen, the brightness intensifies. A very intelligent test person hit on the idea of waving the arm and palm of the hand up and down along the wall of the cage at the level where the strongest thermal radiation is felt. The electrical sensations became intensified, and this phenomenon was also reproduced by others. Dr. Havrevold, who is collaborating in the experiments on the electroscope, believes, and I agree with him, that two things are happening in the rubber. The electroscope reacts by building up a charge when the glove is removed and, under conditions which cannot yet be explained, when it is allowed to rest for a long time on the plate. Long contact of a charged glove with the palms of the hands will discharge the glove in the same way as fresh air does, only much quicker.

There is something else I want to tell you. I have hesitated for some time before doing so, but now I no longer want to keep this from you. Since you hypothesized in a letter to me that life is a radiation phenomenon, what I am now going to say will interest you. When I was certain that the SAPA emit radiation and saw a connection between this radiation and Gurwitsch mitogenetic rays, and after I had, furthermore, undertaken the tests in which, as I told you, I exposed rubber to the sun and exposed photographic plates while applying a magnetic source, I concentrated my work on the human body. In the course of vegetotherapeutic treatment I placed soft pieces of rubber on the lower abdomen and, with some students who are thoroughly conversant with our work, also on the genitals, both directly and through their clothing. After a few minutes, persons who exhibit strong vegetative excitability transmit something to the rubber that produces a deflection at the electroscope. This "something" can be discharged in the shade in fresh air, also by touching the rubber with the palms of the hands. Vegetatively rigid persons, that is, persons incapable of experiencing vegetative streaming, produce only weak reactions, if any at all, at the electroscope via rubber. It was these observations that caused me to write to you that I believe a specifically biological, electrical energy, namely the orgone, must exist. I am deeply convinced that rigidified human organisms, which are incapable of vegetative streaming or sensation, cannot perceive any of the subjective phenomena that characterize orgone radiation. Consequently, they will not have the patience to find their way to the objective phenomena, such as the rubber test. On the basis of observations so far, I have to conclude that the SAPA radiation has uncovered a very important relationship: a remarkable identity exists between vegetative excitability, vegetative energy, and solar radiation. This has always been known to the layman, and it has always been part of the sun myths, but it is a very significant matter to have proved it experimentally. I shall have to postpone detailed analyses of the subject until I have reestablished my laboratory in the States. Similarly, I shall postpone any analyses of the highly informative, theoretically important relationships between the increase in sexuality in the spring, the effect of the sun on living nature as a whole, and the fantasies that human beings have created since time immemorial around these intuitively perceived relationships.

I will remain in Oslo for no more than four to eight weeks in order to wind down my teaching activities. Please allow me to give you a good piece of advice based on the difficult experiences I have had with coworkers who have been taken out of the normal swing of routine work: if you cannot find any scientific assistants who are in some way theoretically or emotionally prepared for these matters, then it would be better to work by yourself. When one spends many months, even years, alone with the subject of one's research, growing accustomed to its peculiarities, learning to perceive them, and gradually feeling totally at one with the subject, then it no longer matters—at least that was my experience—if the experiments go wrong month after month. When I had obtained the first bion cultures, about six months of laborious work went by before I was able to find the bions again. What was I supposed to do with a system of scientific thought that has to believe at all costs that, four times in a row, I had cultured something from sand that by chance were *sarcinae* from the air—four times in a row and each time in pure culture! In fact, I learned that this type of bacterium is extremely difficult to find and occurs only rarely.

I would very much like to have told you a lot more and to have put many more questions to you. Once I have your detailed report, I will try to write everything down as accurately as possible to save you perhaps from pursuing unnecessary roundabout routes.

20 May 1939

I do not keep a diary for the same reasons an adolescent girl does but because these notes on my remarkable existence may someday be of use.

Today Gertrud left for New York with the archives, the instruments, and the furniture.

23 May 1939

I am sitting in a completely empty apartment waiting for my American visa. I have misgivings as to how it will go. I have lost faith in pushing things through rapidly.

I am utterly and horribly alone!

It will be quite an undertaking to carry on all the work in America. Essentially I am a great man, a rarity, as it were. I can't quite believe it myself, however, and that is why I struggle against playing the role of a great man. What have I discovered?

1. The function of the orgasm
2. Character armoring

3. The life formula
4. The bions
5. The electrical function of sexuality
6. Orgone radiation
7. The processes involved in cancer formation
8. The processes involved in rheumatism
9. The processes involved in schizophrenia, including the organic causes of neuroses
10. The sociology of sexual repression
11. The dynamics of fascism
12. The spinning-wave theory

A lot of fine work, and still I can't really enjoy it. I fear for my future!

TO W. F. BON
24 May 1939

Dear Dr. Bon,

After I mailed my last detailed letter to you in response to your queries, it occurred to me that I had never specifically told you the little technical tricks I use in making the radiation visible and the minor observations I make in the process. When I set about making the first observations in the darkroom, everything went wrong until I rid myself of a false expectation. I had assumed that the rays were similar to radium radiation, that they would produce bright flashes when I directed them onto the fluorescent screen. However, no rapid "lightning flashes" were to be seen. Since the only preparations I took into the darkroom were those I had previously checked out through the skin reaction and the sensation of prickling in the vicinity of the skin (palm of the hand or cheek, also tongue), I was very disturbed when, for a long time, I did not see the expected flashes of radiation. I was not aware of what I now see all the time in the darkroom. On the day I telephoned you, the phenomenon had become startlingly clear for the first time. It is quite different from what I had originally expected. Once the brightness images begin to fade in the darkroom, the room at first starts to turn dark again. In the control room the darkness increases and nothing can be seen. In the room containing the preparations, on the other hand, it starts to get significantly *lighter* after about half an hour. Instead of seeing nothing but blackness, one is aware of a strange gray-blue color. What one sees is diffuse but not uniform. It is like a surging and seething, in which the gray-blue color alternatingly becomes more and then less intense. It looks like fumes, fog, or something similar. I have experienced it myself, and most test persons hesitate a long time before describing what they have perceived. Some of them say it is "ghostly." As time goes by, one believes that one is seeing blue "afterimages." But they are not afterimages; instead, very fine deep blue-violet points of light are emitted from the copper walls that are resting against brick walls. They are quite different from "flashes." It looks as if they were slowly floating in the air, moving through arcs or in an undulating fashion. They fly or float slowly through the room. If a fluorescent screen is positioned on the north wall, the surging clouds and the deep blue floating points shimmer as if bundled or clustered together. The motion is not constant but occurs in a very slow rhythm. The same thing can be observed when a photographic plate that has been exposed to orgone for several days is developed. The plate emits a deep blue-violet light in the developer. A pale grayish-blue halo appears more and more clearly around hands, white coats, cotton, and porcelain, but it is diffuse and without distinct boundaries. Several persons who had no idea what was going on drew my attention to the phenomenon with shouts of astonishment. "Your hands are lit up." "Your head is." Havrevold once compared it to the northern lights. On the fluorescent screen one sees what looks like billowing clouds.

I have been working constantly on the technical problem of how to make these phenomena stand out so clearly that even the most un-willing person will see them immediately. As yet, I have not progressed very far, but at least I am trying. I have purchased an apparatus that permits the radiation to be deflected by a mirror and projected onto a matte screen. Instead of the matte screen, the fluorescent screen can be interposed. It is positioned right at the focal point of the microscope system. The preparation is placed at the top, on a plate, so that it is located in the focal point of the ocular. The position can be checked beforehand using light. I also try to place the preparation (open agar plate turned upside down) over the condenser so that the rays are collected by the condenser. It is still not certain which method is better. I am now so well trained that I can see the rays even in the semidarkness. When the room is not completely darkened, one sees the familiar surging and billowing clouds on the fluorescent screen. The points appear black-gray, sometimes also as bright, extremely fine dots and streaks that appear and then disappear again after one or two seconds. In the dark, one sees deep blue fluorescence with a tinge of green on the yellow screen. The sharper the focus, the clearer this phenomenon. The phenomenon can be amplified by using a magnifying glass. Similarly, a magnification effect can be achieved by holding the north pole of a magnet against the screen (the north pole attracts the radiation). I am using and also experimenting with a simple photographic plate. The phenomena are visible on this plate. I also try various combinations, such as placing the photographic plate below the fluorescent screen and so on. Photographic cassettes made of metal also emit the floating blue points of light, which can only be seen in the dark. Here is an attempt to describe the phenomenon:

I use quartz glass lenses. The condenser is also made of quartz glass. I allow the camera chamber of the microscope to "absorb" the emanation for a few hours, because then it shows up more clearly. I can only say that once the phenomenon has been correctly observed, one never forgets it, because it becomes so typical. In the darkroom one often has the impression of being "dazzled" when one stares at the fluorescent screen or the photographic plate. When one looks away, the deep blue rhythmically appearing spot remains visible. But it disappears again after a few minutes. So this is not a subjective phenomenon. Once one looks back at the screen, the spot appears again. Thus, the rays are pulsatingly emitted, very slowly and rhythmically, at the same tempo at which they appear and disappear. The radiation begins weakly, becomes stronger, then starts to fade away again slowly before returning once more. I tried to determine whether the preparations themselves are giving off light. Sometimes I believed I saw this, but I am uncertain. Insulating materials are best suited for absorbing the radiation and causing it to produce the light phenomena. Sometimes, around the north pole of a strong magnet, I see fine shimmering rays like the halo that appears around the north pole during the solar tests. I have not been able to discover why the action of the rays on photographic plates sometimes produces fogging through the cardboard coverings and black paper and sometimes does not.

In diagnostic terms, the prickling and burning feeling on the skin is very important. Three women introduced test tubes into their vaginas and left them there for only one to three minutes. One woman exhibited an extremely strong reaction and experienced a prickling and burning sensation deep inside her. These were women in whom I had found amoeboid cells in samples of vaginal secretion taken following intermenstrual bleeding. These cells were promptly destroyed when they were exposed to the radiation. The radiation is strong when the SAPA are cultured in broth + KCl. They also become significantly larger in that medium.

I am sure you will understand, dear Dr. Bon, why I am writing to you in detail once again. I am very eager to ensure that your efforts will prove worthwhile. You are also performing control tests to confirm my findings, but I am less interested in that aspect. For me your collaboration is not a "control" procedure, but instead I regard it as essential assistance from a fellow researcher who can help explain these peculiar phenomena. I cannot spend all that much time on the purely physicochemical tests because I am very busy with my clinical work. For a long time, my attention has been focused on the orgone radiation emitted by my students and patients. I have noted some very strange facts in this connection. As far as determining the orgone radiation in the bions is concerned, the test that has been performed with rubber at the electroscope and the subjective prickling reaction are sufficient evidence for me.

TO W. F. BON
1 June 1939

Dear Dr. Bon,

Your letter arrived today confirming receipt of my explanatory letters. I am very happy that you have seen the blue shimmer. What you have seen is correct. I, too, originally thought this phenomenon was a subjective deception, but I found out how to eliminate all doubt by constantly looking away from the blue luminous spot. Then, the phenomenon ceases to exist; or I go into another darkroom where there is no orgone. What I do not grasp is why this blue shimmer appears on porcelain, glass, cotton, and the palm of the hand, whereas the culture plates themselves do not seem to shine or only when they are covered with lead or something similar. This is incomprehensible. There are many other questions that have still not been answered. Yesterday I placed gelatin that had been boiled until semisoft in a porcelain dish with KCl in a cage filled with orgone. The result was extremely satisfactory. The entire area was lit up by a bluish light. By working calmly and steadily, undisturbed by futile doubters, we will discover the methods by means of which the light phenomenon can be amplified a hundredfold. In New York, I shall place not dozens but hundreds of agar plates and KCl suspensions in a dark cage with masses of cotton and porcelain.

Yesterday I discovered why some X-ray films did not undergo fogging. The films in question were those that had been wrapped in silver paper: metal reflects the radiation back. I will keep you informed of small observations like this that can clear up areas of doubt. However, we shall have to stand up firmly against the widespread attitude among scientists who feel that such facts ought to be easily and routinely verifiable. I wish I could sometimes give an impressive demonstration of the vast amounts of love and patience I have had to pour into the work, how many nights I have worked through without sleep, in order to obtain this or that result.

9 June 1939
Amplification

Blank sheet of glass, [surface] scratched. Clean cotton attached with paste. One corner of the cotton immersed in glycerin. Covered over with a fluorescing plate.

Flight path of the blue rays.

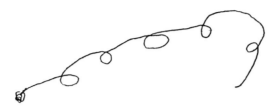

With eyes closed such a pattern is never seen!

The cessation in the rhythm is very marked.

The light point has a cometlike tail. Sometimes it appears as if the light point is swinging into itself.

During retropulsion the ray must retreat into itself. As the flight continues it expands again.

Thus, of necessity a rhythmic pulsation—expansion and contraction—is set up in the spinning wave. Depending on the interval between the spin phases, the expansion can be longer or shorter in duration. (Twelve-year rhythm in the case of the solar spots might correspond to a spin phase.) Then the luminous head disappears in the fog of its own tail.

The question is whether the flight path is a pure parabola or whether it is changed at each spin point.

TO W. F. BON
[*Undated*]

Dear Dr. Bon,

On the question of the blue color of the light and of the "subjective phenomenon," it occurred to me that the orgone radiation acts in particular on organic bodies and therefore must very strongly excite the optic nerves and consequently, like full sunlight, must generate an "afterimage." It is thus conceivable that we really do see blue "afterimages," but in the case of orgone radiation such an afterimage is produced by the effect of a perhaps invisible radiation that reveals itself by generating the impression of blue light. The eye thus reacts with specific sensory sensitivity.

TO ROGER DU TEIL
15 June 1939

My dear friend du Teil,

You can hardly imagine what pleasure your letter gave me. I am ashamed to have to confess that your failure to communicate for several months made me believe that you, like many others in the past, had abandoned my sinking ship. I had written two or three letters to you in Nice without receiving a reply. I am happy to read that you have managed to regain your old situation. There is very little reason to doubt that ultimately we will be victorious. The only question is whether I will live to see that day. The campaigns of harassment directed against me are still going on, most recently with the psychiatric diagnosis of "insanity." This does not matter. Every time I look into the microscope, the pain caused by such meanness is lifted from me.

I am moving to New York. Some of my students there have set everything in motion and are struggling to overcome enormous difficulties. My laboratory and one assistant have already arrived on the other side.

For the time being, my immigration to America means nothing less than my complete financial ruin. Despite all the countless major and minor new observations I have made, I have not published anything, because I must first compose myself before starting the process of rebuilding. I am wondering whether it wouldn't perhaps be better not to publish anything anymore and just send my material to selected colleagues. This is the only way to escape the appalling smear campaigns waged by so-called scientists. The French academy did not publish a report on *Bion Experiments on the Cancer Problem* but instead merely consigned it to their archives. I received a letter from Bonnet in which he confirms that he did not verify your experiments when they were en route from here to Paris and that he "does not understand anything about it." Our Dr. Kreyberg here in Oslo is therefore nothing more or less than a common liar and scoundrel. I do not envy him the position in which he will find himself a few years from now. We must stay calm. I, too, have heard from many quarters that the bion theory is taking hold and has found a great deal of support.

TO ROGER DU TEIL
22 June 1939

My dear friend,

Your letter of 19 June arrived today. You will be interested to know that your line of experimental inquiry, which led up to the question of solar radiation, is not a fluke. I am sending you a report I distributed some time ago to various institutes. It does not yet contain the experiments I have performed here in the meantime on the basis of the SAPA bions. These experiments also led directly to the question of solar radiation. I have obtained some reliable results, which I will summarize in the near future and pass on to you.

In New York, a seminar of psychiatrists and analysts has been formed and I am to be its educational director.

My address in New York for the time being will be c/o Dr. Wolfe, 15 East 86th Street, New York City. If my appointment is recognized by the officials here in Oslo, then I will definitely be in New York in mid-July.

I would like to bid you a warm farewell. But New York is not on another planet, and we will without doubt see each other again soon. *

---

* There is no indication in Reich's archives that du Teil responded to this letter. Reich's subsequent efforts to locate du Teil during the war were unsuccessful and, in 1945, he was told that du Teil had been imprisoned in Marseilles in 1940. According to a biographer of Reich, du Teil survived the war, but apparently he did not contact Reich.

TO THEODORE WOLFE
6 July 1939

Dear Wolfe,

Today I spoke with Raknes, who advised me to go to Kelsey tomorrow and play dumb, to say that I did not understand his notification and to ask for a clear reply.* Above all, I should point out to him that I now have a contract that obliges me to begin work on 15 September. It is in fact doubtful whether the State Department will reply, because the matter has been reported and in the meantime dealt with by the New School. It is therefore still possible that I will get Kelsey to change his mind, unless he personally avoids me the way he did on the last two occasions. I don't know what is wrong with him.

Since Kelsey has arranged a new examination appointment, he is obviously expecting to issue the visa. I simply don't understand what the reply from the department—if it comes at all—could do to change the situation. I did not have any opportunity to explain to him that the seminar work and the New School work are connected. It seems important to me to make clear, both here and over there, that the seminar work comes under the aegis of the New School. Could Dr. Johnson† perhaps write directly to the consul? But I don't want to tell you what to do. If I get to talk to Kelsey tomorrow, I will add to this letter a brief report on his reply.

We should not treat the matter too tragically, no matter how irritating it is. But people believe here that war will break out either at the end of August or in early September. I do *not* think that will be the case.

---

* The American vice consul in Oslo, E. T. Kelsey, had written to say that the New York Seminar for Vegetotherapy (which Reich's American students proposed to establish at the New School for Social Research) did not appear on the Department of Labor's lists of approved American educational institutions and that information about it had been requested of the Department of State. In order to obtain a 4(d) nonquota visa, granted to professors who were coming to the United States solely to pursue their vocations as teachers, Reich had to produce a contract to teach at a recognized educational institution. The contract with Columbia had not come through.

† Alvin Johnson, president of the New School for Social Research.

8 July 1939

Last night and tonight I wandered the streets of Oslo alone. At night a certain type of person awakes and plies her trade, one who these days must view each bit of love with great fear but who will someday hold sway over life. Today practically a criminal, tomorrow the proud bearer of life's finest fruits. Whores, ostracized in our day, will in future times be beautiful women simply giving of their love. They will no longer be whores. Someday sensual pleasure will make old maids look so ridiculous that the power of social morality will slip out of their hands. I love *love*!

14 July 1939

For two days I have been helping to set the type for my first work on cancer.* It's good—not an untrue sentence in it. But it is no joy to work in a vacuum, especially when such truth is involved.

The work on the orgone will be perfectly logical. Practically airtight! The rational progress in my cause is intoxicating. It is like a journey through an unfamiliar landscape where new paths are constantly opening, paths that one never noticed before but that are nevertheless completely familiar. It's as if I had walked them in the distant past. Such is the ongoing discovery of life. If they just don't destroy me along the way!

17 July 1939

I am still sitting in Oslo while the essence of my life lies on the other side of the Atlantic. It's raining and the wind is whistling through the rooftops. I am reminded of my student days when I would listen to the wind and a very peculiar restlessness drove me forward, onward. I was aware of not harmonizing well with people despite my gregariousness. And it has not changed to this very day. I feel comfortable only with my work—or in the arms of a loving woman. None of this world's pleasantries bring me enjoyment. I shall list the things I do not enjoy and therefore do not do:

1. I do not play bridge.
2. I do not have parties, except with good friends.
3. I carry no life insurance.

* *Bion Experiments on the Cancer Problem*, Sexpolverlag, Oslo, 1939.

4. I have never had a permanent home.

5. I do not sacrifice myself for my children.

6. I do not sacrifice myself for my wife. Adults must earn their own living.

7. I do not smile when I'm furious.

8. I cannot make small talk.

9. Except for its practical advantages, I do not value the title of "Professor."

10. I consider most authority figures banal individuals.

11. I find the homage paid to kings laughable.

18 July 1939

Still in Oslo.

Any mention of an objective science becomes utterly ridiculous when one thinks in terms of the natural sciences, because scientific research is not carried on by objective scientists but by living organisms. Science only becomes objective when these organisms are no longer afraid of insight. Otherwise arguments concerning scientific problems develop into a struggle of these organisms either for or against pleasure or nonpleasure. This is invariably the case in questions dealing with sex.

TO GERTRUD GAASLAND BRANDT
20 July 1939

My dear Gertrud,

Your letter just arrived. You ask what I am doing. It is difficult to say. I am extremely depressed, and not just because of the stupid waiting. I am almost choking here as I review my life in Oslo, going over the many errors which I made in my dealings with other people; in particular, I am aware of my complete inability to get people to produce and to simply work as they would normally. It is terribly difficult to maintain a balance when, on the one hand, one hates subservience and yet, on the other hand, that's how work is structured. I have the feeling that things will start moving again, and may even turn out well, but this present upheaval is too much all at once, *if* I wish to hold on to the fact that the work must continue unabated. And it must. I simply cannot live without my work. I have discussed all this very seriously and in great detail with many friends here. They all now realize that they were not rigorous enough; they tell me that they did not do enough, although I don't accept that. It is somewhat ridiculous not to be able to remain in a country with a "socialist government," all because of a scientific publication, and to have to go to America—and coupled with this there is the emigration problem, which really has nothing to do with me in this situation. And on top of that comes the separation from much that had become dear to me, even though it could not keep up with me. In short, this is another one of those difficult phases which require all one's strength, as I have already said, if one is firmly committed to continuing one's work. And that I am.

The reason I haven't written very much is that I thought I had noticed that you had withdrawn a little bit from me personally while you were here, and I didn't want to disturb you. There is so much in interpersonal relationships which comes from deep within us and cannot immediately be fully comprehended. Nevertheless, I am very happy to go on working together and to be good friends with you. You know that I would find it very hard to do without you, but at the same time my ties with other people have in the past cost me so dearly, when they were unwilling partners in the relationship, that I have therefore become somewhat more restrained. Do you understand, Gertrud? Perhaps, one day when everything is going smoothly again, and we're both in a suitable mood, and the situation is right, I will give you some insight into the years and decades of my life before Norway so that you will understand certain things much better than was possible up to now.

It is good that you are making a proper effort to study physics and chemistry. That is where the future lies.

I am expecting to receive the contract sometime around the twenty-third, and then I will immediately get in touch with the consul and telegraph you to let you know what he says. If everything goes well, as I hope it does, I should be able to leave here on 2 August, arriving in New York on the twelfth. So it will take about another three weeks. Keep up your spirits, Gertrud! There will be more unpleasant things than this for us to overcome. What is important now is to tear ourselves away from the old and the decayed. That is probably the most difficult thing to do.

4 August 1939

Tonight Elsa was with me. (We both knew that the separation is both necessary *and* tragic.) There is a part of me that she understood better than anyone else. Her morals are those of a beautiful wild animal that acts in accordance with its nature. I, however, have been appointed professor of medical psychology at the New School for Social Research! I am supposed to acquaint civilization with a part of nature. Thus nature must go!

7 August 1939

It's ludicrous to think what the fate of individuals depends on—and with it the fate of mankind. For instance, a vice consul who fears for his position and holds back information in order to make an impression. At the moment I am dangling between heaven and earth or, better said, hell. If the State Department in Washington cables or writes to the consul in Oslo saying that the seminar at the New School is arranged, then my work will be recognized. If the official *doesn't* cable, then I'm finished—for quite some time. And with me the cancer issue as well.

Elsa has become a distant vision, unreal. I loved her so dearly.

In reading the newspapers I find that the problems they contain are ludicrous compared to the one fact that the sun, the bions, and the human body radiate orgone energy. This is what will determine the future, not current events!

I am utterly alone, utterly, despite all my friends. I lack the character traits necessary to direct an organization. All I'm interested in is what creates life.

If one could only remain honest, i.e., not have to say anything other than what one thinks!!

Or at least remain silent!

18 August 1939

On 11 August I received the American professorship visa. Johnson cabled that the Seminar for Vegetotherapy was being run under the auspices of the New School.

Pilsudski's Polish Line was supposed to leave on 12 August but refused me passage because the Danish police would not allow me to pass through the country with "only" identification papers. Had to quickly pay another $250 in taxes.

Spent 12–17 August with Elsa. Our farewell was in keeping with the seven years that had gone before. Saw the northern lights—I'm sure they are orgone radiation.

Tomorrow morning at eleven o'clock it's off on the *Stavangerfjord!*

21 August 1939

At sea. Today I made a woman happy, but I wanted Elsa. Can't free myself of her.

Just observed the northern lights. There is no doubt that they are orgone energy: blue-green color, intense ionization in the air, the North Pole, not understood to date, slow movement.

22 August 1939

10–11 a.m., bright sunshine, breeze.

Orgone reaction with rubber could not be obtained in moving air. Weakly positive in sun in area protected from the wind. Water seems to absorb large amounts of orgone.

TO ELSA LINDENBERG *
23 August 1939

My dear Elsa,

I am writing this letter so that it will come back by the same ship when it returns across the Atlantic in two days' time. So far the trip has been good and not too rough. In contrast, I have been rocked by explosive emotions. It did not seem important that I was heading out

---

* Written on board ship en route to New York.

to start a new life. Instead, there was a lump in my throat when I thought of everything that I was leaving behind, especially you. Many different elements that are important to me seem to have come together in you. For example, the youth movement, which was so characteristic of an old Germany in which a different kind of youth had begun to emerge. Then there was the political movement, into which had also penetrated a little something of that spirit which had last expressed itself on 1 May 1932. Then there was something earlier, much more intensely experienced: what theater is to a maturing man. And even deeper, and far more exciting, the small blond sister. And over it all, embodying everything, there is Elsa with the slightly dreamy eyes— blond, beautiful, in the middle of some dry studies on character neuroses and cancer—nothing but nasty subjects. Through you I was connected with Berlin and then with the great catastrophe I experienced, with so much loss of energy. Then there was Drammensvejen—the new beginning, the first blossoming of my own scientific research. With it is associated our physicality, which I will probably never find again.

If I finally have thanked you so copiously, it is because I am moved by a vague emotion that only now is capable of being expressed in words.

The pain that our necessary separation brought is all the greater. I begged you to speak, speak, speak, but you could not or did not want to. Didn't you understand, were you incapable of understanding, that whatever the secret was, nothing could be worse than not knowing, not knowing from you, even though I was *absolutely sure* that something was wrong? I just could not handle it any longer and it destroyed my trust.

And I am very, very sad because something that I so deeply wanted to cling to has slipped away from me.

I hope with all my heart that you can still find a corner for me in your heart, that corner which opened up on holidays but in dull everyday life—so logically—was almost always closed.

Elsa, I loved you very, very much—very much indeed.

Farewell.

27 August 1939
Surprise!!

From 26 August onward, hot and humid conditions—no orgone results. Humid air absorbs everything.

28 August 1939
Uneventful arrival in New York. Children in the country. Gertrud is well.

30 August 1939
New York is a real *city*.

2 September 1939
Letter from Annie. Will it work out? Children to call tomorrow.

4 September 1939
Rented a house for the laboratory. 75-02 Kessel Street, Forest Hills.

5 September 1939
Children just called. Eva very reserved, uneasy, but willing at the same time. Lore asked, "May I come along too?"

Annie was self-conscious. I would like to be on good terms with her. At eleven o'clock in the morning I will see her for the first time in four years.

Painful longing for Elsa yesterday. That relationship is so strange. But one does forget.

TO ELSA LINDENBERG
8 September 1939

My dear Elsa,

Your letter has stirred up so much in me. It reflected the mood I was in when I left, a mood that still persists and confuses me. Therefore I will have to make some order of things. First the external events:

Within the space of about ten days, I managed to rent a house for roughly $110 per month outside the city in Forest Hills. It has a large workroom downstairs with adjoining laboratory, a kitchen with gas, and a small laboratory for Gertrud. I set up my bedroom on the first floor; next to it is an as yet undefined room that is very nice and sunny, and opposite, on the same floor, are the bathroom (large and beautiful) and the office where Gertrud is going to work. On the top floor is a single room with a separate bathroom that Gertrud has reserved for herself. We get on very well. She is the same way she has always been, and we are just good friends. Most of the house has already been furnished except the laboratory because I am having tables made for it. As far as prices are concerned, one dollar is roughly equivalent to 2–3 kroner. But in order to make ends meet, I shall have to earn $800 to $1,000. For the time being, Wolfe is my only student. It has turned out that being a professor of medical psychology has nothing to do with the right to practice as a medical doctor, which is granted by a different state institution. To make full use of all the opportunities, I shall take the formal examination required to practice medicine, although I can teach without it. However, Briehl and Wolfe were of the opinion that I would be more independent and protected vis-à-vis the psychoanalysts if I were a full-fledged American medical doctor. I have faced gigantic difficulties in trying to carry out my work properly, because everybody is scared. But things will come together. I am used to this, after all.

The children are putting me to the test to find out if I am as kind as they would like me to be. The situation is a trial of patience. I am very reticent and wait for them to phone. We have spent two whole days together out of seven. Annie is subconsciously very hurt and hostile, but I hope to be able to keep quiet. Thomas is a neurotic windbag who feels physically very inferior to me. Eva has become fat but is as clever as ever. Lore is a delightful girl and very similar to me. She is obviously very fond of me.

New York is huge and totally different from Berlin, simpler and more impressive. People are quiet, not rushed, as I expected; they are friendly and courteous; in a word, they are not yet disappointed or corrupted. Business is all-pervasive, and one has to be careful not to be cheated. Everything is delivered to the house. When we moved in, various businesses descended on us. Everything is very well organized. Traffic is orderly. The large centers are really impressive with their abundance of light and the size of the buildings, as are the crowds around 4 or 5 p.m. Mass-produced articles are incredibly cheap. However, furniture like mine does not exist, nor are the microscopes and other equipment available. They tend to be stolen, and I was advised to protect them from theft by installing an alarm. After I had moved into the house, I discovered something very surprising about it: my predecessors had obviously put a children's playroom in the basement, a room that was larger than my workroom in Oslo. Here I can use both projectors without having to move them about. Benches for at least thirty people can be put into this room, as well as a cage. The room is windowless, an ideal darkroom. The house has three bathrooms, one on each floor. It is entirely surrounded by greenery. One can feel the difference in the quality of the air as soon as one leaves the subway station. The center of the city—5th Avenue—is only about half an hour away. My room is much larger and more beautiful than the one in Oslo; it has five large windows and there is nothing but green outside.

The only bad thing is that I have no idea yet how to organize my real work here.

Because of the enormous distance, the war in Europe appears to us like an unreal dream. Only knowing and worrying about you makes it real for us. I ask you and others to write to me in great detail about what you are doing and to tell me if the war has already had an influence, and in what way. Have any of you thought of coming here? How are Sigurd, Odd, Nic, Raknes, and all the others? You are so terribly far away. It was not until I arrived here that I realized how much I had become at home in Oslo, how many ties bound me to life there, and that by moving here I had just managed at the last minute to avoid a catastrophe, that in fact I fled as a persecuted scientist. I still feel that I am part of Europe, although I am already beginning to take root in American soil. I admit that I often long for the old surroundings, and I am hurt that more was not done to enable me to stay. This brings me to the two of us:

Only now do I realize the full extent of the catastrophe that befell both our lives, just as you probably do. How we had grown together in body *and* character! You say so many wise things about this in your letter, which I need not repeat. I wanted to have a child with you because it would have embodied in enhanced form the qualities both of us possess. It was not to be. I loved you as I had never loved a woman before, and I was very happy with you, despite all the great difficulties. I still sense you physically, but I cannot have you. You feel the same way. I am extremely worried about how both of us will get on without each other. Embracing others with whom we do not have this kind of relationship seems to me to debase our ability to love. I am alone; you are perhaps living without a man. Nevertheless, speaking with total honesty and contrary to these deep and vital interests, I think that parting was the right thing for us to do, for I could not go on living with the secret. This would have continued to poison our love and would have bred distrust. I look for the secret in your features, which give nothing away. But when I feel that something vital is being hidden from me for reasons that I cannot understand, when I sense beyond any doubt that you cannot muster the confidence and the courage to tell me, then I simply *have no choice* but to sacrifice what has been dearest to me in these past seven years. I must let go of all my expectations and hopes; I must become lonely again, embrace without love again, just to get out of a situation that has become untenable and degrading for both of us. The big bad wolf, after being pinched many times, has finally bitten. However this matter resolves itself, whether it ends in a loveless relationship and resignation with another partner, whether in misery or some other way, perhaps in years of fighting for love, things had to happen the way they did for me to save the memory of our great love. And I still say the same thing: "Speak to me as to your best friend!" for I do not want to lose your image from my memory. If we want to go on living one way or another with untroubled minds we have to throw some light on what shattered our relationship. Otherwise for the rest of my life I shall be plagued by the thought that the person I loved most lied to me. I shall never hate you for that, but I shall suffer, and so will you. There is something else as well: My character and the need to give have meant that our love was never enriched by your fighting on my side. As a result, I found myself alone in the most difficult times. Whether this is due to a failing on my part or on yours, I do not know. However, one thing became clear to me in these last few months: neither of us can live without a lover, but what you really need is a husband just as much as I need a real wife. We were fighting against a world of obstacles. Perhaps there would not have been a catastrophe if I had married you properly. I am not sure. As it was, you were never totally committed.

I am convinced that you will see many things more clearly now, and this will change you greatly. I could kick myself when I realize that someone else, not I, will enjoy this change for which I fought so hard. You will acquire the capacity to give yourself as a woman. That will be the result of the catastrophe.

I am very depressed. Somehow a beautiful light in my life has been extinguished. Everything is grayer than before, despite the improvement in my external circumstances. The world appears dull to me. The fire inside me is searching for the hidden fire inside you and cannot find it. I know that I was the one who lit this fire but it hid itself from me too often—and played games with me. You loved me very much and still do. What made you afraid to give yourself fully? That would have been the crowning act. Elsa, I do not wish to reproach you. I only want to describe my inner sadness, although I am aware that it could tempt you to go on playing with me. But this time I am sure of myself. When you make a new start, watch out for your obsession with using a man as a plaything. The question I am now asking myself in desperation is where to take the love I experienced so intensely with you.

Please, Elsa, let me know exactly what work you do, and where and how you work. Do not drink! I have consumed practically no alcohol here, although I did have a drink on the evening before I was going to meet the children. I am glad the Norwegians did not succeed in turning me into an alcoholic after all. Write me openly when you start a new relationship, and be careful if you do.

Elsa, I want to know exactly how you are. If you feel my interest bothers you and you want to make your new start without being disturbed, tell me so openly in your letters. If, however, you would like to help me clarify the events of our lives together, then write openly and clearly.

Tell me what the Oslo group is doing, whether any work has been started, what effect my absence has, etc., etc.

As of now, I still have lots of spare time, since the laboratory is not operating, I only have to teach one lesson a day, and the lectures do not start until next semester. I am a bit worried about money because it will take a few months for me to establish myself.

When you write, please remember there is censorship because of the war, and tell the others. Don't forget to pass on important news of all kinds, such as articles that appear, any continuation of the discussion in the papers, etc. Have everything sent to me. Write and let me know how you get on with our friends.

All the best, Elsa. Stay my good friend. Both of us will need this friendship. With love and kisses.

TO ELSA LINDENBERG
17 September 1939

My dear Elsa,

Four weeks have now passed since I left Norway and it seems like an eternity. I was expecting mail from you and my friends last week when the *Bergensfjord* and then the *Oslofjord* arrived here. These ships still carry mail directly and with relatively few disruptions. But nothing came and my first reaction was not to write until I did have some letters from you. But you know me—I brush such principles aside until it is clear that the other party no longer has any interest. I would dearly have liked to hear what has happened to you in these past weeks. I did receive your telegram. Many thanks!

My whole life is in a constant whirl at the moment. I have just completed all the complicated procedures involved in equipping and furnishing a house, and that has cost an enormous amount of money, more than anyone who later benefits from the fruits of these escape/ new job/relocation upheavals can possibly imagine. It is a very tough time at the moment. And underneath it all I am extremely depressed by this new war. I have personally been through it all before and I cannot believe that twenty-five years of struggling, misery, explanations, efforts on all sides have completely failed to stop this atrocity. Have you heard from your family? If so, what? The political information we get here is the best possible, but in personal terms Europe is so terribly remote.

Once I had got an impression of this enormous city of New York and had found the house, I retired "to the country." For ten days I had no desire whatsoever to go into the center of the city. The house gives one the impression of living in the countryside, as Eva put it. It is very quiet, lonely, and conducive to work. In my large room downstairs I have retained a Norwegian atmosphere. All the furnishings and decor remind me of that country. I still believe that you will walk through the door at any moment. I think of you a great deal and suffer—terribly. All these catastrophic events have produced an enormous depression in me. I am not interested in having much to do with other people. That would merely interrupt the state in which I find myself. I am just allowing things to take their course and I am trying honestly to discover what I could have done better. Again and again I find myself faced with the choice of allowing people to drag me through the mud or keeping to myself. Repeatedly I come up against the gigantic problem posed by my extremely intense relationship with you. And I curse my fate, which has prevented me from finding peace in an area where my emotions run so deep. I envy you that you can go on living and working in an environment that is entirely compatible with my philosophy of life, while I now have to rebuild everything from scratch. People here expect that I will, of course, fit in completely because they suspect nothing. But I feel that I *cannot* fit in. Oh yes, I will have many pupils, I will be honored, loved; after years of hard work I will have rebuilt a group around me that will fight for what is naturally right, but I will never be able to fit in and to settle down in this world. Again I shall exist merely on an island— 75-02 Kessel Street. One of the most optimistic people I know is Dr. Briehl, one of my pupils from ten years ago, who as the son of working-class parents seems to have the proper structural base. He is very helpful and has already found a source for cancer research material. The day before yesterday a young doctor, an internist, applied to study under me. I have submitted a very good lecture program to the New School. I shall be paid a fee of one dollar per lecture and per person attending. In addition, I shall be holding a seminar for physicians, educators, and social workers that will introduce them to the problems of the body-mind function from the standpoint of Freud's libido theory. This theory is in a bad way in the International Psychoanalytic Association. Everybody is running away from it. But there is a group that still clings to it theoretically. On the other hand, the inferior form of psychoanalysis is very widespread.

There are problems with the children. Annie obviously regrets her attitude toward my work years ago; she maintains strict authoritarian control over the children. Lore is frisky and rebellious. On the other hand, Eva has identified completely with Annie. She has become just as fat as her mother, terrorizes Lore, plays the role of the strict mother toward her, etc. The children are extremely "well brought up," restrained, and superficially cheerful. You can imagine that it is not easy for me to stand by as an observer and not intervene in any way. I will probably not have very much to do with them. Perhaps Lore will come to me now and again, as a way of protesting against the strict conditions at home. I would welcome her with all my heart, but at the moment there is a wall between us. It is not set up against me as her father but is merely the usual protective armoring that one finds in people.

It is very good that Gertrud is here. She understands everything and is an extremely good friend. She likes it in the house and is happy to be able to work here. She will take a one-year course to become a medical assistant. Next week my work will start up again. The new equipment has cost a lot of money.

I am dying to know how you are getting on. Sometimes I believe that my absence will help you to see things much more clearly. My need to protect you is still enormous, even though it is no longer very effective. I am close to admitting that it is now I who am somewhat in need of protection. In particular, I see myself faced with the need to give up, and I cannot believe that I have become too old to enjoy things once more with a youthful spirit. I am burning deep inside and I am being consumed by the flames, Elsa. But for the time being I prefer this condition to the other one—being somebody's plaything.

Please write and let me know whether you can receive mail via England. Then I won't have to wait just for the Norwegian boats.

I embrace you. Be brave and think things through.

TO HARALD SCHJELDERUP
[Undated]

Now that I have relocated to New York I must approach you with a request that has important consequences for clearly delineating the existing views in psychological research. The most important changes and amendments in the development of psychology took place during the last six years in Scandinavia. On the theoretical side they have been grouped together under the concept "sex economy," and on the practical side they come under the heading of "character-analytic vegetotherapy." At the core of these changes lies my orgasm theory, which asserts on the basis of clinical experience that disturbances in the autonomic vegetative functioning of orgastic experience constitute the core mechanism that produces and maintains the source of energy for all types of psychological disorders. Character armoring and muscular armoring have been detected and formulated as the most important result of this disruption in the equilibrium of sexual energy. The technique of "character analysis" stands and falls with the recognition of the "function of the orgasm" as the economic principle of psychological functioning. One can have whatever views one wishes on this subject. You have on several occasions publicly disassociated yourself not only from orgasm theory but also from my sociological explanation of the origin of sexual suppression, which is essential for character analysis. Since I am responsible for the cohesion and also for the further development of my theory, and for the time being I alone must bear the odium that attaches to that theory, with all its consequences, I must ask you to refrain in the future from calling your technique "character analysis." You probably never accepted the fundamental principle of my method, even while you were studying with me. Besides, the technique of character analysis has been absorbed completely into the technique of vegetotherapy and, as a result of this progression into the field of the biological and physiological foundations of psychological disorders, it has ceased to exist as an independent technique. The gaps and deficiencies in "pure" character analysis, which is merely a psychological method of treatment, necessitated further development of the technique. Separating character analysis from vegetotherapy, which I have heard is being attempted, is theoretically and practically impossible, because vegetotherapy is nothing other than character analysis in the biophysiological sector and character analysis is vegetotherapy in the psychological realm. This is clear from the most recent insights into the antithetical unity of the body-mind relationship. A mechanical separation of the two practices would accordingly simply confuse the student because it is not based on any theoretical foundation.

I extend to you my best wishes, certain that you will not refuse to help clarify scientific views.

24 September 1939

Freud is dead.

Today someone said that I was his scientific heir.

27 September 1939

Freud's legacy is a heavy burden!

30 September 1939

My pupils repeatedly try to convince me that it would be best to follow *their* path instead of mine. And the past has repeatedly shown me that my path is indeed dangerous but the only one that is right *for me*. Among the people who come to see me, the fear of losing their conventional lifestyle is tremendous.

Yesterday a physician from Columbia Medical Center wanted to discontinue vegetotherapy on the grounds that he was afraid of falling into the hands of a paranoiac. The reason for this: The bion experiments on the cancer problem greatly impressed and terrified him: "Gosh, if that were true!" In other words, it is too frightening to admit; therefore the following has to be true:

1. My publications are not scientific. For example, I do not state exactly *what kind* of control has been employed.

2. I am overanxious.

3. It can't be true because no one verified it.

4. It can't be true because cancer is the most important problem in contemporary medicine.

5. If thousands of other researchers have not been able to solve it, then I cannot solve it either.

6. Consequently I am not to be given any cancer material—and this despite the fact that the pathologist saw my cancerous mouse in alcohol, diagnosed the section, and admitted that he had never laid eyes on a *living* cancer cell.

3 October 1939

Took Lillian [Bye] to task yesterday. That woman, making herself look old at thirty-three, wants to be a bluestocking intellectual and is in love with me because I'm, as she puts it, red-blooded. But she feels that it is high time for me to start exchanging the "red" within me for the "blue." I told her I had another fifteen or twenty years to do that.

Praise God that I am still afire!! As long as I am still hot-blooded, red-blooded, I am *alive*. If Elsa would give me the ultimate, I could find happiness.

What a fool I am. The orgone theory is correct, the cancer theory is correct, vegetotheory is correct. Nevertheless, I am alone. I fear growing older alone.

5 October 1939

Lore was here. Annie set a time limit for the visit. Lore believes that a mother "has all rights over the children and that the father has none."

11 October 1939

Things are going badly for me. I am completely blocked in my work. There is no sense in continuing to putter around with my experiments. I lack the funds, the material, and the coworkers necessary to concentrate everything on *one* crucial issue—for example, the cancer problem. It's enough to drive me to distraction. And thus, essentially, *nothing* is happening! I sit and wait for cancer material, for confirmation from the place where everything is available.

What disgusting times!

14 October 1939

People take wherever they can and give only when it is demanded of them! This statement comes to mind again and again. It is correct.

Should I continue to hand over knowledge, senselessly, without insisting that something be done for the cause? With my responsibilities and obligations? Is it right to do that, even if I were capable of it? Am I still capable? This block is hideous! Despite my knowledge of all the beautiful things that I teach and produce, I am completely uninterested. Whom does it benefit? Mankind? I am tempted to say that it is useless to exert oneself for "mankind"! So that they can beat you down afterward? I am struggling with all my might against this attitude—it leads to the domains where Stalin and Hitler hold sway. These fellows who arise from the masses know exactly how to stir up the filth in man. They know it much better than rulers from the "upper" classes! And the masses have more confidence in them (because they come from their midst) and willingly allow themselves to be controlled by them, more willingly than by aristocrats and the bourgeoisie. And yet in everyday life nothing has changed.

Is there a way to unite the profoundly true, forthright scientific thoughts of individuals with the great emotions existing in mankind as a whole? Or will there always be a gulf between the two?

An uncanny feeling of certainty is beginning to dawn on me—namely, that great and crucial discoveries do not influence the masses directly or very rapidly. My gravest mistake lay in my desire to have my *nascent* insights of twelve years ago transformed directly into social practice. For these twelve years everything has gone against them, progressively and relentlessly. When I hear sacred music today, I think of Jesus two thousand years ago, of what he intended and what became of it. I think of how that which prevails so strongly today, mankind's basic vegetative longings notwithstanding, has nothing to do with the teachings for which he was crucified but is actually their opposite. It's hopeless. The principles of society have yet to be discovered. True, my theory does answer the question of mass fascism, but it is not practicable. And perhaps many will still be crucified before so-called sex economists spring up within "churches" and other organizations, men who will represent the exact opposite of what sex economy really means. It is entirely conceivable that my theory will someday (but when and where?) become social practice, although I will not live to see the day. Discerning people who understand my intentions have prophesied that I will die a lonely death, and I also sense that an evil fate lies in store for me. But to surrender for that reason and try to adjust would mean an even worse death—namely, *the death of my self-esteem*. I must prepare myself for my destiny. Great honor and success may lie ahead, but the end will be wretched.

I must continue to follow my path—and with full vitality. If there were a God, I would cry out, "God help me!"

TO ELSA LINDENBERG
16 October 1939

My dearest, darling Elsa,

Your letter of 1 October arrived two days ago. I have not received the other letters from you. Mail and everything else is getting more and more unreliable. This uncertainty is a characteristic feature of all life at the present moment. People here are very naive and believe that they will not be affected by this war. I do not believe that is the case. I am also firmly convinced that the northern part of Europe will also soon be right in the thick of things. I am overwhelmed with concern, both of a general kind and specifically for you people on the other side of the Atlantic. I am unable to work properly and I just walk around thinking and thinking. I can only accomplish what absolutely has to be done.

You have not really replied to my three letters. Nevertheless your letter was a relief after not having heard from you for so long. Please let me know what you intend to do. You have the possibility of waiting out the war on this side of the Atlantic, and if that is what you wish to do then you must hurry. The war is making the situation even more crucial than the unanswered questions that still exist between us. Do you really want to live this "other" life or can you accept the difficulties of living your life together with me? Is our relationship really over or not? If yes, then we should stop torturing each other; if no, then we should find the courage to start over again and to behave better toward each other. You write that you have changed greatly. How? In what direction? I want to know everything, Elsa, because I cannot stand this state of uncertainty very much longer. If you would tell me clearly and honestly what you think about all this, we could quickly make a decision.

If we both succeed in fully clarifying the past, then there is no danger. All this, of course, presupposes that you are willing to accept leading a difficult life with me and are willing to rebuild your work here with my help and the help of my students. That will not be difficult because the Americans are very receptive to new things. You must understand clearly that living with me in no way means that you have to abandon your personality. In fact the opposite is true, but it would require a particular style of life with which you are very familiar.

However, many things would be different as long as nobody like Kreyberg with all his dirty tricks intervened again. I am yearning for peace
and quiet in which to work; I want a child; I no longer have any
political illusions; I know that what I am teaching cannot become
reality tomorrow or even the day after tomorrow. Therefore I do not
have to engage in daily battles. Nor do I want to anymore. None of
the existing scientific or political organizations has anything to do with
me. In addition, I need your help in my work, your understanding
for physical things, your fine sense of rhythm. I would be the happiest
man in the world if you and I could succeed in smoothing out the
unevenness in our relationship, which arises perhaps from my not
showing enough consideration toward you and from your fear of my
work. But, ultimately, we must control the gypsy in us. If it had not
been for the urgency imposed by the war and the risk that we might
be torn apart for years, I might have waited a while with these serious
proposals until we had both gained a clear understanding of everything
that is still up in the air between us. But then we might face the misery
of discovering that, because of all the common experiences we share,
we cannot live with anybody else. I recently discussed all these difficulties with a very intelligent person, who said to me: "But it is obvious
from your demeanor that you love this woman and cannot give her
up." All I could say in reply was: "But what can I do when she wants
what I want and yet cannot share this life?"

If you clearly feel that my relationship to you is false, artificial, born
of a momentary need, or that it is harmful for your future, then tell
me and I will abandon it.

Now let me tell you a little bit about conditions here in America.

The newspapers are full of stories about the war. The special news
cinemas show authentic film reports from the various theaters of the
war. Everyone is asking whether the States can remain uninvolved or
not. But life here is far removed from the events. People don't really
understand Europe.

One can live a very lonely or a very sociable life here, depending
on what one wants. It is not absolutely necessary to move in "society,"
and it is not even necessary to wear a dinner jacket to concerts, except
in certain seats. One could go to the cinema twice a day and still not
have seen everything even after several weeks. I have been to the
World's Fair three times. There's a lot of life there and many beautiful

things to see but, as you know, I am not very interested in anything but special matters. The exhibition will be extended into next year. I have two six-hour series of lectures that are fully attended each week and one series that is 50 percent full. For the time being I am earning enough for myself and a modest laboratory. In general, everyone who comes into genuine contact with my work is very interested; some are even enthusiastic. A few analysts were here and they told me about the political infighting in the organization. It does not look good.

Yesterday I drove with the Briehls, who are very nice people, to the beach on Long Island, which is about an hour from me and can be reached in approximately one and a half hours from the center of the city. There are several kilometers of sandy beach with large bathing areas. I took my driving test last week and I am going to buy myself a car as soon as I have the money. As I said, having a car here is not a luxury and it costs about a quarter as much as in Europe. Yesterday a new maid came to work for me. She works from about eight in the morning until five in the afternoon for ten dollars a week plus food. The food here is very good and cheap.

My students come out here to me. Whether it will remain like that or whether I will take an office somewhere downtown I do not know. It also depends on whether I receive permission to set up a medical practice in addition to my professorship. Some doctors told me that is possible because I am introducing a new medical technique that is unknown and that nobody else can carry out. I would therefore not have to take the state examination that people normally have to take to practice as doctors.

Elsa, who of our friends would want to come here if war breaks out in Norway? Sigurd? Philipson? We could make inquiries and provide you with information. I do not know whether they will ban all immigration. This war may change an awful lot and tear apart what appeared indestructible and create situations that nobody anticipated.

23 October 1939

I rant and rave, seek and search, am awfully unhappy! Here I sit with a pile of cancer experiments that I can't carry out. My children remind me of frightened little dogs on a leash. They are afraid of me.

Have no woman—and am suffering greatly. Can't go to whores. My pupils in this country are, for the time being, only interested in plagiarism. And all I can do, for the time being, is look on. In the psychiatry department at Columbia University, they are already studying my clinical theory with Wolfe. But my name isn't mentioned and it was not officially planned that I should be in Columbia Psychiatry.

I fear the consequences of abstinence. Can't understand how the medical profession can overlook them. One becomes lethargic and mean.

25 October 1939

Life is amazing! In the evening I sent a telegram to Elsa, and two hours later I found myself close to falling in love with Ilse Ollendorff. * She seems to be compatible. Poor Elsa! Or didn't she write because she has found someone to comfort her? How fervently I wanted to prove that a Jew can be perfectly happy with an Aryan woman!

26 October 1939

Following six ghastly weeks of abstinence, interrupted only by emergency measures, I now feel strong and optimistic again, have confidence and a desire to work. Ilse said my forehead was wider and more powerful this morning than last night. I am writing this down deliberately, not because I want to inform future generations that I embraced a woman, but to prevent some quack or charlatan from daring to claim that the life of all creative individuals "proves that sexual abstinence has a favorable effect on achievement."

Preposterous nonsense!

27 October 1939

I met Ilse Reissner (Ollendorff) one week ago. She had made up her mind to meet me and we established contact immediately. Without being entirely aware of it, she is very clever, pretty, and she has a body that reminds me of Elsa, except that she is brunet. Actually I am extremely happy that she is with me and that I am no longer alone. She could easily become my wife. And now, what about Elsa? Will allow matters to take their natural course.

---

* A friend of Gertrud Brandt's.

29 October 1939

One doesn't work "for mankind." One works against the disquiet caused by things that challenge the understanding. People who are afraid of a thing flee. Those who are not afraid struggle along until they either understand it, can cope with it, or destroy it. People in their present state only disturb one's efforts. It would be stupid to work "for them." "It" is working for them.

Decades later they take for granted the fruits of the work brought to fulfillment for the love of life itself. If one were to work "for man" or "for mankind" there would soon be no achievement at all. That's how poorly our contemporaries behave. One would lose one's sense of that certain living quality which exists in everything, which is highly unscientific, daring, often vulgar and then again loving, which takes all the pleasure it can get, stretches in the sun, sighs in the embrace, and cries when it is sad.

30 October 1939

Did well with the experiments tonight. When I had pleasurable sensations my hands glowed in the darkroom.

I have actually discovered life. It's truly incredible. I, a mere nonentity, a nonacademician, a sexual scoundrel in the bourgeois sense, have made the greatest discovery of the century. Told Wolfe yesterday that I thought I was greater than Freud. But I feel like a baby impudently traipsing over the countryside. In reality, the baby is lost but is fortunately not aware of it. Otherwise it would immediately become afraid in the very ordinary sense of the word—not very smart, and dirty. This great life is so simple that it just outgrew itself and forgot what it actually was. Magnificent!

How logically and honestly life has led me over the past twenty years, led me by the hand, so to speak, *lovingly and faithfully.* It has treated me better than my mother ever did, better than any woman ever could. *It was logical.* It revealed itself to me step by step, rewarding each discovery with still another. It loved me, provided me with the insight and good luck to be able to recognize it. I shall remain true to it. If it would just grant me a little more self-confidence so I could serve it better.

I must continue to struggle without consideration for friends! Must remain faithful to the larger concept that is my guide.

5 November 1939

One must remain decent—and the criterion of decency is one's attitude toward everything that was previously considered indecent out of the cowardly fear of confronting life, of encountering it in all its fullness, confusion, and consistent inconsistency.

Irrational human structure is a plague, an endemic disease. We fight against it, catch it, are infected, murder, commit stupid, mean mistakes, love, and betray love. And yet we are decent, or attempt to be so.

It must be far easier to bear distress with a complete block against the life within oneself than with an unguarded capacity to experience, to recognize and fulfill life, to experience oneself in the light of truth, to agree with everyone while adhering to one's own principles amidst the universal conflict of opinions, to feel the pulse of life, to see loved ones fall, to skirt the edge of an abyss, to see man's great talents ruined—in a word, *to love*.

20 November 1939

The contemporary human creature categorizes the straightforward, uncomplicated, and obvious things that are foreign to him under the heading "genius." Even things that are perfectly natural. When an emotional cripple uses the term "genius," what he means is: a threat to me. He elevates in order to alienate, praises in order to efface. He saves his admiration for the orgy *after* the person has been destroyed. This, in turn, spares his making any effort. The so-called genius is a product of coincidence, a small bit of life that has somehow been salvaged. The tragedy of the genius lies in his alienation from contemporary living, as well as in the average person's fear of life, in the gap between life's fervent emotions and the forms in which life manifests itself—i.e., in mankind's fear of unarmored life, which behaves like an ocean polyp.

28 November 1939

I must quickly make the following decisions:

1. Whether to close the laboratory or make a supreme effort to keep it open.

2. Whether to plunge into a bourgeois life or just continue as I have been.

3. Whether Elsa or Ilse is to become my wife here in the USA. Have a feeling that Elsa would not be able to cope with the situation and am constantly growing closer to Ilse. She's very dear.

4. Whether to continue to have pupils who then desert me or simply withdraw.

Gertrud wants to return to Norway. She either cannot or will not fully devote herself to the work. The situation is abominable.

Too hard for a baby elephant! By God! Is that infantile? No, it's the honest truth!

29 November 1939

Somewhere my political-psychological theory has an enormous loophole where all the facts I try to gather slip through my fingers. The more I attempt to cling to the idea of human decency, the more man behaves in an indecent, unintelligent, stupid fashion. Just take one look at American baseball and all the fuss that's made over it!

1 December 1939

Russia has occupied Finland. I am completely disoriented. Is all this really possible? The communists are either cowards or swine. What is a person to do or think?

15 December 1939

With my knowledge it is not easy to get along with people. Ilse has had two spells of depression without knowing why. She is being put through the wringer. Is probably thinking of marrying me or something like that. Her concept of my greatness is too simple.

After all, I'm entirely alone! It's easy for other people to be kind and sociable. Their organisms are not bombarded by thousands of demands each day.

I. Conditions needed for cancer to occur: Vesicular disintegration of tissues and the formation of protists; poor respiration of the tissues as the cause of the decay; poor charge of the tissues as the cause of the decay. Muscle spasms and loss of charge as a chronic sympathicotonic state. *This is the "cancer disposition."*

II. Its causes: Psychic armoring = physical withdrawal; sexual repression as a result of the foregoing. Consequences: Stasis of electrical energy, spasms to ward off feelings lead to sexual stasis → degeneration of tissue, partial death.

III. The protozoa that form irritate the tissues. The tissues react by producing tumor growths. Cancer cell = agglomeration of defense forces → degeneration → production of destructive bacteria. *Circular effect*: More bacteria → more defense → *more* bacteria → *more* defense → emaciation. The body defends itself against decay at the cost of its own strength.

IV. The tissues in which this takes place are the red blood corpuscles. Their decay produces (a) bions, (b) T-bacilli.

Intensification of decay. Same blood picture as in pernicious anemia. Supply of red blood corpuscles is not adequate. Spiked shapes appear, indicative of the decaying of the blood corpuscles.

Death through self-consumption. Dying in the living organism. The antithesis of blood-charcoal bions and S is the antithesis of life and death. Life defends itself against death. (I am surprised at the wealth of blood-carbon bions in cancer.)

Life destroys itself by drawing its defense forces from *the blood*: it is conceivable that the carbon from the blood is organized like 3e or 10e bions and that these bions penetrate into the tissues where the S are located.

16 December 1939

Dr. Johnson from Presbyterian Hospital brought one mouse suffering from cancer of the breast (right side) for an experiment with bions. I injected 0.3 cc of Lorin III + II subcutaneously. Problems connected with this first injection:

a. SAPA Lorin was seen killing amoeboid ca cells and T-bacilli, not immature ca cells. If they don't attack ca III cells, then the mobile type of bion (PA) should be applied, because these penetrate ca III tissue.

b. Not too much should be injected at once, because of the danger that the detritus of the destroyed cancer tissue would overrun the body.

c. SAPA could cause damage in too big doses.

17 December 1939

The breast tumor seems smaller. *Seems!* Last night it was like that ; tonight it appeared like that . Let us see tomorrow. It would be too much, if true! Johnson said, "All we have so far is *one* healed mouse."

18 December 1939

Lorin 0.4 [cc] injected.

19 December 1939

Tumor has shrunk still further.

A SAPA mouse injected with 0.5 cc SAPA two and a half months ago died today. Lungs full of T and cancer cell structures, like a mouse in the spring. No SAPA in the blood. *Problem:* SAPA destroys tumors. SAPA produces cancer cells. Question = dosage.

When a tumor is present, it is possible that SAPA exhaust themselves in destroying it and act differently than when no tumor exists and they are able to affect fresh tissue.

The question of the harmfulness of the T is still the most important one.

To be transplanted in a new world is still a cross to bear, despite the feeling of being at home in any country. To know the truth and not be able to put it into practice is like watching one's own beloved child die. Seeing loved ones fall by the wayside is worse than living through a pogrom. There is no bloodshed, but it's often worse than sudden murder. It is a *slow* death. Watching the masses sell themselves into such undignified slavery is almost too much for me to bear.

As long as the search for truth in human society is not based on as firm a foundation as the arrogance of the diplomats, peace on earth will never become a reality.

Was just interrupted by I. J. Fox, 6th Avenue, Christmas sale on fur coats. Business—but that's OK.

22 December 1939

This week the first cancer mouse was 50 percent healed of its cancer by means of bions.

It is obvious to me that I have the solution to the cancer problem in my pocket, so to speak. The only thing I don't know is how to get the solution out of my pocket.

I love my work! It is faithful and honest! But people are incredible cowards!

25 December 1939

Ilse will become my wife after all. I still love Elsa but I wish her what she wishes for herself—that is, to be able "to live." There is no "life" here. I wish her much, much happiness.

26 December 1939

And when I have conquered cancer, all this will seem "simple" and "banal"—the sacrifices, the suffering, the struggle, the uncertainties —and highly questionable individuals will be injecting bions that they neither discovered nor suffered for.

30 December 1939

Ilse is pregnant—6th–8th week.* Wasn't able to conceive for years. Now what? Elsa? Guess that settles matters. This *could* be a cause for great joy, but in reality it's an enormous tragedy. Elsa will commit suicide.

31 December 1939

Thus the blood-drenched year of 1939 sinks into its grave. 1940 will probably be no better. However, 1939 saw the birth of an understanding of cancer—the first mice were cured of cancer by means of bions. Silently, far removed from the frenzy of those nature-alienated beings, creative and constructive thinking pursues its steady course. It is erecting the pillars of the future. The privilege of participating in this compensates for all my loneliness, for all the ridicule and calumny. What does all that matter? Doesn't spring water seep through the ground and emerge clear on the surface? Are not the pure, productive contours of the living engraved upon the infant who is born in blood and pain? Doesn't the sun emerge strong and bright when clouds and fog have disappeared? Doesn't each springtime green anew when snow and ice have melted? And even if all life on this earth were to perish, it would still exist on other stars, in other worlds. Undulation and convulsion will never cease! Nor will development! To feel this, yes, to direct it where it can be directed, is Godlike—if "God" is indeed a valid concept. Events such as those in 1939 engender an obligation to *genuine* science.

Good luck in the new year, Willi! You have been pretty brave until now. Stay that way, and bear the loneliness without becoming a misanthrope.

---

* This pregnancy was aborted.

INDEX

abiogenesis, 77; *see also* spontaneous
generation
abstinence, 246
American Consulate, 171
anxiety: in psychoanalytic theory, x; relation to vegetative nervous system,
xi, 7; and sexual stasis, xi
armor, 5, 9, 37, 89, 181, 238; *see also*
character armoring; muscular
armoring
Arrhenius, Svante, 165

Bauer, Victor, 61ff
Beethoven, Ludwig van, 124, 166, 187
Berle, Vivi, 96, 97, 102
bioelectrical experiments, 45, 47, 173,
203; difficulties with, 51; monograph
on, 61; control experiments, 62
bions, 80, 81, 107, 116, 129, 159, 162;
The Bions, 135; cultures, 95, 136,
168, 178, 180, 190; and cancer, 112,
143; injection of, 99, 110, 112, 250;
smear campaign against, 139, 146ff,
161; commission to investigate, 149,
159; radiation effect of, 173, 188ff,
204, 211, 216; SAPA, 188, 196ff,
204, 211 *n*, 223, 250, 251
Bohr, Niels, 189
Bon, W. F., 172, 176, 188, 191, 193,
194, 195, 197, 199, 201, 202, 211,
216, 219, 221
Bonnet, 116, 145, 156, 162, 163, 222
Bornstein, Berta, 30, 38, 44, 51
Brandt, Willy, 183

Brecht, Bertold, 34
Briehl, Walter, 140, 171, 175, 178,
208, 232, 237, 245
Brownian movement, 93, 97, 136, 190
Bukharin, Nikolai Ivanovich, 94
Bye, Lillian, 241

cancer, 66, 76, 81, 99, 105, 110, 119,
120, 240, 241, 251, 252; "postinfection" in, 105; and carbon, 112, 121,
250; causes of, 113, 249; "disposition," 115, 249; early diagnosis of,
122, 130; radium industry, 131; therapy, 143; experiments, 145, 178;
Reich's first work on, 225
character analysis, xiv, xvii, 4, 21, 35, 37,
41, 125, 239; *Character Analysis*, xx
character armoring, xi, 239
Christensen, Lars, 139
Communist Party: and sex politics, xix;
and *The Sexual Struggle of Youth*,
xix; in Denmark, xx
Curie, Marie, 193

Davos, 131
death instinct theory, x, xii, xiv, 3, 11,
21
Debré, 156, 162ff
Deutsch, Felix, 22
dialectic of death and life, 65
dialectical materialism, xiv, 23, 79, 89
*Dialectical Materialism and Psycho-
analysis*, 11, 20